Beethoven: Studies in the Creative Process

LEWIS LOCKWOOD

Beethoven

Studies in the Creative Process

Harvard University Press
Cambridge, Massachusetts, and London, England   1992

Copyright © 1992 by the President and Fellows of Harvard College
All rights reserved
Printed in the United States of America
10 9 8 7 6 5 4 3 2 1

Page 276 constitutes a continuation of the copyright page.

This book is printed on acid-free paper, and its binding materials have
been chosen for strength and durability.

Library of Congress Cataloging-in-Publication Data

Lockwood, Lewis.
    Beethoven: Studies in the creative process / Lewis Lockwood.
        p.   cm.
    Includes bibliographical references and indexes.
    ISBN 0-674-06362-7
        1. Beethoven, Ludwig van, 1770–1827—Criticism and interpretation.
I. Title.
ML410.B4L595   1992   91-24796
780′.92—dc20   CIP
                                                              MN

To Alison and Daniel

Contents

Beethoven: Studies in the Creative Process

Abbreviations

Anderson
Emily Anderson, ed., *The Letters of Beethoven,* 3 vols. (London, 1961). Numbers in citations of Anderson's edition refer not to page numbers but to her numbering of the letters

BJ
Beethoven-Jahrbuch, First series (1908–09), ed. T. von Frimmel; Second series (1953–), Vols. 1–8, ed. J. Schmidt-Görg; Vol. 9, ed. H. Schmidt and M. Staehelin; Vol. 10, ed. Martin Staehelin

BS 1; BS 2; BS 3
Beethoven Studies, ed. Alan Tyson; Vol. 1, New York, 1974; Vol. 2, Oxford, 1977; Vol. 3, Cambridge, 1982

JAMS
Journal of the American Musicological Society

JTW
Douglas Johnson, Alan Tyson, and Robert Winter, *The Beethoven Sketchbooks: History, Reconstruction, Inventory* (Berkeley, 1985)

Kinsky-Halm
Georg Kinsky, *Das Werk Beethovens. Thematisch-bibliographisches Verzeichnis seiner sämtlichen vollendeten Kompositionen,* completed and edited by Hans Halm (Munich-Duisburg, 1955)

MGG
Die Musik in Geschichte und Gegenwart, ed. Friedrich Blume et al., 17 vols. (Kassel, 1949–1986)

MQ
The Musical Quarterly

N I
Gustav Nottebohm, *Beethoveniana* (Leipzig and Winterthur, 1872)

N II
Gustav Nottebohm, *Zweite Beethoveniana: nachgelassene Aufsatze* (Leipzig and Winterthur, 1887)

N 1865
Gustav Nottebohm, *Ein Skizzenbuch von Beethoven* (Leipzig, 1865); trans. by J. Katz in *Two Beethoven Sketchbooks* (London, 1973), pp. 3–43

N 1880
Gustav Nottebohm, *Ein Skizzenbuch von Beethoven aus dem Jahre 1803* (Leipzig, 1880); trans. by J. Katz in *Two Beethoven Sketchbooks* (London, 1973), pp. 47–125

SV
Hans Schmidt, "Verzeichnis der Skizzen Beethovens," *BJ* 6 (1969), pp. 7–128

Thayer-Forbes
Thayer's Life of Beethoven, rev. and ed. by Elliot Forbes (Princeton, 1964)

WoO
Werke ohne Opuszahl (works without opus number) in the listing by Kinsky-Halm (see above)

Introduction

In different ways the essays in this volume attempt to grapple with the same big question: what can we learn about Beethoven's compositional process and musical thought from his surviving sketches and autographs? Since musicians, scholars, and the literate public have been aware of the survival of Beethoven's working papers for more than a century, one would think on the face of it that such a question must have been answered long ago, at least in general terms. But the initiated know how little we really know. Paradoxically, as more and more of Beethoven's sketches and autographs are discovered, reconstructed, transcribed, and studied, the mysteries seem all the greater.

Some of the essays in this book embody attempts to unravel particular problems by looking at individual works from the viewpoint of their compositional background; some focus instead on the nature of the evidence that makes this background available to us. In certain cases I have made moderate revisions in essays that had been previously published, in order to reduce cross-references and some overlapping, but the basic substance remains unchanged, with only a few points brought up to date to reflect more recent scholarship. Several essays are published here for the first time.

Although Beethoven's sketches have attracted wide attention for many decades, the growth of the field has been sporadic and uneven. Ideally, the pioneering work of Gustav Nottebohm in the late nineteenth century should have given rise to a steady stream of transcriptions and studies of the large mass of sketches that Nottebohm revealed in partial outline for the first time. But for reasons inherent in the development of musicological research between 1900 and 1950, this did not happen. There have been some important individual publications—for example, those of Nathan Fishman, Joseph Kerman, and Sieghard Brandenburg—but progress has been slow in the development of a large-scale project that would aim to publish the entire body of the Beethoven sketches in full transcription and facsimile. Such an enterprise was begun at the Beethoven-Archiv in Bonn in the 1950s, but it still has a long way to go and even now is the only major effort of its kind.

Recently the whole field received a vital forward impulse from the first published catalogue of the sketchbooks as reconstructed according to their paper types, watermarks, and other physical evidence. This is the important book by Douglas Johnson, Alan Tyson, and Robert Winter, *The Beethoven Sketchbooks: History, Reconstruction, Inventory* (1985). Yet even this impressive inventory still leaves the large number of single sketch-leaves and bundles of leaves uncatalogued, except as they are now known to belong to larger sketchbooks. And beyond this, the vast bulk of the known sketchbooks and sketch leaves is still awaiting reliable publication in facsimile, let alone transcription.

As for the autograph manuscripts, they have become better known in recent years thanks to increasing numbers of reliable facsimile editions and studies of individual autographs. But here too, in only a few cases have scholars begun to work out the important compositional changes that Beethoven often made in his works as late as the autograph stage. More studies are needed that do this in close conjunction with study of the surviving sketches, so that the two categories of evidence may shed light on each other. Indeed, I have believed for a long time that the study of the Beethoven sketches and that of the autographs may profit from a coordinated approach to both types of sources. Admittedly this is not always possible, as in the present studies on the *Eroica* Symphony, for which a large body of sketches survives but whose autograph has been lost since Beethoven's time. The opposite is true of the Quartet in F Major, Opus 59 No. 1, for which we have the richly informative autograph manuscript but, so far as we know, only a trace of sketch material. Yet in other cases the possibilities exist and should be further developed, for reasons suggested in the first essay in this volume and returned to at least briefly in others.

A special word is needed here about the autograph manuscript of the first movement of the Violoncello Sonata, Opus 69, which is published in this volume in complete facsimile along with commentary in Chapter 2. This marvelous example of what we mean by a composing score has been published twice before—in *The Music Forum,* Volume II (1970), and in the same year in a separate facsimile edition. But both of these publications are now out of print. At the time I worked on the manuscript, in the late 1960s, it was in the private possession of Dr. Felix Salzer of New York, the well-known music theorist and teacher. I can never forget the memorable days I spent in his apartment, poring over the intricacies of this manuscript, with Dr. Salzer always nearby for discussion of new and unexpected points. Just recently, in 1990, following his death, the manuscript was auctioned by Sotheby's, and through the generosity of an anonymous purchaser was acquired by the Beethoven Archiv in Bonn. It is reproduced here once again in full, now with the kind permission of Dr. Sieghard Brandenburg, Director of the Beethoven Archiv, and thus will once again be available to scholars and performers alike. In this connection, another major discovery has been made within the last few years, although it has not yet been formally announced: it is the recovery of the vitally important "Clauss copy" of Opus 69 by Dr. Albert Dunning. I have taken brief account of this discovery in a note attached to Chapter 2.

To study the surviving evidence of the creative process of one of the greatest of composers is in some people's eyes quixotic and foolhardy. And yet for many musicians and scholars, the impulse is irresistible. On the one hand, we sense that the goals of such study will always remain beyond our grasp—that the intensity of vision and depth of imagination that Beethoven brought to bear on his greater and even lesser works entailed judgments remote from casual musical experience. We feel that such problems in their larger scope go beyond the range of even our most dedicated work on sources. And yet we persevere, borne forward by the instinctive knowledge that in doing so we are engaging musical and artistic issues of profound significance. In the process we often find, as musicians have felt since the days of Nottebohm, that tracing the stages of Beethoven's composition of his works can enlarge our understanding of his artistic development in specific ways, and can furnish paradigms for the close study of the complex structure of tonal music in the hands of one of its central masters. We can hardly dismiss the potential extensions of knowledge that lie open to us through the remarkable preservation of his sketches and autographs. I can only hope that these essays may contribute modestly to the enterprise and may stimulate better efforts in the future.

ONE

On Beethoven's Sketches and Autographs: Some Problems of Definition and Interpretation

The autograph of Beethoven's Piano Sonata in A-flat Major, Op. 26, was published in complete facsimile by Erich Prieger in 1895. In Variation No. 3 of the first movement we find the passage shown in Example 1.1. Although at first glance this segment may look like one of the many corrections we expect to find in Beethoven's autographs, on closer inspection it can be made to reveal more than may at first appear. It raises questions that can serve as points of entry into the difficult and still largely uncharted domain of Beethoven's procedures of composition.

Example 1.1   Piano Sonata in A-flat Major, Op. 26: autograph, fol. 4v

The spacing and ordering of the four components in this passage enable us to reconstruct Beethoven's procedures step by step in this phrase, and in doing so we can see that the revisions he made here are peculiar. After writing the B-double-flat upbeat with downward stem at m. 16/3, he continued with the material we see in the first version of m. 17 (A1). The upbeat was followed in A1 by its continuation, repeating the same downward direction of the stems. Whether Beethoven intended before cancelling to add to A1 the bass line we see in A2 we cannot say; in any case, he introduced it only in the A2 version. A1 was then rejected, evidently as soon as written, by means of the crossing cancellation strokes and the familiar "Vi-de."[1]

He then wrote down A2 as the preferred alternative, and we can readily see what it corrects. The stems were now turned upward for the middle voice to bring it unequivocally into the performer's right hand, the double stem was added to prolong the A-flat in mid-register, and the bass was filled in.

But with the next measure (B1), we come to something strange. In the theme of the movement and in the first two variations, the corresponding measures (mm. 17–20) had been divided into two exactly parallel subphrases. But now, instead of following A2 with an immediate and literal transposition of its material, Beethoven not only wrote the upbeat to B1 with downward stem but continued by writing the entire measure B1 as a precise parallel to the A1 version that he had just rejected. This time he even included the bass part. Then revising again, exactly as he had done before, he wrote out B2 as a "Vi–de" substitute for B1 (after still another momentary lapse on the first two beats of B2 that had brought a wrong note on the second beat of the measure).

Of several possible interpretations of the passage, one seems to me the most plausible. Having written A1 and changed it to A2, Beethoven, in a momentary lapse, wrote out B1 without realizing that he was following the A1 version he had just rejected. Then he saw his mistake and changed B1 to B2. The two pairs of graphic operations—A1, A2 and B1, B2—clearly reflect different degrees of concentration. I think, though, that we can go a step further, and that the evidence permits a further distinction. In changing A1 to A2, Beethoven was making a deliberate, conscious alteration in his material; he was working on the phrase as a minuscule problem of composition. But at the moment of writing out B1, he must have reverted to a more nearly inadvertent level of procedure, in which he wrote out a version that had formerly seemed acceptable and was still fixed in memory—even though he had just rejected it. If the first pair reflects a procedure of composition, we can regard the second as forming a process of virtually mechanical reproduction—of "copying"—but in this case copying the wrong measure. Then at B2 he copied the right measure and went on from there.

The critical link in the chain is clearly B1, and the main point of this little example is that the paired revisions are consecutively spaced within the main text, not added elsewhere. It is substantially self-evident that they were consecutively written.[2] Had Beethoven first written A1 and B1 plus their cadences and had only later decided to revise, he would have been compelled to find space elsewhere to do so, either on the same page or on an adjacent one, as he does for all the other corrections of any magnitude in this autograph (and, of course, in many others). What he wrote instead shows an unusual pattern of fluctuation: from measure to measure, from phrase to parallel phrase, between active and passive stages of writing. Had this change occurred in the sketches, it would seem less surprising. But the conjunction of the two versions in one short passage helps to focus attention on the larger context of the passage and, in turn, on the problem of defining and interpreting the concept of the "autograph" as a document of the composition process.

As a rule, when we use the term "autograph" in ordinary discourse we have in mind a familiar abstraction: the "final version" of a composition, ideally complete in all details, as written down by its author. On the basis of this intuitively reasonable category, manuscripts are regularly listed—as in Kinsky-Halm—classified and studied, bought and sold. In the study of them, furthermore, it seems to be an accepted article of faith (and one that would be difficult to supplant) that as a work progresses from first inklings to final realization, it should pass through successive phases of growth and clarification of structure, and of complication of detail in relation to that structure, becoming progressively more definite en route to its goal. Following the historian's bent for discerning genetic patterns, we suppose too that the relevant sources should articulate this progress, that they should ideally reveal a sequence passing from many and far-reaching revisions to fewer and less significant ones, affecting only minor details. In the case of Beethoven, a century-old tradition made up of a certain amount of close study and considerably more popularization of that study has led us not only to regard the progressive refinement of ideas as being his most basic and characteristic trait, but to look for evidence of it in the sketches, and to seek the final product in the autograph. The concluding stage should be the autograph as "fair copy" containing the work in final form, ready to be transmitted to the copyist or printer, with no further corrections required.

But a close look at even the handful of Beethoven autographs so far brought out in complete facsimile shows that they more often frustrate these expectations than fulfill them. The published autographs cover a wide range of contrasting stages of development along the complex paths that must have led to the realization of each work. They make it clear that for Beethoven the term "autograph" embraces no single or uniform concept. In order to come to grips with the composition process in its true dimensions for any given work—let alone the broader shaping forces and tendencies that may eventually be attributed uniquely to Beethoven—we shall have to find a way of determining as precisely as we can how a given autograph relates to the other formative elements in the genesis of a given work.[3] It seems particularly important to stress this for Beethoven, however obvious it may seem, because the vast mass of sketches, although still largely unknown, have attracted so much attention in the past that they have tended to overshadow the potential importance of the autographs as primary documents not only for text-critical and analytical problems but for the composition process as well.

Of the autographs published in facsimile so far, a majority are piano sonatas. They range over a wide area of Beethoven's career: Opp. 26, 27/2, 53, 57, 78, 109, 110, and 111.[4] The chronological span is particularly fortunate because the larger mass of Beethoven autographs of major works is not at all so well distributed: despite some notable exceptions, more autographs of late works are extant than of early ones. This is probably due in part to the changing function of the autograph as a working tool in the course of his career. In his early years, so far as we can tell, Beethoven seems not to have had a single professional copyist at his disposal; he employed them as he needed to, or was able to, and he must frequently have sent his own manuscript to his publisher to be used as *Stichvorlage* (engraver's copy). From what we know of the business habits of many of the publishers of the period, we should not be surprised that many manuscripts seem to have been lost. But in his middle years Beethoven began to use a professional copyist regularly, and from 1807 on (perhaps somewhat earlier) he came to have special preference for a Viennese named Schlemmer.[5] It became his practice to have his works copied by Schlemmer or another copyist, make his own corrections in the copy, and then send the corrected copy to the printer.

Beethoven's autographs were thus designed from the beginning to be read by eyes other than the composer's—a condition that distinguishes them sharply from the sketches—but they may also have had different potential recipients in the early and in the later periods. The early autographs must often have had to be read by engravers unknown to the composer, working far away and beyond hope of contact or control.[6] In later years, working with a dependable copyist close at hand, Beethoven should have been able to count on the copyist's being able to read his difficult handwriting—if the copyist could survive the necessary indoctrination—and when we find that his manuscripts contain highly complicated bundles of corrections, it is obvious that only a copyist well acquainted with his techniques of revision could solve them.[7] The Fifth Symphony autograph is a familiar example; despite a famous error in the Scherzo, it seems to have been well copied from the difficult autograph. As is well known, Beethoven's manuscripts give every sign of his strong feeling for maximum graphic economy and of his using every device that could save time and effort without sacrificing any of the powerful structural properties of his notation.[8] Thus he may well have found that by working with an efficient copyist, he could often solve a problem of revision by methods that now may seem baffling but that could be quickly explained to a copyist of reasonable intelligence. There is some indication that at times Beethoven preferred the copyist to come to work in his own home.[9]

If these assumptions are justified, they imply that for a composer as incessantly bent on revision of detail as Beethoven was, there may have been some works for which an autograph "fair copy" never came into existence at all. Indeed, a true specimen of a "fair copy" is a rare and remote exception among the known or published autographs. Of the latter, only Op. 78 can be characterized as belonging to this class, and it is worth observing that Beethoven's unusual pains in producing this *Reinschrift* might have arisen in part from the exceptional notational problems occasioned by the key of F-sharp major. All the other published facsimiles, and many more partially reproduced or described by various writers, show corrections of various types and degrees of significance. Some embody decidedly mixed stages of realization for different parts of the work in relation to the final version. In the earlier example from Op. 26 we saw an unusual double correction, partly revision and partly regression to "copying." The Op. 26 autograph also contains a number of changes more drastic than this one. For instance, the last eight measures of the Scherzo (mm. 60–67) are revised in the autograph, and the spacing shows that Beethoven revised these measures directly after having written them and before going on to the writing out of the Trio. But on the whole this autograph is a relatively clear and final version.[10] As for other autographs that have truly massive revisions more elaborate than this, I shall mention only one that I have had particular opportunity to study: the autograph of the first movement of the Violoncello Sonata in A Major, Op. 69.[11]

The Op. 69 autograph (see Fig. 2.4) begins with the serenity of a finished work but en route becomes a battlefield of conflicting ideas. It exemplifies a stage of writing at which the larger, well-defined sections of the movement are in manifestly different phases of development. The exposition and recapitulation are worked out in essentially their final form, despite many important alterations of phrases and details, and some discrepancies between apparently parallel passages in the two sections. But the manuscript is in a quite different state for the development section (mm. 95–151). Here the cancellations and revisions not only form a continuous chain of problems throughout the entire section, but they are densely packed into every available space on the page. From the tangled threads of these pages one can unravel two full-length versions of the entire development section, of which the second version (nearly equivalent to the final one) represents a total recasting and exchange of the roles of the violoncello and piano that had been set down in the first version. The second is superimposed upon the first. Yet although many details of register and some elements of figuration are reorganized, the general flow of harmonic, rhythmic, and motivic material in the development remains essentially the same in the two versions. The manuscript shows that when Beethoven came to the stage of writing down this "autograph" version of so richly complex a movement, he had not yet finally decided what the functional relationship of the two instruments would be throughout the entire middle section. Apparently, only when he had written down one version of the development in this autograph did he see how he really wanted the two instruments to be fitted together.

The corrections are so amply spread upon the middle pages of the manuscript that it is hard to imagine at first how even the most astute copyist could have plucked out the second version without excessive trouble, and for this section of the movement one may suppose that Beethoven might have had to prepare another version. But if he did there is presently no trace of it, nor of any other autograph version of the movement. We must remember too that the autograph was apparently set up from the beginning to be final: it contains the full title heading in Beethoven's hand, and even the opening indication of the instruments for each staff, however obvious. It also contains a number of cues and notational elements that seem to be understandable only as implied messages to a copyist. One of these is the use of letter names to clarify uncertain or corrected noteheads. Another is the addition of Beethoven's signature, "L v Bthwn," in the margin of the score, adjacent to a measure in the recapitulation in which he evidently wants to be sure that a dissonant *e* against *f* in the piano part will be understood as his true intention. It seems unlikely, to say the least, that he would have signed his name as a reminder to himself, or added it in a version that he expected to supersede with another complete *Reinschrift*.

Still another revealing passage in the Op. 69 manuscript is the handling of the second subject in the exposition and recapitulation. In the final version of the passage, the piano has an imitative descending prolongation of the local tonic triad (E major in the exposition, A major in recapitulation), moving from tonic to dominant over four measures and followed by a parallel phrase moving in the same way from dominant to tonic. The violoncello simultaneously rises through almost three octaves in purely linear motion, exploring the same extremes of range as the piano but in the opposite direction and by contrasting means of motion. But in the autograph, this version is not yet present at all. Instead we find an intermingling of two readings in the same measures, again one superimposed upon the other, and both of which bring the two hands of the piano in simultaneously descending motion in octaves, not in imitation. Extending above and below the piano staves for the duration of this passage, in both exposition and recapitulation, are wavy lines (in red pencil in the exposition, ink in the recapitulation), a sign that Beethoven often uses to mean "bleibt," that is, to restore a previously canceled reading. Here I take it to mean something else. For we find that in the sketchbook Beethoven was using at the time of concluding work on this Sonata (first offered to Breitkopf & Härtel in June of 1808, along with Opp. 67, 68, and 86), he wrote down exactly the material that is covered by the wavy lines: the piano part only, and only the second subject in its two appearances in final form, first in E major, then in A major. Having evidently decided to change the simultaneous octaves in the autograph version to a one-measure imitation between left hand and right hand, Beethoven apparently could find no clear way to indicate in the autograph itself what he wanted to keep and what should be deleted. So he wrote out the whole passage again in his current large sketchbook, on a blank page that lay open amid sketches for the Pastoral Symphony. I infer that the wavy lines are an indication to the copyist: they tell him to consult the sketchbook for the final readings. The writing of these two phrases in the sketchbook is clear and careful, rather different from the sketch hand that runs through its pages; it ensures that they can be read at once. As I have put it elsewhere, it does not seem to me merely ironic that what is in the sketchbook is the final reading that we would expect, according to common preconception, to find in an autograph, while what is in the "autograph" is, in effect, a series of sketches.[12]

That the variety of different types of evidence mentioned so far permits no simple conclusion about the nature of the "autograph" is for my purposes reassuring. It reinforces awareness of the mixture of contents we may expect to find in the manuscripts, and it supports the contention that to advance in further studies of the Beethoven composition process with any semblance of confidence, one of the major tasks will be to attempt to satisfy ourselves as to what stages of the realization of a given work are combined in a given autograph. Beyond this, the complex character of many autographs also suggests another line of study. Within certain limits, the long-familiar and superficially obvious distinction between "autograph" and "sketch" may begin to break down; or, in some cases, the relationship between the two categories may be most fruitfully understood not as one of antecedent elaboration to finished consequent, but as partially complementary and reciprocally useful areas of work serving different tasks of elaboration en route to a common objective. In other words, for certain compositions Beethoven may have proceeded not simply by first elaborating and refining his ideas in his sketchbooks and only then beginning his autograph, but may have worked more or less simultaneously at both, shuttling back and forth from one work area to the other as he sought to clarify and revise. It appears that in setting to work on some autograph scores, Beethoven was not only writing down practical, readable, and complete versions of finished works, but in some cases he was setting down a work at an earlier stage of realization, in the full notational scope that would make it possible for him to see on paper the relation of details to the whole, and thus to solve certain problems for which he could not yet envisage solutions through sketches alone. From this standpoint some material in the sketchbooks that may otherwise remain elliptical or even inexplicable may conceivably be clarified.

II

If it is hard enough to assign a precise meaning to the term "autograph" for Beethoven, it is still harder to do so for the term "sketch." Again, in a rough and ready sense we know what the term denotes, but when we look carefully at enough of the evidence, we find that this sense will barely do. In speaking of the "autograph" we can at least proceed from the premise that the written object is a complete and consecutive representation of a single composition, and that it is normally a discrete physical unit set apart from material belonging to other works. When it comes to the sketches, we can reaffirm the obvious by saying that as representations of given works they are never complete and rarely consecutive, and that they normally appear in sources combining material for more than one composition. Beyond this we can only rely on threading our way through the maze of ideas that we find in many of the sketchbooks, ranging from the fragmentary to the extended, but always in highly abbreviated notation.

Although only a small fraction of the contents of the known sketchbooks has become available even at this late date, Nottebohm's pioneering essays of a century ago and the handful of publications and studies since then have made their approximate character widely known—one might almost say too widely and certainly too approximately.[13] It is thus a matter of common knowledge that the sketchbooks record not only preliminary studies of a large number of finished works, but also additional matters of all kinds: jottings, themes, larger progressions of ideas, harmony and counterpoint exercises, copies of works by other composers, and all sorts of miscellanea. They also harbor occasional commonplace-book entries: street addresses, fragments of letters, and passing thoughts. What characterizes the main bulk of the musical material is the well-known difficulty of its orthography: the hand is rapid, small, unpredictably given to uneven spacings, often unarticulated by clefs or barlines, and above all frequently uncertain as to pitch and duration.[14]

If there is a familiar and by now widely shared impression about the sketchbooks, it is that they range from the difficult to the undecipherable. This assumption doubtless underlies a good deal of the neglect they have suffered. But despite the admitted problems of determining content and organization, some general distinctions have also been long familiar, and these point the way to more concrete problems of interpretation. The first is that the extant sketchbooks divide fairly clearly into two general types: large-sized sketchbooks written in ink for use at home, and pocket-sized sketch-booklets that Beethoven carried for use out of doors, usually written in pencil.[15] The majority of the extended, intelligible, carefully worked-out drafts of larger sections fall naturally into the first group, and in attempting to make preliminary sortings of these we shall have to separate them from other types. Following a distinction first suggested by Nottebohm, we can readily distinguish these broad categories: (1) variant versions of discrete motifs, phrases, or themes, consecutively or nonconsecutively ordered; and (2) continuity drafts[16] for entire sections, movements, or even entire compositions (in the latter case usually short compositions, such as songs). It goes without saying that many examples only approximate these categories, but the extremes should for the most part hold. Examples of the second category are familiar—the drafts for the first movement of the Second Symphony in the Landsberg 7 sketchbook and those for the first and second movements of the Pastoral Symphony in the Pastoral Symphony sketchbook.[17] As for the first category, consecutive variants of a basic theme are perhaps most familiar, and a sample is provided by the group, incomplete as it is, published by Nottebohm for the theme of the song *Sehnsucht,* WoO 146, from the sketchbook of 1815 owned by William Scheide.[18] The nonconsecutive category requires no examples.

We can also see that the variety of contents in the sketchbooks reflects a variety of purposes. In part the sketches reflect active creative work on definite compositions. In part they seem to be experimental, to represent the trial of ideas and possible combinations, perhaps apart from larger contexts. And in part they seem to reflect a lifelong impulse to deepen the well of memory by storing thoughts which might prove of value sooner or later, and which might be lost in other preoccupations unless put on paper—as Beethoven himself is said to have confessed to Gerhard von Breuning.[19] One of the most astonishing things about the sketchbooks is that we have them at all. That Beethoven kept them so carefully through all the vicissitudes and alleged confusion of his daily life and affairs in Vienna and all his moving from place to place suggests that in holding on to the growing mass of these volumes he was deliberately constructing the mirror of his own development.[20] He is perhaps the first major composer who, by keeping his sketchbooks so assiduously throughout his working life, made it possible for him to look back at any time over the details of his own development as reflected not only in the finished works but in their formative background.

The foregoing observations may prepare the ground for an excursion into other territory, based on what was suggested earlier about the possibly complementary relationship of sketch and autograph in some works. Again, we need to consider the problem apart from the familiar straitjacket of the usual terminology and the portrait of the subject established by Nottebohm. We are accustomed to seeing the sketches as being typically one-line drafts compressing material of upper and lower range into a single staff, sometimes shifting register without explicit change of clef. But there are many instances in the sketchbooks in which Beethoven expands the single staff to two and sometimes more staves, to make clear the relationship of upper line and bass or to work out a contrapuntal problem. Extended passages of this kind mark the point at which the sketchbook method begins to expand toward the role of rudimentary score. At times he must have required separate sketch sheets for just this purpose—the broadening of single-staff material into two- and three-staff versions. But there are limits to what can be expressed in any compression, above all within a sketchbook that was a unit from the beginning and had a limited number of pages. It was always possible in a sketchbook to work out the rudimentary score of portions of works for piano alone, or sonatas for piano and one instrument, or trios, or even a string quartet. But to incorporate into a sketchbook the full rudimentary score for an orchestral composition, requiring ten to thirteen staves on each page for many pages, ought to have been impossible on grounds of size and length alone. Had Beethoven wanted to fit in such a score, for some reason, it would have meant abandoning the typical spatial freedom and the diary character of the sketchbook—that is, giving up its function as a sketchbook. From this practical premise we can infer that rudimentary scores for orchestral compositions required him to use one or more separate fascicles from the beginning, no matter how early in the conceptual process the score was initiated.

From the few facsimiles and the very limited bibliographic information we have, it is hard to say how many examples of such rudimentary scores remain, but I should like to call attention to one that seems particularly revealing. It is the sixty-page score, completely autograph, of the projected first movement of a piano concerto in D major.[21] Beethoven worked on this movement in 1815, but after writing out this score and a number of sketches of different types he cast it permanently aside. Had it been finished it would have been not only his sixth piano concerto, but the last of all his concertos. Its failure to come to realization undoubtedly signals a sharp break in Beethoven's development at this time. The autograph contains the exposition and development section but breaks off just after the beginning of the recapitulation. In the stage represented by this score, the basic material of the exposition is continuous but in the process of alteration, while that of the development is often in doubt even as to its basic continuity. The main point is that everything is laid out here in full orchestral score considerably before the full flow of events is complete or conclusive in many significant aspects. The movement begins firmly and securely; it then gives way to a patchwork of cancellations, insertions, corrections, and rescorings. In several places barlines are drawn through the page, but the main text is left entirely blank. This suggests that Beethoven did not simply work on the movement by progressing steadily forward, but moved back and forth from one segment to another, no doubt as solutions to particular problems gripped his attention.[22]

Since I can only offer here an abbreviated summary of a complicated problem, I should like to stress two particular points about the autograph of this movement. The first is that this rudimentary score not only represents a stage of composition very close in conception to what we have traditionally thought of as the "sketch stage," but is actually more primitive in portions of its musical content than some of the sketches for the work that we find in other sources. This strongly reaffirms the idea that the score was begun very early, to give scope and space for the working out of details, and it suggests that some of the sketches in compressed form may represent more complex phases of realization of certain motifs and themes that were made later than the version we find in the score, that is, after the score version had been broken off.

The second point concerns Beethoven's method of laying out the score but also has implications for the composition process. The manuscript contains another element of continuity aside from the score itself: a small but legible "cue-staff" (as I am provisionally calling it) that runs through almost the entire manuscript at the bottom of each page, below the full orchestral score. It begins on p. 6 of this sixty-page score—that is, just after the opening subject has been introduced and the first orchestral tutti is beginning—and runs intermittently to p. 12; then it runs continuously from p. 12 to p. 53 (the end of the development section), breaking off at the sketch for a main cadenza by the solo piano. Since the score occupies thirteen staves on each page of sixteen-staff oblong paper, it was a built-in condition from the outset that there would always be three staves blank at the bottom of each page. On first glance, this "cue-staff" looks as if it might be a line of jotted revisions of the complicated orchestral material that has been put down on the only available space on the page. But it is soon clear from the format and content of the "cue-staff" that it cannot be a chain of corrections, because it rarely reflects the numerous cancellations and changes of its material that are given above in the score. This makes it look as if it had been entered earlier. Indeed, from several pages of the manuscript we can tell that the "cue-staff" could not have been inserted after the instrumental material above, but must have been put in first. This is discernible in several pages of the development, most tellingly on one page (p. 49 of the manuscript) that comes just at the point of connection between the end of the exposition and the beginning of the development. This passage effectively brought Beethoven to the end of the track for this version of the movement, although he pushed mechanically on a little way into the recapitulation. On p. 49 we find the barlines drawn freehand through the page for six measures, but no music whatever except the "cue-staff" across the bottom of the page. Further, the notes of the "cue-staff," here and on virtually every page, correspond to those of each measure above it, presenting the leading voice of the material at any given moment; and each group of notes in the "cue-staff" is grouped in such a way that they fit fairly centrally into each measure. This suggests how the score was set up: first Beethoven drew the barlines; then he filled out the "cue-staff" at the bottom, perhaps for only a few pages at a time, perhaps for much more; then, using the "cue-staff" as a guide, he distributed his material into the upper orchestral staves. In short, the organization of the score proceeded from the bottom of each page upward into the orchestral fabric—from the "cue-staff" to the instrumentation of its content.

Thus the function of the "cue-staff" seems in part to have been a practical one: to serve as an aid to the composer's eye in the physical process of laying out a score. But it also seems important to stress that the score being laid out was being assembled not only physically, but also intellectually—that the "cue-staff" furnished a readily available and conveniently visible abbreviation of the basic material, and one that gave scope for second and further thoughts about the elaboration of its ideas into the orchestral fabric. In its format, content, and certain details of notation, the "cue-staff" in this score is identical to the linear sketches with which we are familiar from many sketchbooks. In effect, the "cue-staff" is a sketch-line that has been transferred from sketchbook to rudimentary score. It looks like a kind of "missing link" between the two types of sources and, consequently, between the two types of work areas. The "cue-staff" uses some figured bass numerals; here and there it expands to two staves to encompass upper line and bass, and to three and more to encompass its own corrections. In all these aspects it resembles the typical sketchbook line. Near the end of the development, where the whole movement was breaking down, Beethoven in fact abandoned the scoring process altogether and devoted himself to elaboration upon the "cue-staff" in several versions, using for this purpose the lower six staves of the page; here a new continuation is labeled "meilleur," again a typical sketchbook entry.

Without attempting to base sweeping conclusions upon this example— above all one that Beethoven abandoned—I would point out nevertheless that the evidence offered by this score is not unique among the known orchestral autographs. The few that have become visible so far provide some corroboration and suggest directions for further research. Among other autographs containing similar marginal jottings that may have compositional significance I can mention three, all obviously finished works: the Violin Concerto, the Scherzo of the Fifth Symphony, and the Kyrie of the *Missa Solemnis*. The unusual organization of the autograph of the Violin Concerto results, of course, from the special problem of the variant versions of the work as a concerto for violin or for piano. In an admirable study of the text of the concerto, Alan Tyson observed the sporadic use of the lowest staff in the first and last movements of the autograph version for jottings that resemble, in purpose, what I am calling a "cue-staff."[23] The autograph of the Fifth Symphony, long available in facsimile, shows a similar use of the lowest staff, beginning at the fugato in the Scherzo, where the contrapuntal scheme seems to have caused special difficulties at the autograph stage. Brief passages in other movements of the symphony had required occasional use of the lowest staff of the autograph for local jottings, but only the fugato of the Scherzo contains the consistent use of the "cue-staff" as a kind of sketch-area throughout the section, expanding to two and three staves as entrances pile up in the contrapuntal web. The further relationship of the Fifth Symphony autograph to the surviving sketches, which are known to include a *Partitur-Skizze* (score-sketch) for the Scherzo, remains at present an open question.

Still another recent facsimile presents an even more striking case, this time from the last period: the Kyrie of the *Missa Solemnis*.[24] Here we can detect a type of "cue-staff" at the bottom of the score in Kyrie I and II, but not in the Christe. Its presence or absence coincides with the variations in appearance of these sections with regard to autograph corrections. The material of the two Kyrie sections (of course, the material of Kyrie II partly recapitulates material of Kyrie I) was evidently in a far less conclusive stage than that of the Christe at the time of writing out the score. The distinction is visible in both large-scale changes and in more refined features of the notation. In Kyrie I we can see evidence of a drastic process of revision, involving many kinds of changes: the deletion of entire leaves, the crossing out and cancellation of the entire content of pages that remain; the addition of measures to a page that had already been completed in an earlier version; and the numerous alterations of detail. The "cue-staff" runs through the entire Kyrie I and II, and, again characteristically, it presents the main thread of the principal material for the movement. There is some evidence to suggest that it was among the first elements entered into the score, perhaps the very first. It goes without saying that even the most elementary problems in the genesis of this work have barely been touched as yet, let alone thoroughly examined in terms of the relationship of one part of the autograph to another, or of either to the sketches. But the autograph alone is suggestive, and the continuity and prominence of the "cue-staff" are fully apparent.[25]

If the course of further study were to show that the procedures partially visible in these works can reasonably be interpreted in relation to their sketches as forming a complementary process anything like that of the unfinished concerto of 1815, one may speculate on the possibility of establishing an outline portrait of certain aspects of Beethoven's composition procedures over a vast portion of his development—the evidence at hand alone runs from about 1805 to 1820. At the same time, it is clear enough that merely to pose this possibility is to be reminded how far we are at present from being able to realize it, and how sorely the entire field—for Beethoven, but not only for Beethoven—requires a broadening of availability of source materials, and strengthening of concepts with which to interpret them. Eventually, one hopes, much more source material will become accessible in usable form. As it does, the problems of evaluation will inevitably become even more complex than they are now. But it would not be surprising to find that one of the most fruitful dimensions of such study may lie precisely in the interrelations between sketches and autographs, and that the "cue-staff" to which I have referred as a factor in several autographs may form one of the bridges that connect them. It seems reasonable to think, however, even as matters stand, that the more we are able to see the autographs and sketches not as independent objects but as partial and detached segments of larger wholes, as symptoms of processes whose goals were not the writing of manuscripts but the making of compositions, the more likely it is that we will be able to apprehend their content at its true level of significance.[26]

TWO

The Autograph of the First Movement of the Sonata for Violoncello and Pianoforte, Opus 69

Remarkably few of the primary manuscript sources of Beethoven's works have been made accessible in reproduction, despite their acknowledged importance. Valued deeply and universally as artistic possessions, the Beethoven autographs have been coveted, hoarded, revered—and at times dismembered—but rarely published in the complete facsimile editions that would stimulate close study of their contents. It is true that a fair number of single pages are distributed widely through a thicket of Beethoven publications. But the entire group of complete manuscripts produced to date consists of eleven works: eight piano sonatas (Opp. 26, 27/2, 53, 57, 78, 109, 110, and 111); two symphonies (the Fifth and the Ninth); and the Kyrie of the Missa Solemnis.[1]

For the sketches the situation is roughly comparable: apart from single leaves, three complete sketchbooks have so far been issued in full facsimile.[2] Yet even if these sketchbook publications have attracted less attention than they deserve, they nevertheless reinforce awareness of the great potential importance of their musical material, and a program for their publication is in the course of realization. But outside of circles of specialists, the comparable documentary importance of the autographs has remained obscure and largely unsuspected, not only because of the absence of publications but because of the widespread and mistaken assumption that their contents probably represented the "finished" versions as supposedly translated into the "official" versions of the nineteenth-century Gesamtausgabe.[3]

The reproduction here of the entire extant autograph of the first movement of the Sonata for Violoncello and Piano in A Major, Op. 69, adds an important Beethoven work for chamber ensemble to the small circle of published autographs.[4]

The Autograph and Related Sources

Before proceeding to a description of the manuscript and the sources related to it, I should say a word about terms. "Autograph" is inevitably the basic term of this discussion. While everyone knows the commonsense meaning of the term, and while there is no reason to doubt that the musical document reproduced here is the only known source that corresponds to that meaning, there is good reason to recognize that the term in its customary usage is loose and somewhat ambiguous, at least for Beethoven's works.[5] The typical function of the term is as an abbreviated designation (and that is its use here) for what might be termed "the last finished version of a work written down by its author"—the *Fassung letzter Hand*. But the conveniences of terminology should not obscure the complexities lurking in the concept framed by the words "last finished"; and for complexities of this kind, the material associated with Op. 69 forms a masterly example.

The earlier history of the manuscript is not fully documented, but in its essential outline it is clear enough. According to Kinsky-Halm, its first owner after 1827 was the publisher Domenico Artaria,[6] but whether the manuscript as Artaria knew it consisted of the entire sonata or only the first movement we do not know. By the end of the century, at all events, the separate existence of the first-movement autograph is an established fact, as is its change of owner. While the bulk of the Artaria collection of Beethoven manuscripts eventually passed to the Berlin Library, this manuscript became the property of Heinrich Steger of Vienna, an enthusiastic collector of Beethoven treasures.[7] Steger exhibited the first-movement autograph at an international exposition on music and theater that was held in Vienna in 1892, and the manuscript probably remained in his possession until the dispersal of his holdings between 1904 and 1907. At about this time it evidently passed to the Wittgenstein family of Vienna,[8] from whom in turn it came into the possession of Felix Salzer. Neither internal nor external evidence gives any clue to the earlier fate of the corresponding autograph leaves for the Scherzo, Adagio, and Finale of the sonata, nor is anything known of their present location.

The manuscript as it exists is a complete musical and physical unit. Unless the first movement could possibly have been set into score before the other movements were ready for that stage, this manuscript should have formed part of a larger unified manuscript containing the entire sonata at about its own stage of development. But it shows no sign of separation. The entire first movement is fitted onto the nine leaves preserved here, with the last measures of the movement occupying most of the last available page (9v) and leaving only part of its last system vacant. In their physical features the leaves are wholly uniform, in contrast to some Beethoven autographs. They are organized as two four-page gatherings, with an additional leaf glued carefully to the last page of the second gathering to form folio 9r-v. (See Appendix I for a tabulation of the physical characteristics of the manuscript.) It is possible, but not demonstrable, that the added leaf at the end of the second gathering was originally the first member of another binary gathering, and that the putative folio 10 could have begun the Scherzo. All we can tell from the available evidence is that Beethoven worked here with one gathering at a time: first he filled out the first gathering in direct sequence, then continued directly on the second, then either cut folio 9 from an original bifolium to finish the movement, or used the whole bifolium and left it to pious posterity to cut the present folio 9 away.

In setting up the score of this composition on the page, Beethoven's choice of format was no doubt determined in part by obvious notational conventions, but in part too by the size and type of paper on which he was working. And the selection of paper, here and elsewhere, does not seem to have been entirely haphazard. Among the preserved autographs, oblong paper of the type used here is by far more common than tall, narrow paper, especially in chamber music.[9] Even with regard to the choice of number of staves, Beethoven's decisions in the autographs do not appear to have been as unsystematic as the legends and traditions would lead us to suppose. Our view of the situation may be somewhat colored by the unequal survival of sources from all periods: from the early years, when he was making his way as a composer and tended to publish from his own manuscripts, we have few complete autographs; from the middle and later periods, when he was a celebrated artist, we have a great many.

What we have shows some tendency to associate types of paper not merely with the spatial requirements of particular works but with categories. For piano compositions Beethoven evidently preferred oblong eight-staff autographs, in which each page is entirely filled out by four two-staff systems of music, with no intervening staves left blank. The published facsimiles of Opp. 26, 27/2, 78, 109, 110, and 111 all show this arrangement, the use of which compelled Beethoven to extreme solutions when he found that he had to make corrections after all. But in the *Appassionata* autograph, on the other hand, he used the twelve-staff oblong format with intervening blank staves between systems. The difference in relative clarity of the corrections is obvious at a glance. The oblong twelve- or sixteen-staff type is also the one favored strongly for the quartets, orchestral works, and compositions for pianoforte with single instrument, the latter requiring three-staff systems, as here. By choosing this type of paper for a three-staff score, Beethoven was able to set up either three or four such systems on each page, thus assigning to each page-unit a substantial quantity of musical content that could be perceived as a single visual field, and also permitting him to leave a blank staff below each system throughout the manuscript. The blank staff not only helps to clarify the note-field by separating the systems but provides useful and at times essential space for corrections to be made en route. The central folios of the Op. 69 autograph make evident the practical advantages of this format.

It is quite obvious that this manuscript is very far from being a fair copy, but determining the bearing of its various segments on the final form of the movement is more difficult than it might appear. The first page of the manuscript looks deceptively like that of a final version in fair copy, with its bold and well-spaced strokes free of disfiguring erasures or cancellations. But as one progresses through the following pages of the exposition, the signs of recasting begin to spread and multiply. In the area of the development (folios 4r–5v), they become a dense tangle of changes and revisions involving compositional reconstruction on a massive scale; then in the recapitulation and coda they subside again to relative clarity.

The unequal relationship of the various sections of the manuscript to the final version in itself undermines the simple conceptual distinction conveyed by the handy terms "sketch" and "autograph." While some parts of the score are sufficiently clear and final to imply that they could have been copied intact from an earlier source, others exhibit in full force the procedures of reconstruction typical of far less conclusive stages of composition.[10] In many passages, two or more stages of decision are superimposed one upon another, so that these are at once the equivalent of one or more "sketches" plus, in some instances, a "final" version, all on the same page and even, at times, in the same measure. It may begin to appear, even in advance of the specific evidence to be considered, that "sketch" and "autograph" are broad generic categories at best, and that they cannot be stretched too far. Like many other terms in the professional vocabulary, their value is simply that of abbreviated designations by which we can reduce to manageable simplicity some of the more ramified complexities inherent in the continuum of evidence, evidence in this case of a process of composition and of reconceiving musical structure that must have been in some significant sense a continuous and unbroken line of development.

Despite these reservations, however, something fairly definite can still be said, namely that the version represented by this manuscript can be described as "advanced" for the exposition and recapitulation (though these, too, are not entirely parallel) and "less advanced" for the development. But the central characteristic of this entire version is that it constitutes for the whole movement that phase of realization at which Beethoven felt himself ready to commit the work to paper in its entirety in a fully consecutive score and in all details, while doubtless also realizing as he was doing so that he would still have many vital changes to make. It is this characteristic that makes the manuscript the best approximation we have of what we usually mean by the "autograph," and that helps us to assign the manuscript its appropriate place among the sources that bear directly on the origins of the sonata. Since these include not only musical manuscripts but early printed editions and even letters, it will be best to proceed by supplying here a brief catalogue of the known primary sources.

Manuscript Scores

Source A. The present manuscript (the autograph score of the first movement, to be referred to hereafter as the "Salzer autograph").[11]

Source B. A contemporary manuscript copy of the sonata reported to contain corrections, title, and dedication (to Baron von Gleichenstein) in Beethoven's hand, sometimes called the "Clauss copy."

This copy was apparently the printer's source for the first edition of the sonata, and was given to Breitkopf and Härtel in 1808. Nottebohm in 1868 described the manuscript and listed it as being in the possession of Consul Otto Clauss of Leipzig.[12] But Kinsky-Halm reported no information about it beyond Nottebohm's reference.[13] The loss of this copy is especially severe since it evidently represented the next stage of composition—presumably the only one—beyond the autograph but before the first edition, and it may well have been made by Beethoven's copyist working directly from the Salzer autograph.[14]

Related Manuscripts, Including Sketches

Source C. London, British Museum Add. 31766, folio 31v (see Figure 2.1).

An isolated entry for Op. 69 in the large sketchbook devoted mainly to Op. 68 and Op. 70, Nos. 1 and 2, which has been published in transcription by Dagmar Weise.[15] The entry is for Op. 69, first movement, piano part only, mm. 37–45 and 174–182 (beginning of the "second group" in the exposition and recapitulation), and it differs from all other manuscript entries listed in this section in several respects. It is an isolated portion of Op. 69 in a larger sketchbook devoted to other works. It is not a sketch but is really a part of the same phase of writing represented by the Salzer autograph, and is even in a sense beyond it; beyond doubt, it relates to the Salzer autograph in the most direct way, as will be seen. It is written in the calligraphic hand normally used for fair copies, not in the rapid hand familiar from the sketches. Its connection to the autograph stage—though not to the Salzer autograph in its particulars—was first noticed by Nottebohm: "Doubtless these passages were written during the preparation of the fair copy."[16] For a preliminary view of the "fair copy," see the relevant passages on folios 2r and 6v of this autograph.

Figure 2.1   Folio 31v of sketchbook (source *C*)

Source D.   Vienna, Gesellschaft der Musikfreunde, Sketches for Op. 69, MS 59.

One leaf containing sketches for Op. 69, first movement, was described and published in part by Nottebohm.[17] He describes the Op. 69 sketch as forming part of a "set of sketches made up of four gatherings that belong together . . . 16 pages." He further describes its contents: one page of sketches for the Fifth Symphony, Scherzo (page 66); then twelve pages of sketches for the Leonore Overture, No. 1; then a sketch for Op. 69, first movement. He concludes: "From the order and character of the sketches mentioned and transcribed here, it appears that the Overture Op. 138 was begun when the C-Minor Symphony was fairly close to completion, and that when it was substantially finished in sketch form, the Sonata Op. 69 was still in an early stage of its conception." This remains to be verified by much further research.

Source E.   Bonn, Beethoven-Archiv, MS Bodmer Mh 76.[18]

Three folios, oblong twelve-staff format, in ink throughout except page 5 (ink and pencil). Page 4 is blank. How much of the material in these pages is actually related to Op. 69 is open to question. Max Unger describes the contents briefly as follows: folios 1 and 2: Op. 69, first movement, and "Nur wer die Sehnsucht kennt" (second version); folio 3: Op. 69, second movement.[19]

But prior to Unger's description, an auction catalogue of K. Henrici had listed and described two of the same three folios. The correspondence of pages is as follows: Henrici, pages 1–2 = Bodmer Mh 76, folio 1r–v; Henrici, pages 3–4 = Bodmer Mh 76, folio 3r–v. The correspondence is clear not only from the written description but from a facsimile of "page 1" (Bodmer folio 1r) in the catalogue. It thus appears that the center folio (2r–v) was restored to the manuscript after 1928, presumably while it was part of the Bodmer collection. Henrici's catalogue had described the contents in this way: pages 1–2: sketches for string trio; page 3: blank; page 4: sketch for Op. 69, second movement (differs from published version).[20]

Although Unger's catalogue of the Bodmer collection is one of the most painstaking products of a great authority on Beethoven manuscripts, I find after close study and transcription of the opening leaves that I am more inclined to agree with the Henrici description than with Unger's. Although folios 1r and 2r are laid out in three-staff systems like those of a sonata for piano and solo instrument, I am not able to associate any of their material directly with Op. 69, and agree that their linear content and figuration patterns suggest interpretation as a string trio sketch. Here is a provisional view of the contents: folios 1r, 1v, 2r: sketches for an unidentified string trio (?) in A major (almost all on three-staff systems, no clefs); folio 2v, staves 1–6: sketch for Op. 69, first movement; folio 2v, staff 7: entry for WoO 134, second version;[21] folio 3v, staves 1–7: sketch for Op. 69, second movement, with trio sketch wholly different from the final trio; folio 3v, staves 9–12: pencil sketches, almost illegible.

Source F.   Bonn, Beethoven-Archiv, MS BSk 57.

One folio (2 pages), oblong twelve-staff format, ink. Folio 1r: sketches (mainly single staff) for Op. 69, first movement. Folio 1v: sketch entries, apparently for Op. 69, third movement (Adagio) at an early stage of composition. Other jottings on folio 1v perhaps for other works as yet unidentified.

Source G.   Paris, Bibliothèque du Conservatoire (on deposit at the Bibliothèque Nationale), Beethoven MS 45.

Two folios, oblong sixteen-staff format, with all four pages containing sketches in ink. Folio 1r: sketches for Fifth Symphony Scherzo (mainly on single staff). Folios 1v–2v: composition sketch for Op. 69, first movement, mainly on three-staff systems, and largely following the outline of the entire exposition of the movement.[22]

Source H. Copenhagen, Library of the Royal Danish Conservatory of Music (no signature).

Two folios (four pages), oblong twelve-staff format, ink. Folio 1r: no music; at lower right-hand corner is a note showing the presentation of the sketches by Niels W. Gade to the Danish composer J. P. E. Hartmann, with the date "14 Mai 1878." Folios 1v–2r: three-staff sketches containing material in the same format and closely related in content to the first pages (folios 1r–2v) of the Bodmer Mh 76 sketches (source *E*). Quite possibly these Copenhagen pages originally belonged together with Bodmer Mh 76 as part of a larger gathering. Both sketches are interpretable as part of a string trio, using here some of the material finally developed in Op. 69, first movement. Folio 2v: abandons the three-staff systems of the preceding pages and contains single-staff sketch jottings relating to the opening motive of Op. 69, first movement.

Source I. Berlin, Deutsche Staatsbibliothek, MS Landsberg 10, pp. 47–51.

Five pages of sketches for Op. 69, Scherzo and Finale only, not the first movement. Partially described by Nottebohm.[23] This "sketchbook" is actually a mixture of originally separate pages and gatherings from different periods and originally different sources. Its contents range from c. 1805 to c. 1817, some pages having originally formed part of the sketchbook in the British Museum, Add. 31766 (see source *C*).

Earliest Editions

Source J. Grande Sonate / pour Pianoforte et Violoncelle / . . . Oeuv. 59 [sic] . . . Chez Breitkopf & Härtel / à Leipsic. Plate No. 1328.[24]

Source K. Grande Sonate / pour Pianoforte et Violoncelle / . . . Oeuv. 69 / Chez Breitkopf et Härtel / à Leipsic.[25]

Source L. Sonata / per il / Clavicembalo con Violoncello / . . . (Op. 59) [sic] a Vienna / presso Artaria e Comp / No. 2060 . . .[26]

Letters on the Text of Opus 69[27]

Source M. Letter to Breitkopf and Härtel of July 26, 1809 (Anderson No. 220).

For original text, see Appendix II.

Source N. Letter and misprint list for Op. 69, sent to Breitkopf and Härtel c. August 1, 1809; received August 11 (Anderson No. 221). See facsimile published here as Figures 2.2 and 2.3, and Appendix II.

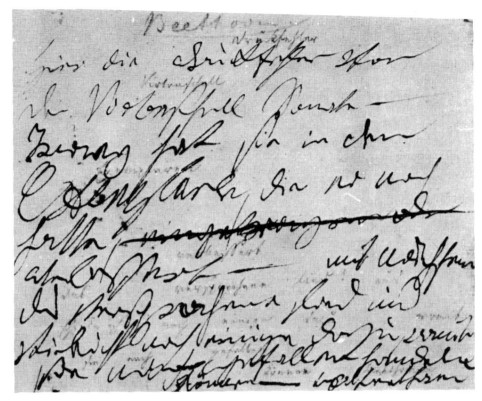

Figure 2.2 Letter, August 1, 1809 (source *N*)

Source O. Letter to Breitkopf and Härtel of August 3, 1809 (Anderson No. 223).

See Appendix II.

Although one of these sources, *A,* is incomplete and another, *B,* is missing, this list nevertheless includes the entire known body of primary sources for the sonata. For an exhaustive study of the early history of the work, the whole network of materials would have to be taken into account, but for more limited aspects of study the significance of particular sources will vary a good deal. Thus, to establish a definitive controlled text for the sonata (and strange as it may seem, no fully accurate edition has yet been published!), the sketches (sources *D* through *I*) are likely to be less essential than the other sources. While this commentary ought to contribute to establishing a final text for the work, it is not thought of as supplanting the detailed text-critical notes that will eventually have to accompany an authoritative edition, and not all textual problems are raised for discussion here. Rather, the primary focus of this

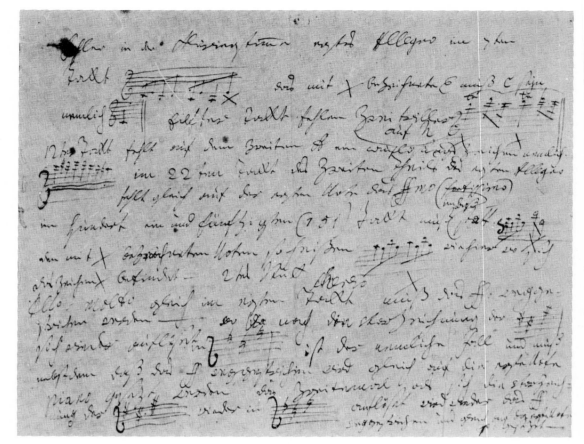

Figure 2.3a   Misprint list (source *N*)

study is upon the Salzer autograph itself. The following discussion will attempt to determine something of its genetic and musical significance and to shed light on it from both earlier and later sources.

Perhaps the easiest way to sort the material initially is to divide it along categorical and apparent chronological lines, with sketches and isolated entries on one side and manuscript scores and early editions on the other. Whatever shortcomings this classification may have, it offers the convenience of distinguishing the first fully consecutive score (the Salzer autograph) from earlier drafts (whether single-staff sketches or rudimentary scores) and from later and more nearly final versions. To simplify the discussion, the network of provisionally assumed connections among the sources is brought together in Table 2.1.

Tacitly assumed in the left column of the table is that the single-staff

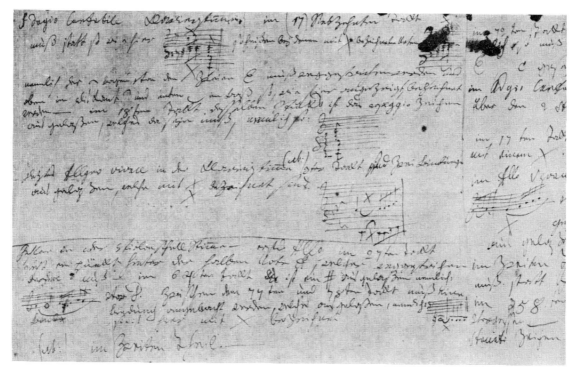

Figure 2.3b   Misprint list *(continued)*

sketches *F* and *D* represent the earliest extant versions of the material, a view based more on their musical content than on consideration of their single-staff format, though both must be taken into account. Between these sketches and that of source *G,* I put sources *E* (or a part of it) and *H,* which are so closely connected in content that they may well have originally formed a single sheaf of sketches, and whose contents suggest an intermediate phase. That sketch *G* is a decidedly more advanced stage is evident not only from the internal character of its material but from its provision of a consecutive "composition sketch" for the whole of the exposition. Since the later sketches listed on the left side of the table either contain material for the Scherzo or the Finale, or are not really interpretable as pre-autograph sketches, I infer a plausible line of derivation from *G* to *A*—in short, from a rudimentary three-staff score to the developed score that has reached what we instinctively call the "autograph" stage. The musical implications of this inferred connection will be taken up later.

In the right-hand column of the table, the consecutive ordering of sources and their implied derivations are more easily confirmed by external evidence. I assume that source *B*—the lost Clauss copy—was made for Beethoven by a

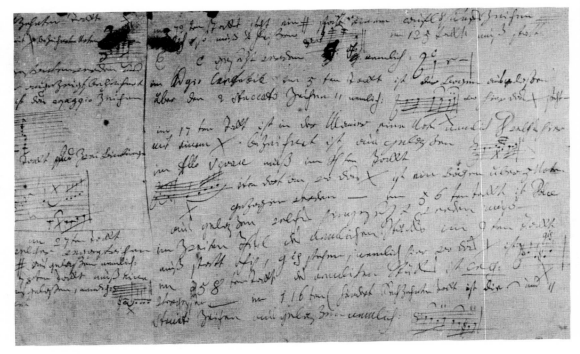

Figure 2.3c Misprint list (*continued*)

professional copyist, presumably his long-time favorite, Schlemmer,[28] and that it could have been made directly from source *A*. Difficult as such a task may now seem, there is evidence from other autographs copied by Schlemmer that he could pick his way through apparently trackless passages in Beethoven's autographs with astonishing skill; the Fifth Symphony is a convincing case. The step from copy *B* to the first Breitkopf and Härtel edition, source *J*, is supported by inferences from the correspondence on Op. 69, and the step from *J* in turn to the later editions and to Beethoven's highly revealing letters and misprint list is once again a chain of inferences from fairly unambiguous evidence.

Perhaps more puzzling are the crossing lines of connection suggested in the table for these pairs: sources *A–C, C–B,* and *E* (folio 2v)–*B*. The special character of the single entry in *C* has been mentioned already and will be further developed; it supports not merely a link in material but chronological coincidence between them. As for *E*, I assume that only a portion of its contents coincides with the autograph phase represented by *A*, and this portion would appear to mesh with certain problems of reconstruction in the middle section of the movement at the autograph stage.

Of the period over which the preparatory sketches extend, little can be said

Table 2.1. Relationship of sources for Opus 69: A provisional stemma

Sketches and isolated entries
in sketchbook sources

```
1807–1808          F        1st movement

                   D        1st movement

Perhaps          ⎧ E   3v   1st movement
originally       ⎨
united           ⎩ H        1st movement

                   G ———    1st movement          Complete MSS and other primary
                                                  sources
                   I        2d and 4th movements  → A   Salzer autograph
                                                        |
1808               C   31v  ————————————————      → B   Clauss copy
                                   1st movement          |
                   E   2v   ————————————————      →     J    B & H 1st ed. (April 1809)
                                                        |
                                                        L    Artaria, 1st Vienna ed. (per-
                                                             haps also April 1809)
                                                        M    Letter (July 26, 1809)
                                                        |
                                                        N    Letter and Misprint List
                                                        |         (c. August 1, 1809)
                                                        O    Letter (August 3, 1809)

                                                  →     K    B & H 2nd ed. (1809)
```

Note: A dotted line indicates possible chronological order; a continuous line indicates definite chronological order and possible derivation.

in the current state of knowledge. There have been adventurous guesses, but none of these sketches can really be dated with close precision. The account in Thayer-Deiters-Riemann, based on Nottebohm, included the assertion that the sonata was sketched "years before its completion" [29] and was taken up and finished quickly in 1808 as a means of compensating Beethoven's close friend, Ignaz von Gleichenstein, for the failure to dedicate the Fourth Piano Concerto to him, as Beethoven had originally intended to do. [30]

Minimally reasonable inference from the evidence permits us to say this much. The sonata was probably nearly finished—perhaps entirely finished—when Beethoven offered it for the first time to Breitkopf and Härtel on June 8, 1808, along with Opp. 67, 68, and 86 (Anderson No. 167). About four weeks later, Beethoven reaffirmed the offer; the negotiations culminated in a contract dated September 14, 1808 (Anderson, p. 1427), and in publication of the sonata in April of 1809. But even though there is no evidence to support Thayer's reference to sketches "years earlier," the physical association of the Op. 69 sketches with sketches for other works of 1807–08 makes it reasonable to assume that the sonata took considerable time to germinate, and that the likely period of its composition is "middle of 1807 to the middle of 1808." Nottebohm, in an earlier essay, remarked in his usual cryptic manner that Op. 69 was finished by "January, 1808" but gave no reasons; yet in his *Zweite Beethoveniana* essay on the "Pastoral Symphony" sketchbook, he simply dated the sonata as "first half of 1808." [31] Of long-range importance is the association of work on Op. 69 with sketches for the Fifth and Sixth Symphonies, the Leonore Overture, No. 1, and the second setting of *Sehnsucht,* WoO 134. But only when the long-awaited and urgently needed comprehensive publication of the sketches is considerably further advanced will we be able to clarify the apparent signs of cross-fertilization with the other major projects of 1807 and 1808.

As for the entire larger conception of this sonata, it is worth reflecting on it from another point of view. That it occupies a principal and even central place in the literature of larger works for violoncello and piano is by now an established and familiar critical commonplace. What is less obvious is the absence of a clear-cut and relevant tradition of works for this combination that Beethoven could possibly have known or recollected—even to dismiss—in approaching the composition of this work. The definitive model provided by the Mozart violin sonatas had no contemporary counterpart for the violoncello, and the older Italian tradition, culminating in Boccherini, scarcely seems relevant. The somewhat surprising fact is that Beethoven's own first sonatas— the two of 1796, Op. 5, Nos. 1 and 2, apparently written on the occasion of his trip to Berlin for performance by Jean Louis Duport and himself—are actually the first sonatas for violoncello and piano by a first-rank composer of the period. And in the light of the preponderant importance of the piano in both these works, the solutions found in Op. 69 for the problems of range, relative sonority, and matching of importance of the two instruments in the entire texture emerge as an achievement equal to that inherent in the originality and quality of its purely musical ideas. It should not be surprising in this sense to discover in the autograph that matters of range, register, and balance play a primary role throughout the complex revisions of its material, and it is not surprising either that these should dominate in a work in which the problem of establishing an adequate balance of function between these two instruments is faced for the first time by a major composer in a major work.

The Autograph and Final Text

Although the primary focus of this study is on the autograph itself (see Figure 2.4 at the end of this chapter), some consideration of its bearing on the final text of the sonata is not only appropriate but, in the actual state of that text in current editions, essential. Even a casual glance at the facsimile should dispel the fantasy that all one need do to establish a true reading is to "look at the autograph"; yet even when all the relevant evidence is considered, the problem of determining a fully authoritative text for the first movement will be extremely difficult. And in this instance the evidence is comprehensive enough to make the traditional and almost continuous mishandling of the text of the sonata even less excusable than it is in more obscure cases.

As is well known, once Beethoven began to use a professional copyist for the preparation of his works, it was his habit to make corrections in the copyist's version and submit it to the publisher for engraving. While this is not the place to do more than mention the intricacies of his relationships with his many publishers, the evidence at hand reinforces his profound concern over establishing the best possible versions of his works in print. Repeatedly and emphatically, in his correspondence with Breitkopf and Härtel and with other publishers, he insisted that they exhibit the courtesy and common sense to send him a preliminary proof of a new piece together with their working manuscript before making an entire press run, so that he could make needed corrections in time.[32] Despite the obvious advantages of this proposal, greed or laziness on the part of the publishers guaranteed that it should virtually never be carried out, with the consequence that much of Beethoven's correspondence with his publishers reflects his well-known and entirely justified exasperation over their incompetence.[33] More than once, on finally receiving first copies of newly printed works, he set to work at once to proofread them with great care, and on several occasions he sent the publisher a list of needed corrections to be entered in remaining copies or in subsequent runs.[34] At times he proposed to publish such lists separately for the benefit of the purchasing public, but in fact he never did. Since the publishers seem in general to have been no more attentive to the insertion of corrections than they had been to avoid errors in the first place, vivid blunders abounded in many earlier and later editions of his works,[35] and a great many were uncritically taken over into the Breitkopf and Härtel Gesamtausgabe and later editions.

For Op. 69, it is safe to assume that the copy from which the engraver worked was the Clauss copy, with Beethoven's added corrections, and that he delivered it to Breitkopf and Härtel's agent in Vienna for transmission to Leipzig not later than September of 1808, when the publication contract was signed. Letters of January, February, and March of 1809 indicate that the sonata had not yet been published.[36] After it did come out, in April, Beethoven seems not to have noticed the state of its text until three months later, when it was pointed out, he says, by a friend. Notable too is that in his first letter mentioning the text of Op. 69 (letter to Breitkopf and Härtel of July 26, 1809) he also mentions his deep disturbance over current conditions in Vienna, which was then under French siege: "Since May 4 I have managed to produce very little that is coherent, virtually only a fragment here and there. The whole course of events has affected me in body and spirit."

In this same letter (source *M* in my list), the relevant passage is as follows (my translation; see Appendix II for the original text):

> Here is a goodly serving of printer's errors, which, since I never in my life trouble myself any longer about things I have already written, were pointed out to me by a good friend (they are in the violoncello sonata). I shall have this list copied or printed here and noted in the newspaper, so that all those who have bought the work already may obtain it. This again confirms what I have experienced before, that works published from my own manuscript are the most correctly engraved ones. Presumably there are many errors in the manuscript copy which you have, but in looking over the music the author actually overlooks the errors.

Although the misprint list he made (see Figure 2.3 and Appendix II) was never published, it is preserved in the Beethoven-Haus in Bonn as part of the Bodmer collection.[37] Not only is it an important document for this work and evidence of Beethoven's capacities as a proofreader, but it seemed especially useful to include it here because of misreadings in the only available German text of the list,[38] and because of some discrepancies between various published readings of the text of the covering letter.[39] The misprints pointed out by Beethoven number twenty-three in all. The original letter and misprint list were also published by Max Unger in 1935 with an excellent commentary,[40] but the periodical in which Unger's study appeared is difficult to obtain, and I know of no evidence that his essay has resulted in any corrected editions since it appeared; nor is it faintly imaginable that more than a few of the most conscientious performers, who need it most, have had access to it.

A close comparison of the misprint list with the earliest editions sheds considerable light on Beethoven as proofreader. These documents leave no doubt about his capacity for painstaking care in producing the best possible readings of his work, and show something of his method. He proceeds by taking first the piano part and then the cello part, clearly because the earliest editions—and apparently most later ones up to about the 1840s—provided no score at all but only separate piano and cello parts, with no cue staff in the piano part. Scrutiny of the earliest editions does turn up a few details—probable errors—that Beethoven did *not* include in his list, but these serve only to reinforce his explicit recognition of his own limits as an editorial consultant for his works. Since he must have been deeply engaged in far more significant problems, the task of correcting his publisher's mistakes some three months after the edition had appeared must have been even more distasteful than it would have been prior to publication. Now it was simply a matter of attempting valiantly to rid his work of needless errors and inconsistencies. That the task really was futile is shown by the lack of evidence that Breitkopf and Härtel did anything at all about the errors he pointed out. Kinsky-Halm describes the second issue of the first edition (also 1809) as one that "contains the corrections which Beethoven sent them in late July 1809," but I know of no evidence to support this claim. Of the two complete copies of this edition I have seen, only one shows any handwritten corrections at all, and it covers only two of the twenty-three errors listed by Beethoven; the other has no corrections at all.[41]

Relatively unambiguous are the errors Beethoven specifies in the misprint list that arise from incorrect notation of pitch (misprint list Nos. 1, 3, 5, 9, 13, 15, 16, 18, and 21), or auxiliary signs (Nos. 2, 4, 10, 11, 14, 17, 19, 20, 22, and 23), or duration (No. 12). But his discussion of the apparent dynamic for the opening of the Scherzo (and its subsequent returns) is so curious that it warrants special mention. Evidently sticking close to their original copy, Breitkopf and Härtel had placed a p on the upbeat to m. 1 and an ff on the third beat of m. 1, producing a remarkable reading (Example 2.1). Beethoven's first cor-

Example 2.1

rection (misprint list Nos. 6, 7, and 8) is to remove the ff at m. 1 and at the returns (mm. 197 and 393). The difference is obviously of drastic importance for the whole movement; but by the next day he had changed his mind once more. Now, he writes, the ff should be restored in all these places. Thus, so far as the evidence shows, his final stated intention was to have the piano's first phrase ff in all three of its statements, contrasting with p at the cello repetition nine bars later—but every edition since the early ones has made the piano's passage $p,$ as if they were following his first misprint list but did not know of the letter that followed two days later. However improbable the ff reading may seem, it represents his apparent last intention.[42]

Finally, I should like to add a word on the possible role of the Salzer autograph in the first-movement misprints listed by Beethoven. In his first letter to Breitkopf and Härtel he observed that "the copy you have" may contain errors, thus readily admitting that the errors might have been made by the copyist and overlooked by him, not made by the printer. But it is interesting to see that of the ten first-movement mistakes he discovered in the piano and cello, *only one* can be traced to his own autograph reading: No. 3, in which the autograph also lacks the natural on the a in the piano cadenza. For Nos. 1 and 2 the autograph clearly agrees with his correct readings in the misprint list, while in No. 4 the copyist might have missed the ff at m. 115, though it is hard to see how; as for No. 5, the autograph version has a different figuration, hence the origin of the error is post-autograph. And none of the cello part errors in the first edition is traceable to the autograph. A few inconsistencies that are *not* mentioned by Beethoven have also plagued later editions and performers, and at least one to be discussed later (concerning mm. 36 and 173) remains unsolved. But despite the maze of cancellations and revisions that cover the autograph and despite the troubled later history of the text of this work, the autograph contains remarkably little that is really uncertain or imprecise. It presents an essentially pure text.

Revisions and Layers of Correction

To facilitate reference to the facsimile from here on, the following methods of abbreviation will be used: folio number/staff/measure number will be indicated in that order—for example, 4v/3/5 means folio 4 verso/staff 3/measure 5. Reference to measure numbers alone indicates the measure numbering of the entire first movement, with the convention that the first and second endings have the same number; I count the whole movement as having 280 measures. References to internal subdivisions of measures are given in terms of quarter-note units, for example, measure 38/3 means measure 38, third quarter. Hereafter, Pfte = pianoforte; Vcl = violoncello.

Methods of Correction

To sum up, the Salzer autograph is perhaps the most essential link in the chain of sources leading from early sketches to the finished version of the first movement, but it is also a score in a mixed stage of development. In part it is a developed score close to the finished product, in part a "composing score" representing more than one layer of elaboration within itself. The reader interested primarily or exclusively in the analytical side of the manuscript will find that even to perceive its content he will have to thread his way through the labyrinth of corrections and puzzling entries that bear on the content; while the student who may be mainly interested in the autograph as a genetic document will discover that to piece its material together requires a consistent view of the musical structure of the movement. And both need a firm base in perceiving its methods of graphic procedure.

A close look at the manuscript as a whole reveals three types of corrections: consecutive, local, and vertical. By "consecutive" I mean the replacement of one passage (at least a full measure in length) by another which is set down directly after it on the same staff or staves. Considering the unsettled appearance of many of its pages, it is surprising to find only one such correction in the entire manuscript: in the coda, mm. 248–250 (8v/13–15/2–4). Here Beethoven first wrote the Vcl part out to the very end of the page; he then went back to fill in the last system of the Pfte, but inadvertently omitted a measure (the equivalent of m. 248). Discovering the lapse after a measure and a half, he crossed out the last three measures on the page, marked a "Vi-" to show the beginning of an omission, and rewrote the passage correctly at the top of the next page. The change was so immediate and obvious that he did not even bother with the "-de" at the top of folio 9r that would have completed the word "Vi-de."

This consecutive correction depended, of course, on immediate recognition of his own lapse of attention in a sequential passage. It was easily made. But the majority of the corrections need not have been immediate, did not result from a direct evaluation of an original version as being plainly and mechanically "wrong," and arose not from lapses in writing but from studied reformulation of the material. They are revisions at the compositional level, and if there is anything anomalous about them it is only that they should have been packed so densely into a single score.[43]

By "local" corrections I mean those which rectify a local passage by cancellation and insertion of a new version next to the ld (within the same measure) or by overlaying the new reading on top of the old *on the same staff*. Looking carefully through the manuscript, one sees that this is the primary method used for minor changes in the exposition, for instance for the last Vcl triplet in m. 26 (1v/9/2), where two versions of the triplet were in turn canceled and a third inserted in the remaining space. Similarly, many of the changes in register that abound in the movement, especially in the Vcl, were handled in this way (for example, 1v/13/4 and 2r/1/1–3). It was used again to replace triplets with pizzicato quarters at mm. 65–70 (3r/staves 1 and 5), despite the difficult appearance that resulted. Corrections by overlaying or close adjacency were the most rapid and most obvious methods used by Beethoven, presumably while working at considerable speed. He resorted to vertical corrections involving extra staves and "Vi-de" signs only when compelled to do so because the original staves were filled in beyond even his ambitious hope of legible addition.

"Vertical" corrections, as I am using the term, are those using the intervening staves originally left blank, with "Vi-de" to mark the connections to the main staves. There seem to be two ways in which Beethoven used the extra staff for new material: first, to indicate an alternative to what he had written on the main staff; second, to put down a replacement for it. The difference is simply determined: when Beethoven wrote in an alternative reading on the extra staff, he left the earlier version intact; when he wrote in a replacement, he crossed out the original. Apart from possible lapses, I take the latter to represent more decisive revisions, while the former represent a less settled stage at which more than one reading could still be considered; in short, they resemble the functions of the sketches. Examples of the two procedures are not difficult to find. I have tried to list them all in Appendix III, which shows all uses of intervening staves within the manuscript, with an indication of what they alter or replace and which sort of reading they represent. Again, these changes center on the development. By following the indications in the appendix, the reader ought to be able to thread his way through the central part of the manuscript and should be able to associate the facsimile pages with each of the transcriptions given here.

One other method of correction remains to be mentioned; it is distinguished not by spatial assignment but by writing implement. While the bulk of the manuscript is written in brownish ink with revisions in a darker ink, there is some use of red pencil for further corrections, *but only in the first few pages of the manuscript* (folios 1v–3v). The use of the red pencil seems to represent a separate pass through the manuscript by Beethoven, a pass that he did not carry all the way but only through the exposition. Presumably, this was because the development pages were already too well populated by inked-in changes, and perhaps also because he may have expected that he could depend on his very able copyist, Schlemmer, to carry red changes in the exposition over into parallel passages in the recapitulation. The red pencil was useful for correcting notes or accidentals, to reinforce certain passages (for example, 3r/2/1), or to cancel (for example, 2r/11/2). Most revealing of all is Beethoven's use of it for the wavy horizontal lines on 2r, between staves 6–7 and 7–8. These turn out to have a special meaning—to indicate to the copyist that another version of these measures (mm. 38–45) was to be found not in the autograph itself but on a separate page elsewhere. As mentioned earlier, this interpretation receives the most positive confirmation when we find precisely these measures for the Pfte written into a blank page in the sketchbook Beethoven was then using, listed here as source *C*. It is only by examining the autograph that this entry becomes truly meaningful, and we need to recognize it not as a "sketch" but as an external component of the autograph itself.

Exposition and Recapitulation

Initial clues to the underlying musical importance of the Salzer autograph are furnished by the study of certain passages in the exposition and recapitulation, even though the equivalence of content in the two sections is limited at the stage of writing represented by the autograph. Not all passages that were to be parallel in the final version of the movement are parallel here in all details, and not all are corrected in the same way. Some of the differences shed further light on the processes inherent in the writing of the movement; to give a precise account of these, it will be necessary to relate their readings not only to one another but to the final text of the movement. At the same time, it should be kept in mind that for certain discrepancies we are faced with an insoluble dilemma. When we find disagreements between apparently parallel passages in exposition and recapitulation, it is sometimes difficult to decide if these are intentional and calculated subtleties, or if they are due to lapses in inserting corrections intended for both sections but actually inserted only in one—or simply to undue haste in writing, especially in sections of the recapitulation that may have been conceived as mechanical repetitions of their counterparts in the exposition, but into which errors infiltrated during the process of writing.

Measures 25–26 and 164–165. At mm. 25–26 radical changes are made in both Pfte and Vcl. In the first version, the Pfte had octaves in the left hand, with triplets in the Vcl (see Example 2.2a). Before abandoning this version entirely,

Example 2.2a Op. 69, mm. 25–26, stage 1

Example 2.2b Op. 69, mm. 25–26, stage 2

Beethoven took the trouble to touch up the voice-leading at the end of m. 26 in the Vcl, twice revising the final triplet as shown in Example 2.2a. He then overlaid a second reading upon both measures (Example 2.2b), which reorganizes the registral layout of the lower voices, makes the Vcl the bass to the Pfte, transfers the triplets to the Pfte and to a different register, and clarifies the sonority by removing the triplets from the Vcl at low register. The second version agrees with the final one; and it is doubly instructive that at mm. 164–

165, the parallel passage in the recapitulation, *only the second version* is present, with no trace of revision and without the further revision in the Vcl that Beethoven would later insert (probably by altering the Clauss copy). From this example two possible hypotheses flow: (1) Beethoven could have reconceived mm. 25–26 as he was writing a new version of the material at mm. 164–165, and then decided to go back and revise mm. 25–26 in the light of the version desired for the recapitulation; or (2) he may have revised mm. 25–26 at once, or at least while still working on the exposition, before writing down mm. 164–165 and perhaps before he was entirely sure in just what details the recapitulation would differ. In cases of this sort, where second choices in the exposition appear as first choices in the recapitulation, the recapitulation represents a later stage in more than the obvious sense.

Measures 33/1, 34/1 and 170/1, 171/1. In the exposition the first triplet in each measure is d♯–f♯–b; in the recapitulation it is g♯–b–d. Whether the variant is intended or not is left undetermined by the context, since either version offers plausible local voice-leading. The earliest printed editions maintain the two readings, as does the GA; in the absence of other evidence, the problem remains open.[44]

Measures 35–36 and 172–173. The problem here is similar to the one preceding, but is more conspicuous and more vital to the structure of the movement. In contrast to the previous problem, here the disagreement is between autograph and printed editions.

In the autograph, mm. 35 and 36 are *not* identical to each other in pitch-content, and the distinction is clear from positive notational evidence, not merely inferred from elliptical or imprecise use of signs. At m. 35 the Pfte triplets bring c♮ and a♯ as neighbor notes to b; in m. 36, as the Vcl picks up the figure, Beethoven changes the c♮ to a bold and clear c♯ on the first triplet of the measure. The reading in the autograph not only lets the change in linear contour reinforce and coincide with the change in sonority, but it effects a transition from the implied E-minor $\left(V^{6-5}_{4-3}\right)$ preparation of the preceding measures to the culminating tonicization of E major at m. 37, anticipating the E-major resolution by means of the c♯ at m. 36.

Exactly parallel is the autograph reading at mm. 172–173. Measure 172 has f♮ and d♯; m. 173 alters to f♯ and d♯.[45] Neither passage shows erasures or cancellations.

The first edition and almost all subsequent editions I have seen, including the GA, give c♮ at both m. 35 and m. 36, but f♮ at m. 172 followed by f♯ at m. 173.[46] On this reading the exposition and recapitulation are *not* parallel, and generations of players must have noticed the distinction without being able to determine what the evidence shows. If they did notice the problem, they were more astute than the editors of the many editions showing the discrepancy, since none ever alluded to it before Tovey in his edition of the sonatas. Of the two obvious interpretations, one is imperiously offered by Tovey in a foot-note.[47] At m. 173 Tovey puts the f♮ on the staff but adds a "♯?" above it, and writes: "It is quite characteristic of Beethoven, as of Haydn and Mozart, to produce an intentional change here, and the passage is not referred to in his own list of misprints. But the question must remain open." A look at the autograph might have punctured Tovey's grand confidence in his knowledge of what was "quite characteristic" in Beethoven's handling of such details, at least at the autograph stage. Again, the loss of the Clauss copy makes it im-possible to judge whether the autograph readings at mm. 36 and 173 were later intentionally changed as Beethoven reconsidered the details of the move-ment. As for the misprint list, there is no doubt of its value for the final text of the sonata, but it will also be seen that Beethoven himself acknowledged his limitations as a proofreader in connection with it. While we cannot doubt the validity of those points that are explicitly brought up in his correspondence, there is plenty of room for doubt about those left unmentioned, and it con-tributes nothing to assume that because Beethoven was careful he must have been infallible. Tovey, then, is right—the question must remain open. But the Salzer autograph brings positive and convincing evidence that at a late stage of composition of the movement, the two passages in exposition and recapit-ulation did match, and did have the chromatic, nonrepetitive reading, not the simple repetition found in the editions. In the present state of the evidence, this reading is the best available, and only contrary evidence from the Clauss copy could challenge it.

Measures 37–45 and 174–182. This passage has been cited earlier for its special method of correction and its link to the Pastoral Symphony sketchbook (source C). Now to the corrections themselves.

An important assumption in the version of this passage given in the auto-graph is that the Vcl part at mm. 37–45 and 174–182 is by this time fixed in form, and in all but one detail represents the final version. This is of interest both with regard to the strategic location of the entire passage (as the begin-ning of the "second group" in the exposition at the moment of the first deci-sive motion to the dominant) and also with regard to the nature of the material devised to articulate this motion: in the Vcl, an ascending scale pattern ex-panding through almost three octaves, coinciding with a descending har-monic prolongation of the E-major triad through a nearly comparable range in the Pfte. The whole is organized into two four-bar complementary phrases moving I–V and V–I. It was only at the late stage of correction represented by red pencil that Beethoven changed a single detail of the Vcl: he altered the repetitive b♮ in m. 44 to d♯.[48] With this stroke, he abandoned the parallel with m. 40 but achieved a local linear crest for the phrase and also a reading of considerably greater motivic significance for the movement (compare mm. 44–45 with 89–90 and 91–92 and their recapitulation complements).

Example 2.3a Op. 69, mm. 37–45, stage 1 (Pfte only)

Example 2.3b Op. 69, mm. 37–45, stage 2 (Pfte only)

To the established Vcl material, he apparently began by adding the octave upbeat figure in the Pfte shown in Example 2.3a, but abandoned this after only a measure. The notation of m. 37 in the Pfte makes it difficult to be certain of priorities, since neither version is amply spaced within the measure. But I assume that Example 2.3a constitutes an earlier idea for the Pfte entrance at this point, reinforcing the tonicized e at m. 38/1 and suggesting a descending arpeggiation by means of the renewed attack at m. 38/3. This idea is lightly sketched again at bar 42 (2r/10/4), where two d♯'s in the rhythm ♩ 𝄾 ♩ 𝄾 are faintly visible in the right hand in a tiny hand, as if this possibility lingered as an afterthought.

The second stage suppressed this in favor of the arpeggiated descending triad of Example 2.3b. This version of the Pfte material, in simultaneous octaves, is simpler in articulation than the final imitative version that was to supplant it; moreover, it explicitly effects an exact rhythmic correspondence between Pfte mm. 38–40 and Vcl mm. 1–3—in short, between the principal subject of the entire movement and this significant thematic landmark in the course of its subsequent unfolding. The correspondence is made less obvious in the final version of mm. 38–40, not only through the more complex articulations of Pfte m. 39 that arise from the imitation, but through the suppression of the eighth notes at Pfte m. 40/4. It should be noted too that the descending version in simultaneous octaves was entered into both the exposition and recapitulation before further changes were made in it.

The process of elaboration becomes perfectly clear, however, when the next step is closely examined. Evidently having decided to convert the descending arpeggiation in octaves to a one-measure imitation, in both first and second phrases, Beethoven must have found that there was no clear way in which he could change the autograph to show precisely what he wanted to keep and what to delete. So he crossed out everything in the Pfte from mm. 38 to 45 and from mm. 175 to 182 in ink, leaving only the parallel measures 41 and 45 and 178 and 182 intact—as if to hold them temporarily open—and then turned to the red pencil for clarifying marks. He crossed out the alternate arpeggiation (from stage 1) at m. 40 in red pencil, reinforced the cancellation at m. 44, and then added the long horizontal wavy lines above and below the Pfte from mm. 38 to 45. In effect, these wavy lines are a direction to the copyist: they tell him to consult another version of these measures, for the Pfte only, in another source. And this turns out to be the blank page in the sketchbook—the principal sketchbook Beethoven was then using—on which he entered precisely the equivalent of what is crossed out on this page, and precisely what is covered by the wavy lines: only the Pfte, mm. 38–45 and then mm. 174–182 (where the wavy lines are in ink but mean exactly the same thing, since Beethoven used no red pencil in this manuscript after folio 3v, for some reason).

Figure 2.1 shows folio 31v of the sketchbook (our source C), with its two entries for these measures; it is obvious that they exactly fit the corresponding pages in the autograph. Writing for a professional eye, Beethoven put down only what was necessary. As mentioned earlier, he wrote in the hand normally reserved for fair copies intended for the eyes of others, not the rapid sketchbook hand intended for himself.[49]

Measures 65–70, 71–76 and 202–207, 208–213. In the later exposition, this is the first larger segment to undergo considerably more than partial or local correction. To clarify the web of corrections visible in folios 3r and 7r-v, I shall center discussion on the exposition transcriptions given as Examples 2.4a, 2.4b, and 2.4c, with the expectation that on the basis of these the reader will be able to make his own comparable observations about the recapitulatory details on folio 7r-v, where the revisions are simpler and clearer. The three examples are also offered as paradigms for later examples in which two or more layers of composition are derived from a composite transcription. The transcriptions in Examples 2.4b and 2.4c are meant to follow from 2.4a in this way: Example 2.4a is a complete diplomatic transcription of mm. 65–76, giving all possible detail; Example 2.4b extracts from 2.4a what I take to be its first stage of composition; Example 2.4c represents a similarly extracted second stage.

Even a first glance at these revisions suggests both distant and nearby connections and associations. From the main course of events in the exposition in its final version, it is obvious that mm. 65–70 represent a well-defined, emphatically articulated phrase-segment that begins a new area of the exposition after its first large-scale tonicization of the dominant. The stage of motivic development reached at mm. 65–70 is reconfirmed at mm. 71–76 by means of the instrumentally interchanged repetition that has also been used for every previous larger phrase-segment in the movement. Of the uses of interchange in the movement more will be said later; it suffices now to emphasize in the final version the intensification of the first statement (mm. 65–70) at mm. 71–76 by change of sonority, expansion of register, and the progression from triplet to sixteenth-note figuration. In this entire movement, as in other Beethoven works of this period, a primary means of foreground sectional contrast is through the identification of successive segments with successive prevailing rhythmic units, taking these at times in graduated diminution, and with the area of maximum diminution coinciding with maximum metrical accentuation and with a rise to a higher dynamic level.

With the final effect of mm. 65–70 and 71–76 in view, it becomes doubly instructive to see that, at an earlier but still autograph stage, the rhythmic organization of the two passages was essentially identical, with both in triplets, and that even the revisions for mm. 71–76 introduced sixteenths only partially and in local alternation with the prevailing triplets. Still more surprising is the recapitulation: at mm. 208–215 there is as yet no sign of sixteenths at all, and only the first layer of composition is represented!

More distantly associated with mm. 65–70 is the earlier transition passage at mm. 25–26, already described in this section. In both passages the first conception of the material included low-register triplets in the Vcl in a strongly articulated forte context, with supporting left-hand octaves in the Pfte. In both, the basic exchange of functions is between Vcl and Pfte left hand, with considerations of sonority and spacing apparently combining to influence the redistribution. At the same time, an important difference distinguishes the first-stage Vcl triplets. At mm. 25–26, they embody the relatively simple functions of repeated rising arpeggiated triads in the familiar 2-plus-1 phrasing that ensures each one a down-bow attack. But at mm. 65–70, they are ex-

Example 2.4a   Op. 69, mm. 65–76 (complete): fol. 3r–v

Example 2.4a   (continued)

Example 2.4b   Op. 69, mm. 65–76, stage 1, fol. 3r–v

*Alternate reading of final triplets in bar 65 is [music notation] agreeing with bar 66.

Example 2.4b (continued)

AUTOGRAPH OF THE FIRST MOVEMENT OF OPUS 69

Example 2.4c   Op. 69, mm. 65–76, stage 2, fol. 3r–v

Example 2.4c (continued)

*I interpret the l.h. at bars 73–76 as follows: "col Violoncell in 8" represents an intermediate stage continuing what I allocate to "stage 2" in bars 71–72; "16tel in 8en" represents a later decision to transfer the written-out triplets to sixteenths, continuing the r.h. at bars 71–72 but extending the sixteenths to both hands.

panded to include differentiated types of diminution: triadic arpeggiation in both directions (m. 65); chromatic neighbor-note figures (mm. 65/3 and 66/1), and the rising figure with detached repeated note (𝅘𝅥𝅮𝅘𝅥𝅮𝅘𝅥) at mm. 68–70. That the last was still experimental, though, is shown by mm. 205–207 (see the facsimile, folio 7v/1/2 and 7v/4/1–2), where it has two forms, the one in Example 2.4b being the second, corrected, version.

Close comparison of Examples 2.4a, 2.4b, and 2.4c with one another, with the final version, and with the facsimile (folio 3r) should yield some insight into the problems of interpretation offered by the most difficult passages in the Salzer autograph. For all that Example 2.4a strives to reproduce the present state of the page in all its ramified detail, it will inevitably fall short of representing the material in its true completeness, since many of the subtle nuances and visual cues of the original handwriting are lost in transcription.[50] The chain of rapid cancellation strokes leaves the contents clear enough at staves 1, 3, 5, and 7; but in staves 9, 11, and the very end of 14 it covers the writing so densely as to make decoding difficult even after close study of the original. Intact even though partly obscured are the words used on folio 3:

a. 3r/1/3: "pizz" (determined not only by the final version and the context but by comparison with the appearance of the term in other scores).[51] At 3r/between 8 and 9/3, the swirling flourish may stand for "arco," which would fit m. 71.

b. 3r 11/1: under the arabesque of cancellations lurks the word "bleibt," referring to an earlier stage at which Beethoven had first canceled the left hand, then decided to let it remain, then canceled it once more.

c. 3r 14/right margin: again the word "bleibt" is canceled.[52]

Another sample of notational detail that can only be understood by reference to the original writing is the hint of successive stages of decision regarding the Vcl at mm. 65–68, after the triplets had been transferred to the Pfte left hand. In m. 66, a half note, e, is canceled and replaced by the quarter notes e, b; but in mm. 67–68 three successive half-note heads are partially filled in to convert them to quarters. The half-note pattern was doubtless the first step in replacing the triplets; in turn it was displaced by the quarter-note pattern. Did the idea for a unique change of Vcl sonority to pizzicato to intensify the articulation coincide with the quarter-note stage?

For mm. 65–70 the interrelation of Examples 2.4b and 2.4c seems clear enough. To what has been said already, it need only be added now that we can attach importance to the change in register in the Vcl as well as the change in durations, that is, the replacement of the low Vcl e and d♯ (mm. 65–68) by pizzicato an octave higher, presumably with a view to reserving the lowest register until its effective arco attack at m. 71.

For mm. 71–76 the situation is much more complicated. Stages 1 and 2 show two readings for the Vcl, changing its octave (I assume from low to middle register), while the Pfte problems include both the handling of the triplet-to-sixteenth-note progression and the function of the left hand throughout. In the first stage, Beethoven worked out triplet patterns (staff 10/ 3) resembling those of the Vcl at stage 1 (mm. 65–70). He also planned to bring both hands in octaves from m. 71 onward—thus the writing out of the left hand at mm. 71–72, with the intention of continuing "in 8" as marked at the end of m. 72, left hand (3r/11/4). At a later stage Beethoven considered strengthening the bass register, presumably to bring out the new position of what had formerly been an upper line (mm. 65ff.). To do so, he marked "Vi-" for the left hand at m. 71 and added the "left hand" interpolation visible on staff 12 just below the triplets. This second possibility lasted a little longer, as expressed in the verbal direction below mm. 73–74: "col Violoncell in 8"— but eventually it too gave way to a return to the idea of restricting the Pfte to the upper register only, in octaves, with the Vcl as sole bass support. I assume that at this stage of events the sixteenth-note "Vide" entered the right hand at mm. 71–72, with the first version spelled out above at staff 8—and that to this last autograph stage alone belongs the direction at m. 73: "16^{tel} in 8^{en}." "Six-teenths in octaves" does indeed represent the final decision for the Pfte at this climactic passage in the exposition, but it is apparently the product of a process of shuttling back and forth among various plausible stages of decision, the remnants of which can still be exhumed from the maze of cancellations across the page.

Finally, it is worth speculating about how the final version of mm. 71–76 (and 208–213) was put down and clarified. While the last stage of mm. 65–70 and 202–207 in the autograph is virtually the same as the final reading, even the last versions visible for mm. 71–76 and 208–213 are not. The sixteenths of the final version are partially added for mm. 71–78, though they are not fully worked out on the page; but for mm. 208–213, as we saw, there are no sixteenths stipulated at all. We are left to assume either that Beethoven made extensive alterations in the passage in the Clauss copy, or else that he may have worked out the details for the copyist on sketch-sheets that have not been preserved.

Measures 77–83 and 214–220. Further discrepancies between exposition and recapitulation appear in these measures, the last revised passages to be dealt with here apart from those in Appendix IV. The Pfte figures at the *ff* measures 77–78 do not at first appear to be revised from an earlier stage. But they are. Originally both hands were to be in triplets throughout these two transitional measures, and the four sixteenths entered at the beginning of mm. 77 and 78 were actually triplets continuing the first-stage triplets of mm. 71–76. The conversion to sixteenths simply necessitated the adding of a fourth member at the end of each group—but only in the exposition was the addition carried out.[53] Again Beethoven failed to take the trouble to change the parallel passage in the recapitulation, either because he was working rapidly or because he knew that he could rely on the good sense of his copyist. Whatever the reason, mm. 214–215 (7v/14–15/2–3) remain in unmodified triplets.

Similarly curious is the revision of the Vcl at mm. 80 and 82, along with their later counterparts. On the original conception of mm. 71–78, the *pp* interchange beginning at m. 79 had furnished a continuation of the previously established triplet figuration. But with the introduction of sixteenths in mm. 71–78, the decrescendo from *ff* to *pp* with continued sixteenths brings a slightly more palpable contrast at m. 79, a more effective sense of a new departure, than the triplet transition could have done. Thanks to the change in figuration at m. 79, any sensitive pianist recognizes the need for an expressive extension of the first note of the measure, not only to heighten the significance of the descent through two octaves by a slight delay in its initial downward motion, but also to sharpen the distinction between the sixteenths of m. 78 and the renewed triplets at m. 79.

As for the Vcl at m. 80, it contains no fewer than three versions of its answering pattern within the same measure, and a fourth sketched lightly below in a tiny hand (3v/8/1).[54] The first idea was to begin the ascending Vcl triplets on b (the triplet is visible in the left center of the measure), but after one triplet this was canceled in favor of a version starting on d♯ and rising directly to the fixed goal, g♯. Yet the preferred voice-leading remained that of beginning the Vcl ascent on the pitch just being reached by the descending Pfte; thus the new trial on b once more, curving chromatically through a♯ to c♯ and down to the g♯. Then the final idea for the Vcl contour is sketched below, with its grace-note turn suggesting a long-range connection with the turn in the Vcl cadenza at m. 24, which produces a similar change of direction after an ascending six-note scale pattern. The d♯ version at m. 80 paralleled the first stage at m. 82, beginning now on g♯, and the change to a version a third lower, with letters added for clarity, needs no transcription. It is worth noting, however, that in the final version the Pfte remained fixed in register at mm. 79–82, but the Vcl was transferred up an octave once more, again showing that registral adjustments in this sonata were matters of continuing concern down to stages of revision extending considerably beyond the autograph.

The Development

Measures 95–151. In what has been seen so far, the passages revised—however varied in length, function, and type of revision—have formed delimited units that can be readily distinguished in a context that is basically clear in content and direction. The corrections in the middle section, on the other hand, form a long and continuous chain of problems that extend across this entire area of the movement. With the close of the exposition at m. 94, the beginning of the middle section at mm. 95–101 unfolds from the second ending in a form that is essentially the final one for this phrase, free of major changes. But, starting in the next measure, mm. 101–102 (4r/9–11/3–4), the entire section up to m. 152 displays alterations in every measure, and these reveal nothing less than the total recasting of the roles of Vcl and Pfte throughout the section.

Even in advance of the details, one wider conclusion can be anticipated. In the exposition, the revisions affected smaller units within a scheme essentially established in all major respects. But in the development, the revisions represent a wholesale conversion of this entire area of the movement from one means of instrumental realization to another. What is remarkable in these revisions is not simply their close relevance to the considerations of balance, sonority, register, and instrumental functions that arose in the exposition as small-scale problems, but also that such massive reconstruction with regard to these parameters could be accomplished by Beethoven in an autograph without his finding it necessary to radically recast the material itself.

Once this principle of revision is seen, however, the rest is comparatively easy, and even the most formidable corrections begin to fit together. It thus becomes possible to distinguish two major phases of composition in the section, phases I have sought to represent as Examples 2.5a and 2.5b, and 2.6a and 2.6b, as follows:

Stage 1 of mm. 101–114	Example 2.5a
Stage 2 of mm. 101–114	Example 2.5b
Stage 1 of mm. 115–151	Example 2.6a
Stage 2 of mm. 115–151	Example 2.6b

But before proceeding to consideration of the transcriptions, a close look at the facsimile of folios 4 through 5v is needed to obtain a clear view of the physical features of the notation of this section and of the character of its corrections. These corrections, even more than those of other parts of the manuscript, make it possible to reconstruct Beethoven's procedures over extensive musical terrain and in illuminating detail.

The first clear hints are offered by the corrections that begin at m. 102 (4r/9–11/4). From here through the entire last system of folio 4, Beethoven first wrote out in all detail both the Pfte and Vcl (as in Example 2.5a), then turned back to the beginning of this phrase and began the process of interchange and revision that led to stage 2. While the Pfte is clear enough in the last system of folio 4, the Vcl is crowded with cancellations of stage 1 and the insertion of stage 2 in overlay upon it. Having used the intervening staff 12 for a left-hand change of register at m. 102, Beethoven was forced to make purely local corrections in the Vcl throughout mm. 103–106. This point deserves very close attention, for it is a good deal more revealing than it might first appear, owing to the means of continuation. At the top of folio 4v Beethoven continued the procedure of systematically canceling stage 1 and fitting in stage 2, taking advantage of originally blank measures (for example, the Pfte 4v/2–3/1–2) for maximum clarity, but using "Vi-de" vertical corrections when it became necessary.

Most revealing is folio 4v. In the first system (staves 1–3), all corrections are local.[55] In the second system (staves 5–7), the first "Vi-" appears, for the Vcl, with its replacement "-de" directly above on staff 4 (4v/4/1–3). But at the third system, the "Vi-de" replacement for the Vcl that had been on staff 4 is continued not on an extra staff but as *uncorrected material on the main Vcl staff* (staff 9). That is to say, the Vcl from m. 101 to m. 113 shows two complete stages—an original and a total revision; but beginning at m. 114 *the previous revision line becomes the main text for the Vcl part*. This implies that all the corrections from m. 101 to m. 113 must have been made before m. 114 was written, and that the process of correction and reversal of the instrumental roles was not wholly a later decision but one that emerged in the course of working out this section in the autograph. Then, in what follows, new interchanges of material between instruments necessitate new vertical corrections that go even further afield. Yet the reason for dividing the transcriptions of the middle section into two units of unequal length (mm. 101–114 and 115–151) should now be clear.

A glance at Examples 2.5a and 2.5b suggests strongly that stage 2 followed quickly upon stage 1, and that its main features of correction superseded the earlier readings even before a few details of stage 1 had been entered in full. Indicative of incompleteness in Example 2.5a is the handling of mm. 105–106: I read the half-note succession in the Vcl as representing stage 1, a reading then transferred to the right hand in stage 2. This leaves the right hand blank in stage 1 (apart from the remote possibility of an intended doubling in octaves in stage 1), with no rests discernible. The obvious result in stage 1 is a breakdown in rhythmic activity at mm. 105–106 that could scarcely have been allowed to stand, even if the interchange of instruments and consequent rewriting had not enlivened it; the solution is the connecting Vcl phrase in quarters that begins at m. 104/4. Curious also in the two versions of Example 2.5 is the change in register at mm. 104–105, as a result of the instrumental interchange; also the double-stops in the Vcl that are lightly sketched in at mm. 111/4 and 112/3 in stage 2 (Example 2.5b)—unidiomatic for the instrument even as rolled arpeggios, and sensibly suppressed at a later stage. Worthy of mention too is an unsettled detail in pitch reading: at m. 114, where both Pfte and Vcl seem in both versions to converge on the triplet succession that leads to the firm tonicization of E minor at m. 115/1, the pitch readings in the two instruments do not agree. The Pfte has an explicit g♯ at the third beat of m. 114,

Example 2.5a Op. 69, mm. 101–114, stage 1, fol. 4r–v

while the Vcl has no sharp (but does imply it, because of the natural at m. 114/
4). In the final version, Beethoven deleted the Pfte doubling in m. 114 altogether and left the preparation wholly to the Vcl—but the first edition and the
GA have a natural at m. 114/3. While this reading anticipates the tonicization
of E minor as resolution of the second half of m. 114, it lacks the interesting
ambiguity of a major-minor approach to a minor tonicization, which might

AUTOGRAPH OF THE FIRST MOVEMENT OF OPUS 69

Example 2.5a *(continued)*

have formed a subtle parallel to the problem at mm. 35–36 described earlier at a similarly decisive move into the tonicization of E major.

Comparable means of interchange between stage 1 and stage 2 are visible in Examples 2.6a and 2.6b, which present the entire remainder of the development section; they can be read as the direct continuation of their counterparts in Examples 2.5a and 2.5b. Among many suggestive details, several points of interest claim priority.

First to be considered is the treatment of diminution at mm. 115–116, in which the firm tonicization of E minor coincides with the reintroduction of sixteenth-note motion in *ff,* the highest dynamic level yet reached in the movement. Within stage 1 the first substage of m. 115 must clearly have consisted in the assigning of sixteenths to the Pfte right hand (mm. 115/2 through 116/1), with the clarifying letters "g e g e" over m. 115/2 and oblique repetition marks in the right hand at mm. 115/3–4 and 116/1. But these Pfte sixteenths were then canceled in favor of the arpeggiated Vcl sixteenths, and although I include both Vcl and Pfte sixteenths as part of stage 1, the Vcl figuration must have been entered after that of the Pfte; since the Vcl sixteenths are crowded in

Example 2.5b Op. 69, mm. 101–114, stage 2, fol. 4r–v

*NB curve in slur over r.h., to bring it under cancellations in Vcl; this helps to show that the latter were already present when the slur was entered.

Example 2.5b (continued)

† R.h. as in stage 1: did Beethoven forget to cancel here? Later editions have whole rest in r.h.

on the left and right sides of the clarifying letters over the right-hand six-teenths at m. 115/2, the Pfte sixteenths must already have been present. Important for stage 1 in both its substages is the cessation of the sixteenth-note activity: in the version of mm. 115–116 in which the Pfte did have arpeggios, these continued as a primary representation of the upper voices all the way to m. 122, while the Vcl was to abandon its sixteenths for the new developmental figure derived at long range from the thematic unit that dominates the entire movement, here used in imitative alternation with the left hand. In other words, in stage 1 the Vcl and Pfte were to exchange sixteenths at mm. 115–117 ff. The evidence that Beethoven considered this possibility beyond a moment's thought is provided by the clarifying letters at mm. 115, 117, and 119, which would hardly have been needed for a version that was at once suppressed.

In stage 2, the alternation plan is abandoned in favor of the consistent relegation of independent developmental processes to each instrument. The Vcl is

Example 2.6a   Op. 69, mm. 115–151, stage 1, fols. 4v–5v

now definitely assigned the function of supplying bass and mid-register har-mony in intensified rhythmic activity by means of its sixteenth-note arpeggios throughout the segment—the only extended sixteenths in the entire Vcl part—while the Pfte develops the sequential imitation of the basic quarter-note figure in both hands, balancing both in octaves. Stage 2 (mm. 115–122)

Example 2.6a (*continued*)

is eminently clear in purpose and realization, and the contrasting motivic and rhythmic functions of the two instruments are admirably matched to their contrasting registers and sonorities.

Especially curious is a sidelight on Beethoven's procedures at mm. 117–122 that is provided by one of the extant sketch-pages for the movement (our

Example 2.6a (continued)

*Assume this barline added at stage 2. †Grace notes unclear.

AUTOGRAPH OF THE FIRST MOVEMENT OF OPUS 69

Example 2.6a (continued)

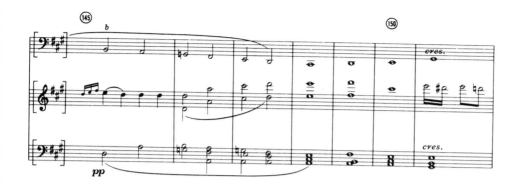

source *E*). On folio 2v of this set of pages, we find an isolated entry (Example 2.7). Typically for Beethoven's monolinear sketches of the most rapidly written type, it lacks clefs and clarifying marks of articulation altogether. But we can supply these without too much speculation, and when we do, the result is as shown in Example 2.8.

The sketch represents, in linear compression, mm. 117–122, showing the chain of transpositions of the primary motivic figure in both Pfte and Vcl and incorporating elements of what I am calling stages 1 and 2. In all probability, this fragmentary entry represents a rapid jotting made while the work on this part of the autograph was in process—indeed, when it had run into trouble. Once again, one sees the use of a sketch-page as a clarifying addition to a problem that had already reached the autograph stage; and once again, one sees how an apparent sketch is really supplementary to a concurrent autograph rather than being a simple predecessor of the autograph stage.

Although many significant aspects of revision are discernible in the remainder of the development section, I shall restrict what follows to discussion of four principal points. These will once again focus mainly on stages 1 and 2 of the autograph, as represented in Examples 2.6a and 2.6b.

The first point concerns the striking effects of revision on Beethoven's treatment of register in this part of the movement. Beginning at m. 117, the essential change from stage 1 to stage 2 involves the exchange between Vcl and Pfte right hand, and their interchange effects important modifications in the registral location of comparable material. Thus at m. 117, the sixteenth-note arpeggios that had been the uppermost voices in stage 1 become bass and mid-register support in stage 2, while the Vcl line of stage 1 (mm. 117–122) is transferred from an interior role to the prominence of the right hand in high register, where it is doubled in octaves. Registral considerations are even more

Example 2.6b Op. 69, mm. 115–151, stage 2, fols. 4v–5v

*The two oblique repetition signs are visible just below the Vcl staff.
†This octave crossed out because of poor spacing(?)
‡Material on cue staff seems to correct both stage 1 (sixteenths) and stage 2 (several versions) in this measure only; next measure = stage 2, then transferred to r.h. staff.

Example 2.6b   (continued)

Example 2.6b (continued)

in evidence at later points in the development, and the post-autograph changes that resulted in the final version clearly reflect Beethoven's special pains with this aspect of the setting. Measures 123–126 and 129, compared in stage 1, stage 2, and the final reading, will supply an adequate initiation to these subtleties.

On the rhythmic side, this portion of the autograph contributes further in-

Example 2.6b   (*continued*)

*Renewal of bass clef not visible but to be assumed.

sight into the genesis of the final version in ways that supplement what we have seen in the exposition. The treatment of triplets and sixteenths in the later part of the exposition (especially mm. 65–79) is the background to the revisions in the development. Especially prominent is the rising sequential transition figure at mm. 123–126, which prepares the decisive and significant tonic-

Example 2.6b (continued)

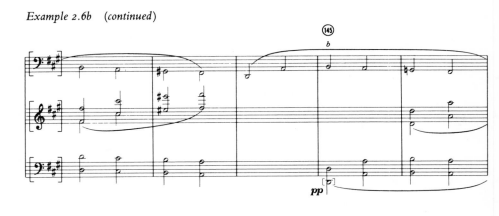

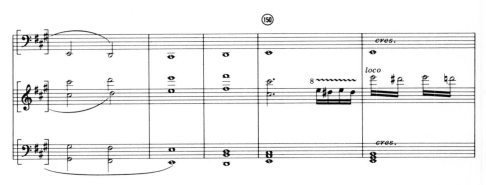

Example 2.7   Source E, fol. 2v, staff 6

Example 2.8   The same sketch with clefs interpolated

ization of C♯ minor at m. 127. From all the evidence at hand, it appears that from his first advanced conception of this part of the development, Beethoven sought to clarify the larger phrase-segmentation of the section on a rhythmic basis. The sequence of phrase-segments forms a series in which the choice of predominant rhythmic units permits a steady path of elaboration within the movement, and also permits the association of segments separated from one another by considerable intervening terrain (for example, mm. 107–114 and 127–136, which form a crucial parallel).

The climactic effect of the Vcl sixteenths at mm. 115–125 is the decisive contribution of stage 2. In stage 1 the Pfte sixteenths had simply and abruptly shifted to triplets in the Vcl at m. 123, perhaps too crudely breaking the continuity developed at maximum diminution (sixteenths) in the preceding passage. In the stage 2 version, the Vcl sixteenths proceed all the way to m. 125, and at m. 123 the Pfte joins its triplets against the Vcl sixteenths to heighten the activity leading to the cadence at m. 127. But at a still later stage Beethoven must have considered the sixteenth-plus-triplets combination insufficiently developed for his purposes. As part of his final conception of the whole passage from mm. 115 to 127, he converts every available unit to sixteenths: the Pfte right hand at mm. 117–122 is transformed from its relatively relaxed and cantabile right-hand statement (Example 2.9) to the octave diminution of this

Example 2.9

figure in sixteenths that is used in the final version. Comparably, the sequence at mm. 123–126 is converted from triplets to sixteenths, thus also articulating the return to triplets at m. 127 and supplying a clearer association of the long-range poles of the development section, mm. 107 and 127.

Finally, an element unique to the autograph version deserves mention. It appears in stage 1 only, at mm. 140–141: a brief linear segment in the right hand, as a trailing-off continuation of m. 139 (Example 2.10). This short segment is introduced here for the first time in the movement, and its evident function is to effect a transition from the dotted even eighth notes of mm. 137–139 to the sustained augmentation in even half notes at mm. 140–147. Nor

Example 2.10

was it merely to have a local transitional use: in the coda, near the very end of the movement at mm. 270–271 (9v/6/1–2), Beethoven found a similar use for this segment in a passage reintroducing half notes after quarter-and-triplet combination, but he suppressed it at m. 270 once he had determined to do so at mm. 140–141. Its removal at mm. 140–141 only enhances the care with which the process of gradual augmentation of rhythmic values unfolds toward the end of the development section, and the care with which the segmentation of larger phrases is associated with specific units of rhythmic activity at every step of the entire section.

The Genesis of the First Phrase

In dealing here primarily with the opening phrase of the movement, I have tried to single out the element that seems most obviously to exert a far-reaching influence on the larger design of this remarkably subtle movement. At the same time, I must explicitly dissociate these remarks from what would be expected of a thoroughgoing analysis of the comprehensive flow of events in the entire movement. The requirements of such an analysis should go far beyond what is possible in this commentary on the autograph, and should deal at length with matters that can only be hinted at here, including the larger linear and contrapuntal structure of the movement, its means of harmonic articulation, and its phrase-structure. It should also, of course, encompass the entire sonata, not merely the first movement, and should do so in the context of Beethoven's other major works of this period, one of the most productive of his career. The extraordinary and even now too little-known analyses of major Beethoven works by Heinrich Schenker are not only the most exhaustive published works of their type,[56] but—despite their diversity and whether or not the Schenkerian approach is taken—they stand as models of a consistent and powerful attack on a broad range of musical problems.

Within the boundaries of this commentary, then, I would suggest as an essential point of departure for this movement the restriction of its opening six-measure phrase to the Vcl alone, with the subsequent engrafting of a complementary six-measure phrase in the Pfte (mm. 6–12). With one stroke, this opening phrase (mm. 1–12) establishes certain conditions that bear significantly on the remainder of the movement: it presents the primary motivic material for the movement as components of a self-contained linear segment first associated with the Vcl alone in low register, and it immediately establishes a balanced, complementary relationship between the two instruments for which even a crude outline shows a symmetrical partitioning of the first twenty-four measures, divided into two larger phrases:

1. Vcl solo (mm. 1–6)—$\frac{\text{Pfte}}{\text{Vcl}}$ (mm. 7–11)—Pfte cadenza (m. 12) to ⌒

2. Pfte solo (mm. 13–17)—$\frac{\text{Pfte}}{\text{Vcl}}$ (mm. 17–23)—Vcl cadenza (m. 24) to ⌒

While the entrance of the Pfte at the upbeat to m. 7 divides the first twelve measures into six plus six, the complementary entrance of the Vcl at the upbeat to m. 17 avoids what might have been considered too square-cut a symmetry within the larger division of phrases. Significant in this connection is the sketching-in of the Vcl doubling in the autograph during the entire first part of the second larger phrase (mm. 13–16) (1r/13/1–4) and its eventual exclusion from these measures. Reserving the Vcl instead for a reinforcing entry at m. 16 not only contributes to the larger symmetry of mm. 1–24 but assists in the exploration of range, which is the other major aspect of organization at the opening of the movement.

Although the structural and expressive quality of the opening phrase has hardly escaped Beethoven commentators, I know of no discussion of it beyond the most perfunctory. Yet a close look at the movement yields some observations on the phrase that seem to me as inevitable as they are obvious. The first is that its establishment of the tonic within its first four measures is not at all a simple expression of the tonic triad, but one in which the tonic-defining opening interval is immediately and strongly colored by its continuation implying vi (m. 2), articulating the progression i–iv en route to v as early as possible. Second, the entire first phrase (mm. 1–6) forms an intervallic and motivic sequence whose components and derivations will have a pervasive importance for the course of the movement. Third, the internal formulation of the phrase exhibits a high degree of sequential differentiation: no two of its measures or subphrases are identical in their rhythm, just as no two subphrases are identical in length, shape, or even point of attack within the measure. Nor do all statements of the motive, as expressly grouped in the autograph, show exactly the same phrasing. At the four main statements of the opening phrase (mm. 1, 13, 152, 254), the articulation varies not only from one to another but even between Vcl and Pfte, though this may not have held fast in the later version of the copy; and both curious and suggestive is the appearance of the phrasing ♩· ♪ ♪ ♪ ♪ ♪ only *after* its exploration in the development.

One consequence of such subtlety of articulation in the opening phrase is the sense it conveys of the slow unfolding of connected motives within the linear stream. This impression is enhanced by the continuity of the Vcl sonority, the entirely nonpercussive legato of its phrasing, the dynamics *p* and *dolce,* the emphatic *ma non tanto* after the tempo marking, and even the time-honored performance practice, familiar to every cellist, by which the first four measures are fingered entirely on the Vcl G-string rather than crossing from G- to D-string on the rising fifth (a–e)—a procedure parallel to the G-string opening of the first movement of Op. 59 No. 1, mm. 1–2.

As for the genesis of the opening phrase, the full details of its development will have to await the complete presentation of the sketches; but two of them are nevertheless sufficiently clear and sufficiently important to warrant discussion here. These are the sketches listed earlier as sources F and G. Although I regard them as representing a stage well beyond the earliest jottings for the movement, their versions of the opening clearly predate and anticipate that of the autograph in an enlightening degree. In considering them, it ought to be kept strongly in mind that the opening phrase of this movement is, by the time of the autograph, firmly fixed in its rhythmic and linear form, in comparison to many of its derivations and many other elements of the movement.

Source F (folio 1r) presents a fairly clear consecutive single-staff sketch for the exposition, of which the opening is shown in Example 2.11. Further down on the same page we find a transformation closer to the final version, which preserves the syncopation of m. 4 but suppresses the internal symmetry of m. 3 (Example 2.12). From these it is a further step to source G, which offers a three-staff composition sketch for the whole of the exposition, and of which the opening up to m. 24 is given in Example 2.13.

Despite the apparent omission in m. 3, which is evidently due only to Beethoven's working at top speed at the very beginning, the final form of the first phrase is reached. What follows then supplies the basic outline of events to be elaborated in the autograph: the quarter notes at mm. 7–9 continue the prevailing units of the opening without the significant diminution that is to be supplied in the left hand; and the cadenza in m. 12 is given only as a flourish of the pen. But the fundamental material and the basic procedures of the opening, including the instrumental exchange and the expansion of its range, are all but fully presented, although the finer details have yet to be worked out. In connection with the first sketch given here, from source F, it might be noted that its resolution to e at m. 6 explicitly provides a resolution in the same register as the d in m. 3, which in the final version remains undisplaced in its own octave. The source F version anticipates therefore the registral rearrangement that was outlined by Schenker in his analysis of this phrase,[57] an analysis laden with implied subtleties that cannot be taken up here beyond noting a few details. The inferred a♯ and consequent VII♯³ of m. 2 in Schenker's analysis clearly result from the explicit presence of this harmony at the corresponding place in the recapitulation, m. 154. While this helps to strengthen his further reduction of this analysis through two more levels, it nevertheless obscures a distinction critical to the foreground of the movement, in which the difference between the totally linear I–VI of the first phrase and the triplet-accompanied

Example 2.11 Source F, fol. 1r, staves 1–2

*Words after NB are difficult to decipher, and I am indebted to Dr. Hans Schmidt of the Beethoven-Archiv in Bonn for the following suggested interpretation: "NB im 3ten aus S 1."

Example 2.12 Source F, fol. 1r, staff 4 (excerpt)

and accordingly harmonized I–VI#³ of the recapitulation is more than a mere detail. Indeed, it could be argued that the combination of Vcl theme and Pfte triplets at mm. 152ff. not only reinforces the structural functions of the opening of the recapitulation, but the whole course of events in the movement from m. 1 to m. 152 forms a process of development from a first expression of the basic thematic material to a more complex expression of it—from purely linear to linear-contrapuntal, from partial harmonic ambiguity (mm. 1–3) to resolution of ambiguity (mm. 152–154).

To scrutinize the exposition in the light of its opening phrase and with an eye for connections is to see a significant influence of that phrase on the contour or rhythmic form of every primary motivic idea introduced en route at important structural junctures. It is not necessary to quote elaborately; such

Example 2.13   Source G, fol. 1v, staves 1–9 (mm. 1–24)

*E and d perhaps present as faint traces in Vcl, bar 3/1–2.
†Lowest note of l.h. written a step lower.

AUTOGRAPH OF THE FIRST MOVEMENT OF OPUS 69

Example 2.13 (continued)

connections are visible enough at the following points: m. 25, Pfte right hand (the brief tonicization of A minor on the way to the preparation of the dominant area of the exposition), where the relationship is obviously one of contour; mm. 38–45, Pfte, the arpeggiated portion of the "second group," whose final version reveals, as mentioned earlier, a virtually complete rhythmic identity with the opening phrase; also m. 89, Vcl, in which the characteristically compressed "closing theme" is given close motivic associations with the opening of the first phrase, expanding its opening interval to a minor sixth but maintaining the element of rhythmic association.

In the development, new treatment of the initial motivic material results, as Schenker observed,[58] in new formulations that are open to elaborative possibilities of a new kind. The principal figures are shown in Example 2.14. Figure a is the primary unit of articulation throughout the development, significant especially as the element linking the two parallel passages, in f♯ minor and c♯ minor (mm. 107–114 and 127–136), that furnish the main balancing areas in the whole section. Figure b appears in this form at mm. 140–143 and 144–147 as the last new figure in the development and in effect the last new motivic unit in the movement. Its associations are complex: in rhythm and partial contour it connects with mm. 95–98 at the inception of the development, while it associates through contour alone with mm. 25–26, the A-minor area of the exposition. The special effect of mm. 140–144 seems to derive from the si-

Example 2.14

a)

b)

multaneous coordination of several factors: the progressive augmentation of prevailing metrical subdivisions in the second half of the development (note, for example, sixteenths at mm. 115–126; return of triplets at mm. 127–136; eighths at mm. 137–139; half notes at mm. 140–147, and at last the whole-note augmentation at mm. 148–151, just prior to the return); the elaboration of the initial rising fifth of the movement through unison and octave imitation, in which its measure 1 combines with measure 2 when used in this form, taking advantage of the contrapuntal possibility that is carefully worked out in sketches and in the autograph itself (Example 2.15).

Example 2.15

A later consequence of this is the Vcl augmentation at mm. 240–243 and again at mm. 244–251; also the final imitation of this type (Vcl and Pfte left hand) at mm. 270–272, elaborating this combination for the last time in the movement.

The last aspect to be considered is that which capitalizes on use of range. Here, too, a few words must stand for a great deal, and it should not be surprising that the same points of major structural articulation appear once again. The initial feature of greatest importance here is the expansion of range that follows upon the specific restriction of the opening phrase to the Vcl in low register. In the course of mm. 1–24, the first large segment of the whole exposition, two expansions of range occur: (1) in mm. 1–12 the Vcl contour woven around the single octave E–e builds to the four octaves separating the Vcl E from the Pfte high point first reached at m. 10. Crucial to this procedure is the persistence of the Vcl E in mm. 6–12 as bass to the Pfte, and corroboration of its importance is provided by the complete linear exploration of that

AUTOGRAPH OF THE FIRST MOVEMENT OF OPUS 69

range, once established, via the four-octave descent of the Pfte in the cadenza at m. 12; (2) at mm. 13–24 the opening material is restated in the three lower octaves of the total span; then, as the Vcl joins it, it expands to the same four-octave span once again at m. 24.

Of the innumerable ways in which such a movement capitalizes on links and associations of register, I can only allude to a few, especially those that form prominent parallels to the procedure established in mm. 1–12, with its direct expansion of range, from a limited sector to the whole spectrum, as part of a single larger phrase. This sort of range-expansion links the opening with the "second subject" at mm. 38–45, the Vcl rising in linear scale-steps through two and a half octaves while the Pfte descends simultaneously through three; the rapid exchange of rising and falling scale-patterns (in triplet diminution) at mm. 79–82; the range-expansion from two to four octaves within four measures at mm. 95–98; and, most important of all, the parallel upward expansion (in *pp*) at mm. 140–143 and 144–147—now moving up from low point to high point through four octaves again within four measures, and now brining each successively articulated octave in each new measure, owing to the imitation.

Having seen this much of this mode of association throughout the movement, we can turn back at last to the autograph, the main subject of this essay. At the beginning I alluded to the clear and uncanceled state of the first page (mm. 1–17), the serenity of which assures us firmly that it had reached a definite and virtually final state. From what we have seen of the first phrase, it could be argued that not only its general character but its motivic construction is suggested by the broad physical spacing of mm. 1–5 across the first system, which forms an example of what Paul Mies has called Beethoven's "hörmässige Schreibart"[59]—his "auditory method of writing." What Mies is referring to is visible in many aspects of Beethoven's musical handwriting, which can be seen as a means of notation whose graphic properties mirror the spatial and organizational properties of their musical contents and even suggest something of their appropriate style of performance. Similarly impressive is the immense space accorded the descending Pfte cadenza in the third system of folio 1r, which occupies as much space in its system as four measures do in the preceding systems. Spatial too is the grouping of triplets in the transition to the dominant in the exposition: one observes on folio 2r in the second system the relatively close crowding of the Pfte triplets at m. 35 and the expanded space accorded the Vcl repetition (*with its change of mode*) at m. 36, as if to imply a slight broadening-out as the dominant of E is prolonged prior to resolution at m. 38; if this seems doubtful, consult folio 6r for a precisely similar spacing in the corresponding measures in the recapitulation. Beams and slurs play equally prominent roles, as Schenker insisted long ago; witness the long arching slur over the entire Pfte phrase at mm. 51–54 (2v/system 2) and slurs at later passages, including mm. 140–148 (both instruments), 175–182 (Vcl), 188–195 (Pfte), and in the coda throughout the last two pages.

Brief and scattered as these examples may be, they nevertheless reinforce what ought by now to be a widely acknowledged truism, namely that in musical masterpieces the means of organization of content and the means of expressing that organization in graphic form are bound up with each other in the closest possible way.

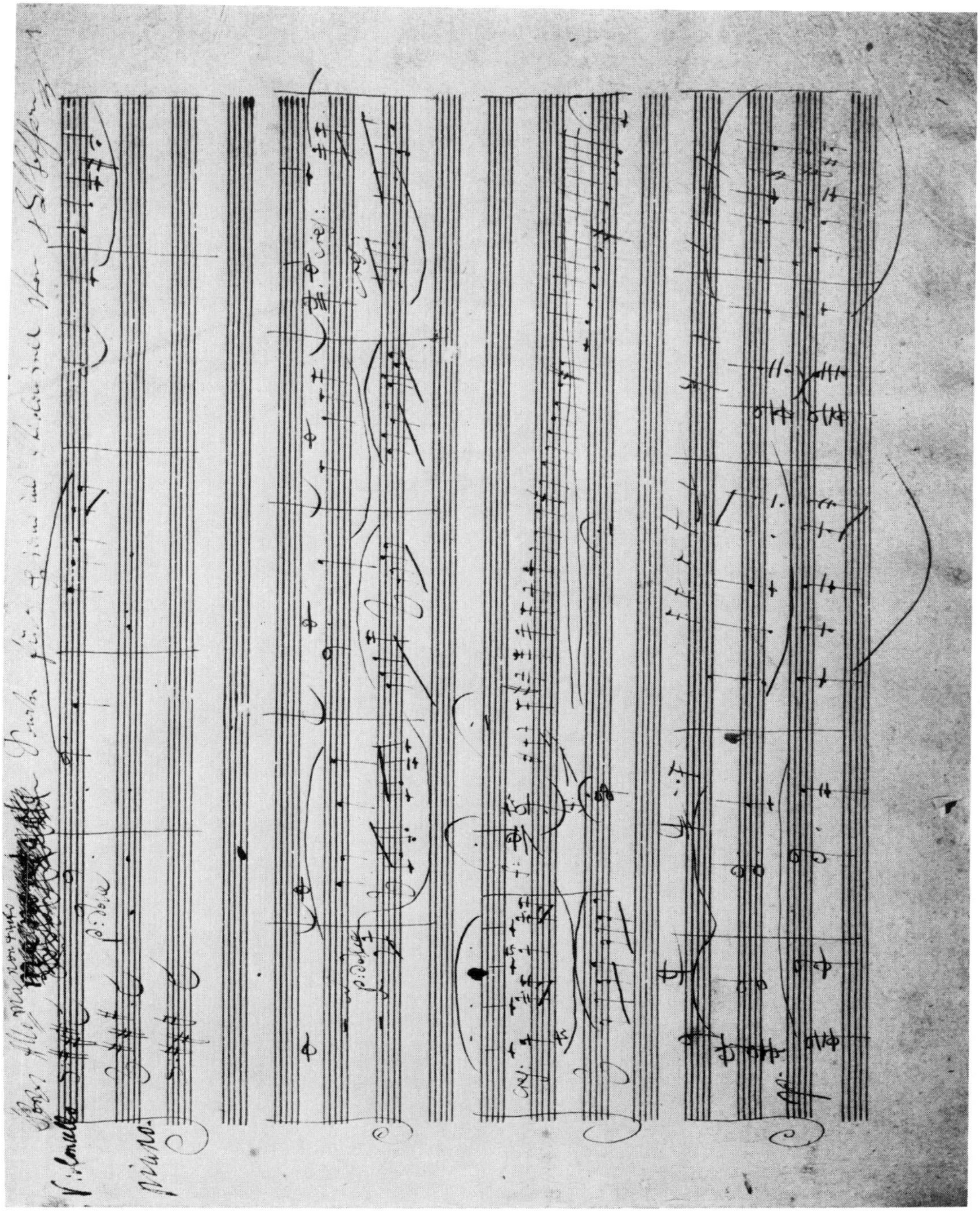

Figure 2.4a Autograph of the first movement of Beethoven's Sonata for Violoncello and Pianoforte, Op. 69: 1 recto (mm. 1–17)

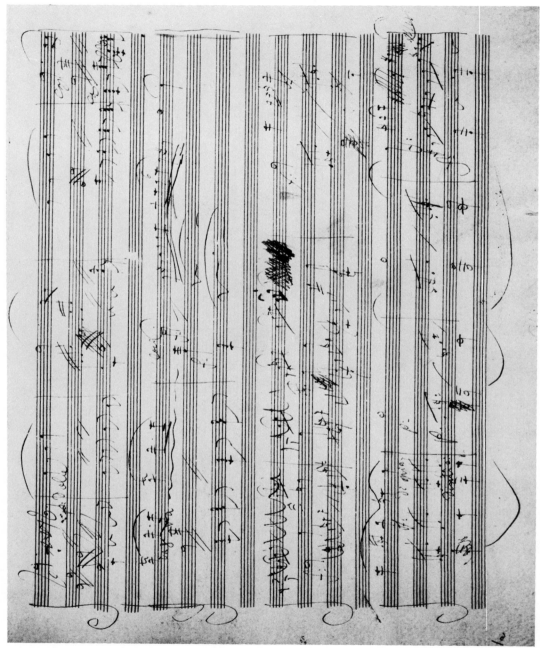

Figure 2.4b I verso (mm. 18–31)

AUTOGRAPH OF THE FIRST MOVEMENT OF OPUS 69

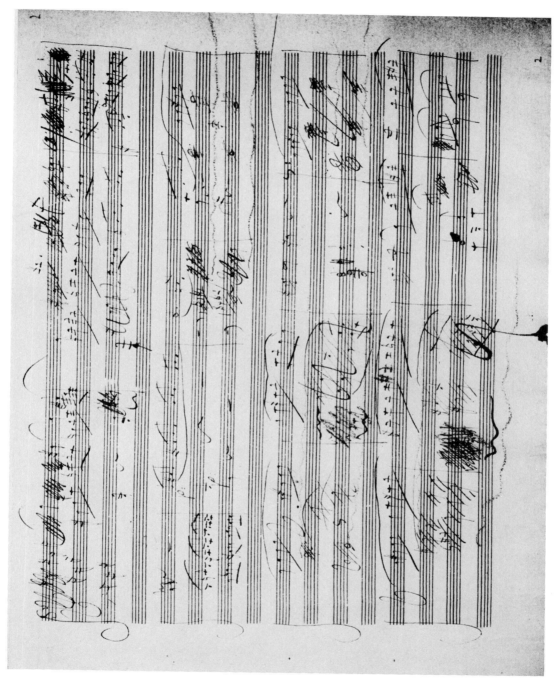

Figure 2.4c 2 recto (mm. 32–46)

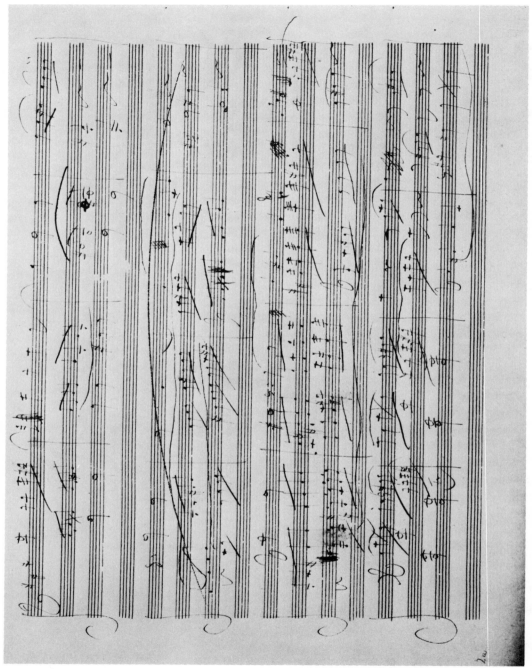

Figure 2.4d 2 verso (mm. 47–62)

AUTOGRAPH OF THE FIRST MOVEMENT OF OPUS 69

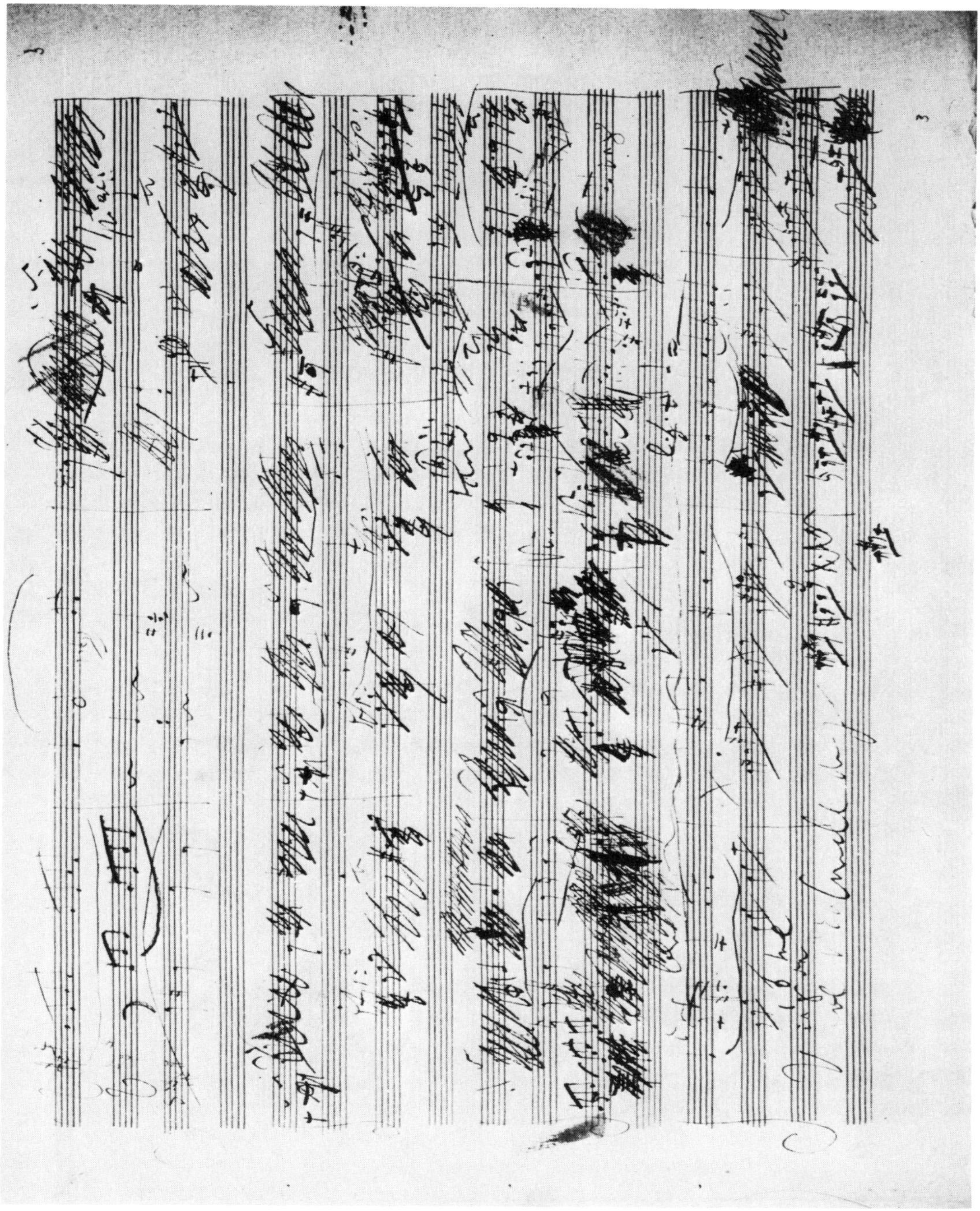

Figure 2.4e 3 recto (mm. 63–76)

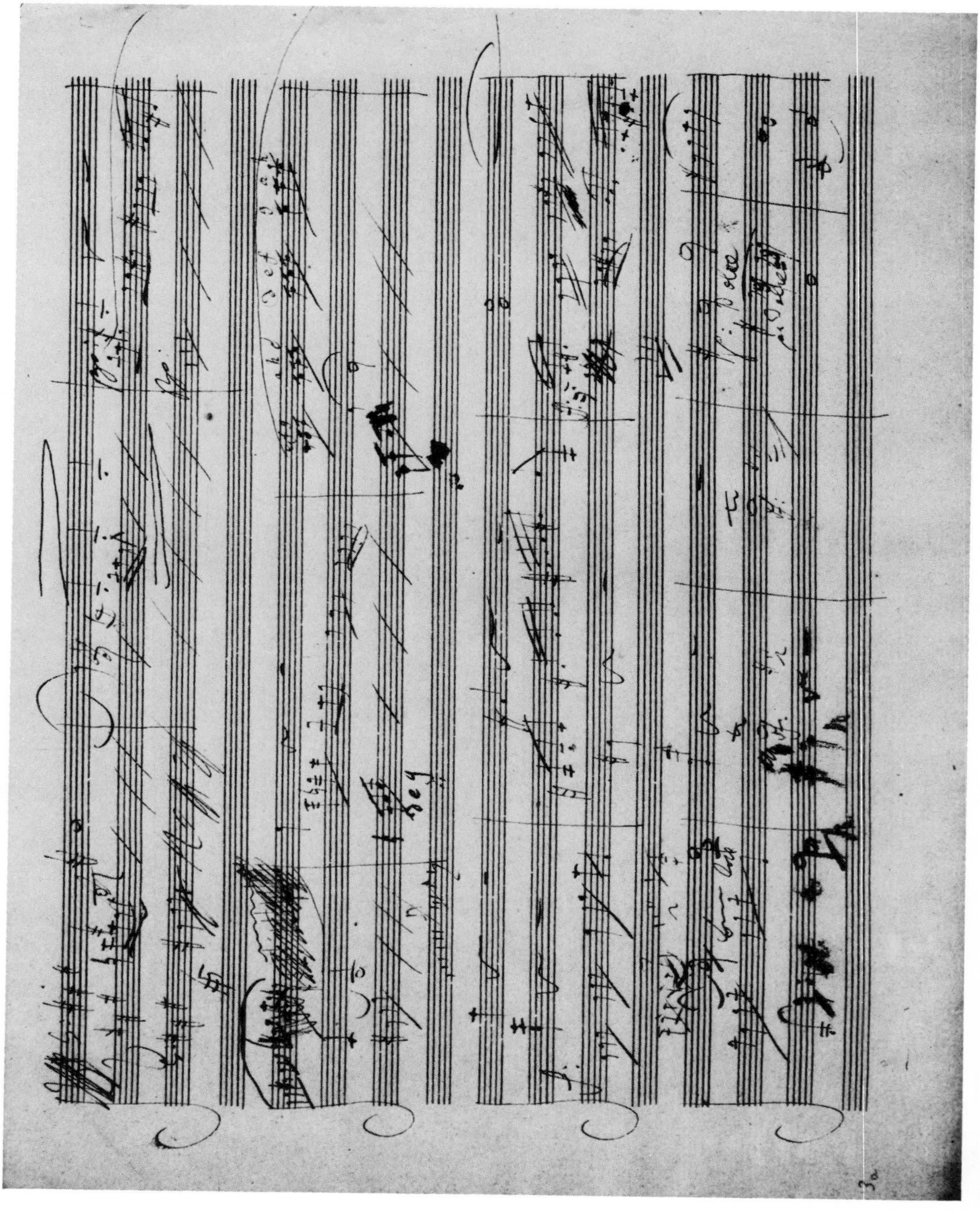

Figure 2.4f 3 verso (mm. 77–90)

AUTOGRAPH OF THE FIRST MOVEMENT OF OPUS 69

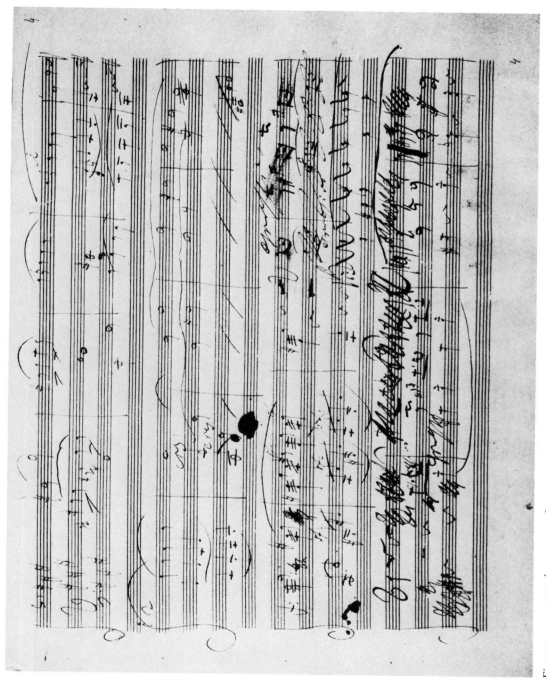

Figure 2.4g 4 recto (mm. 91–106)

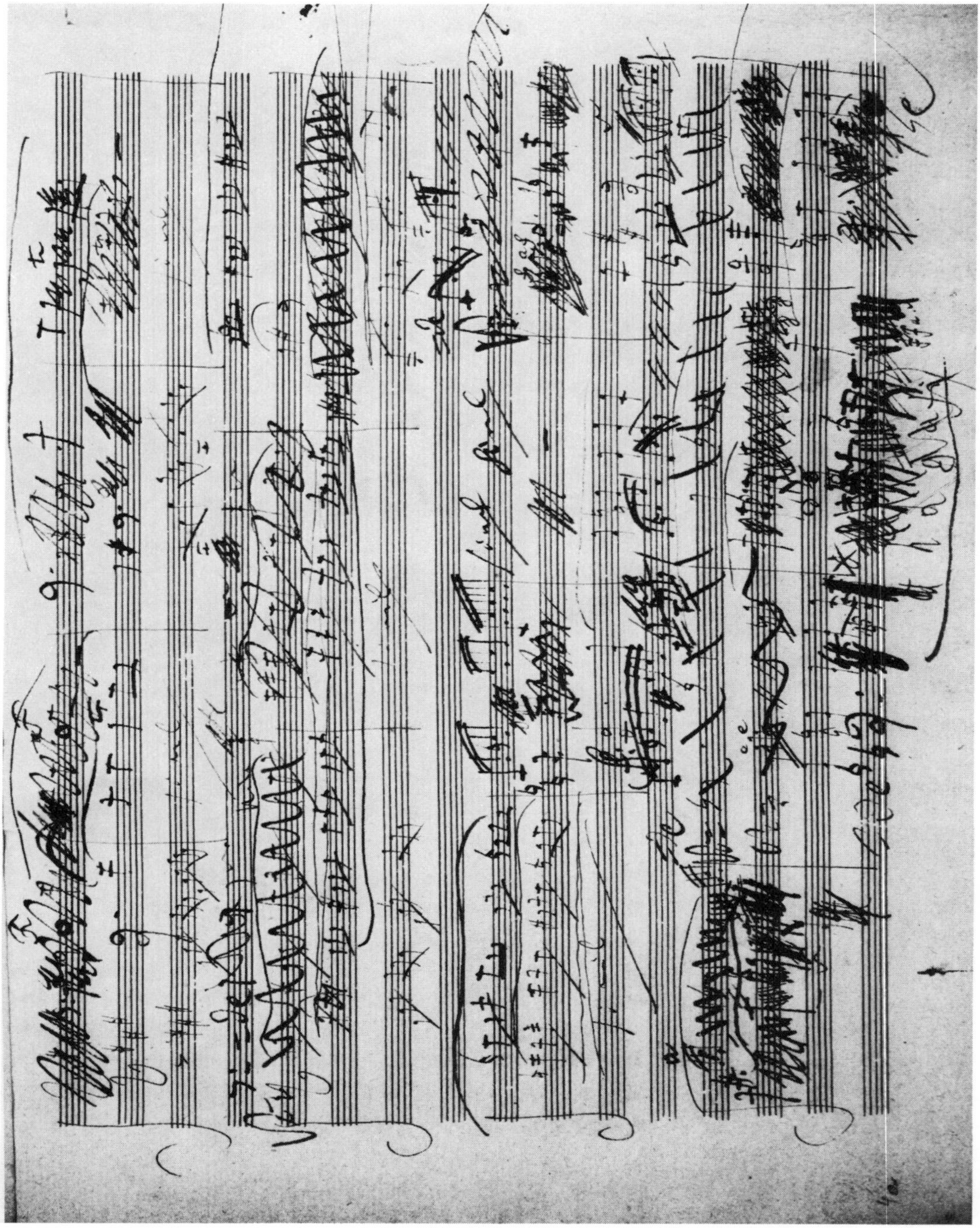

Figure 2.4h 4 verso (mm. 107–121)

AUTOGRAPH OF THE FIRST MOVEMENT OF OPUS 69

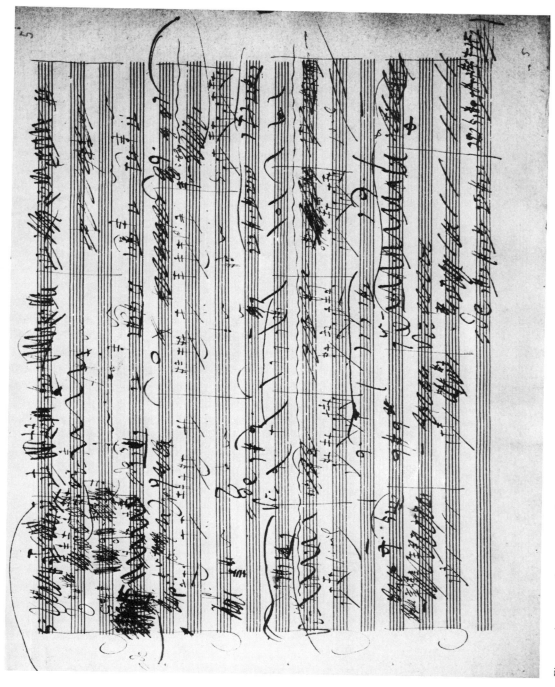

Figure 2.41 5 recto (mm. 122–136)

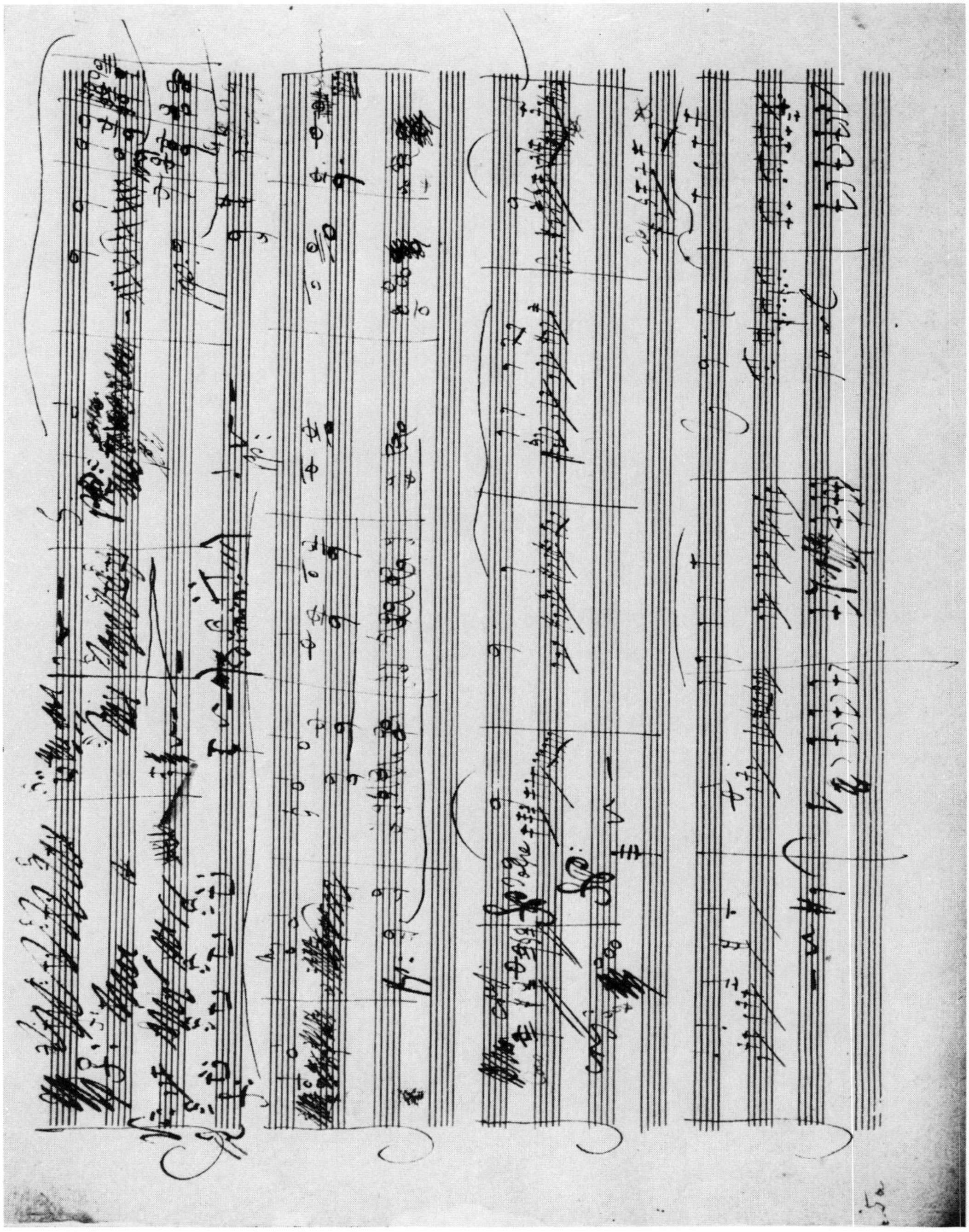

Figure 2.4j 5 verso (mm. 137–160)

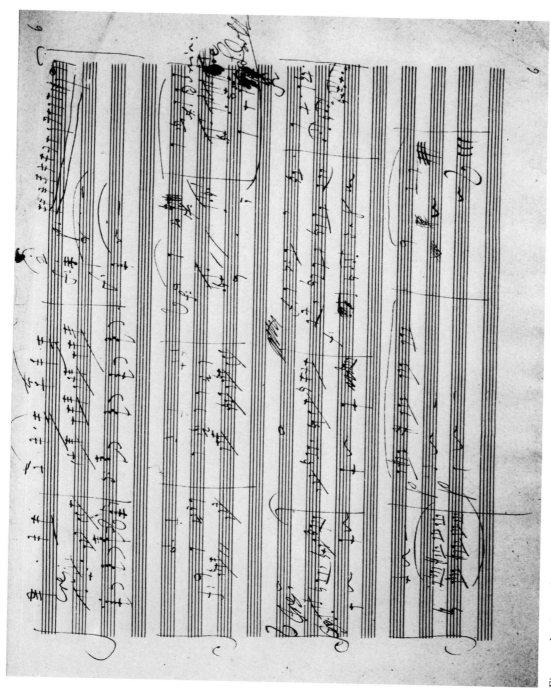

Figure 2.4k 6 recto (mm. 161–174)

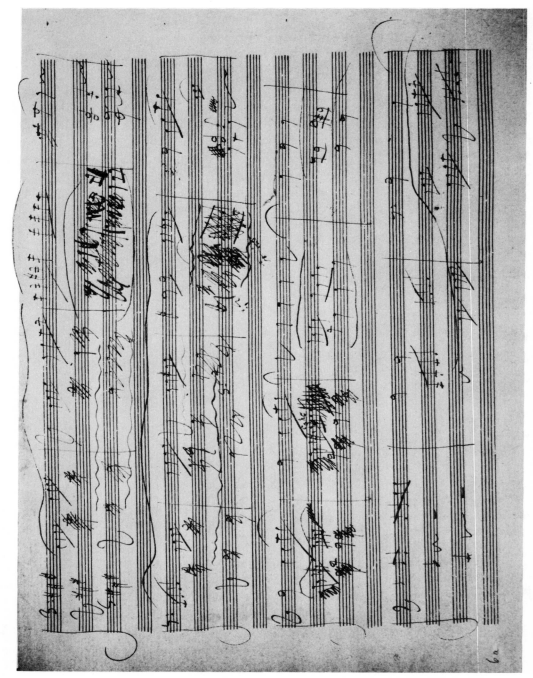

Figure 2.4 6 verso (mm. 175–189)

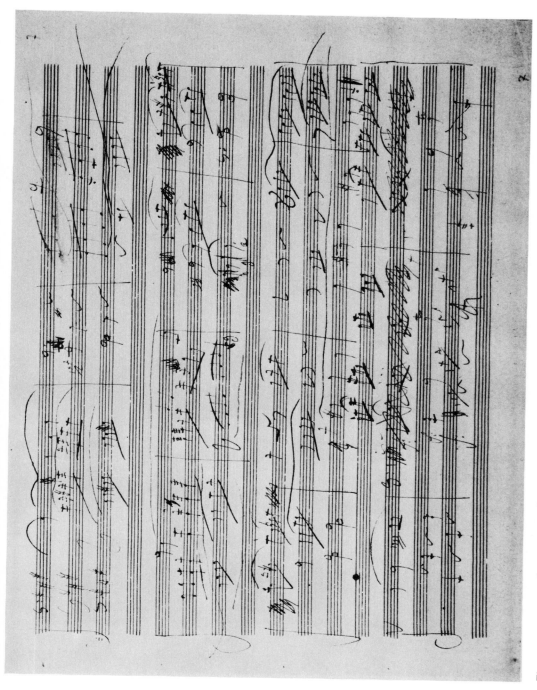

Figure 2.4m 7 recto (mm. 190–203)

Figure 2.4n 7 verso (mm. 204–216)

AUTOGRAPH OF THE FIRST MOVEMENT OF OPUS 69

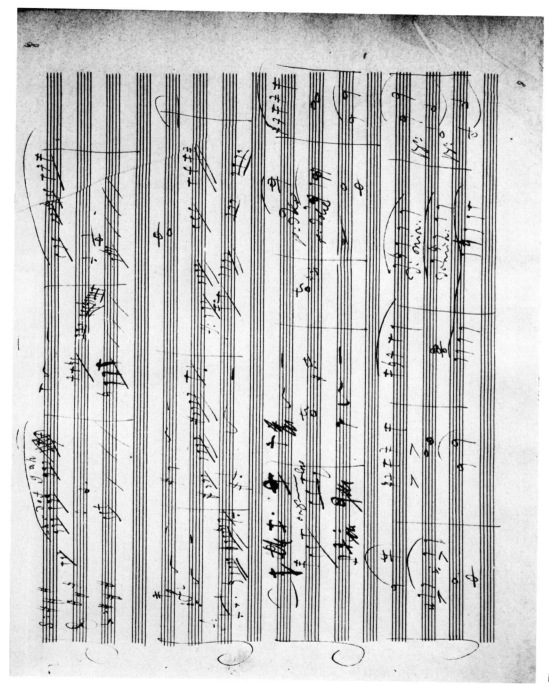

Figure 2.40 8 recto (mm. 217–232)

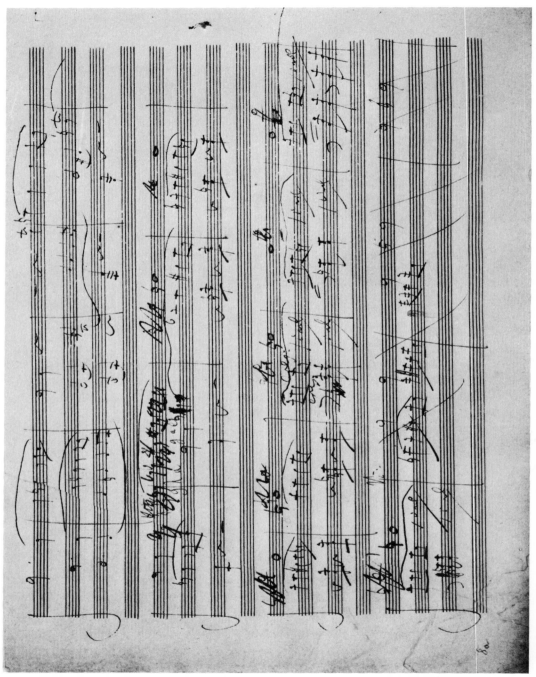

Figure 2.4p 8 verso (mm. 233–250; 248–250 canceled)

AUTOGRAPH OF THE FIRST MOVEMENT OF OPUS 69

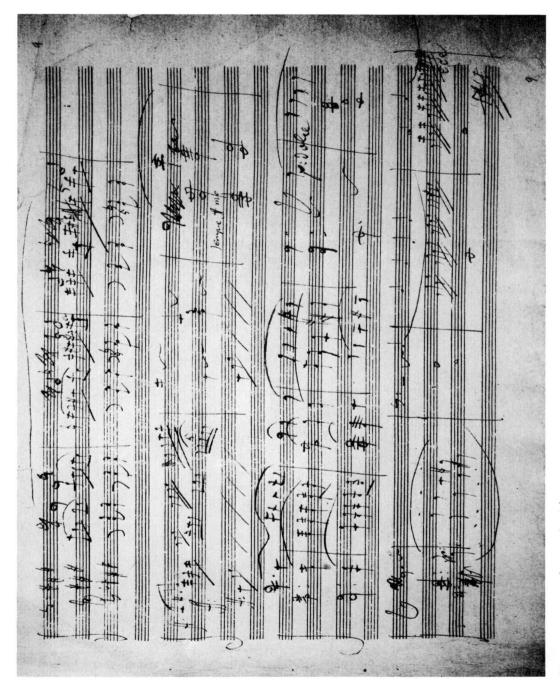

Figure 2.49 9 recto (mm. 248–264)

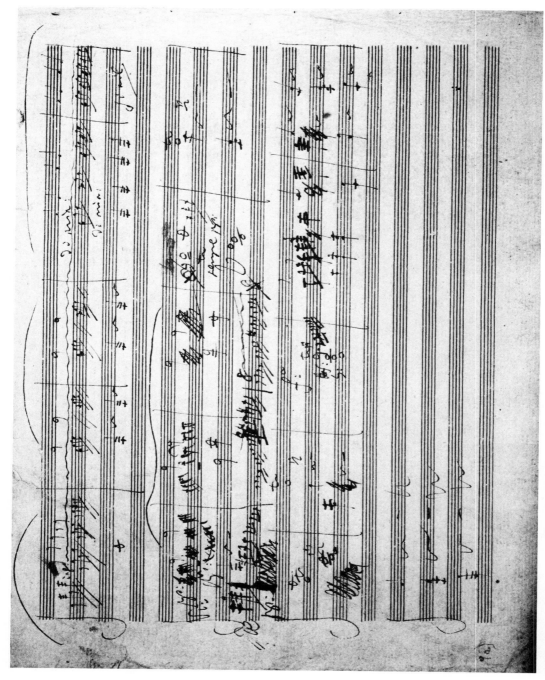

Figure 2.4r 9 verso (mm. 265–280)

AUTOGRAPH OF THE FIRST MOVEMENT OF OPUS 69

Beethoven's Sketches for *Sehnsucht* (WoO 146)

Nothing in the broad span of Beethoven biography or historiography has found a wider and more uncritical acceptance than the view of his creative work as being normally a process of assiduous labor by which once commonplace musical thoughts were transformed by gradual stages into artistic substance. This is often contrasted with the supposedly automatic flow of creative imagination characteristic of a Mozart. Thus the poet Stephen Spender, in an essay first published in 1946, says:

> Some poets write immediately works which, when they are written, scarcely need revision. Others write their poems by stages, feeling their way from rough draft to rough draft, until finally, after many revisions, they have produced a result which may seem to have very little connection with their early sketches.
>
> These two opposite processes are vividly illustrated in two examples drawn from music: Mozart and Beethoven. Mozart thought out symphonies, quartets, even scenes from operas, entirely in his head—often on a journey or perhaps while dealing with pressing problems—and then he transcribed them, in their completeness, onto paper. Beethoven wrote fragments of themes in note books which he kept beside him, working on and developing them over years. Often his first ideas were of a clumsiness which makes scholars marvel how he could, at the end, have developed from them such miraculous results.
>
> Thus genius works in different ways to achieve its ends.[1]

The basis for this prevailing view is, needless to say, the sketchbooks; or rather, those essays about the sketchbooks that have filtered out into the popular literature about Beethoven. Few scholars and even fewer amateurs have actually worked closely with the inner contents of even one Beethoven sketchbook, and scholarship in this field since the late nineteenth century has been remarkably monolithic.

The standard view, repeated by Spender, is drawn, no doubt indirectly, from Nottebohm's pioneering essays, which were first published in the 1870s and 1880s[2] and have been supplemented since then by all too few later studies and transcriptions.[3] In many particular cases this view may, indeed, turn out to be valid and entirely convincing, but in the absence of close study of particular works and their genetic backgrounds, it lacks depth and substance. Enough is known of the chronology of Beethoven's works to suggest not a single mode of compositional procedure but a broad spectrum of structural problems to which a variety of approaches must have been necessary. At one end of the spectrum, for example, is a work allegedly composed in a single night—the Horn Sonata, Op. 17—and at the other is the Ninth Symphony, the first hints for which (at least the idea of a setting of the "Ode to Joy") date from even before the period of Beethoven's arrival in Vienna in the early 1790s, and which in a more specific sense was sketched for at least eight or nine years before its completion in 1824.[4] The purpose of this essay, then, is to take a close look at one of the most frequently mentioned examples of Beethoven's elaboration of a single thematic idea in a single sketchbook—his sketches for the song *Sehnsucht,* WoO 146.

II

Despite the conservative and even recessive character of the German song literature as Beethoven approached it, this piece shows considerable breadth of conception and careful modeling of details. It is one of Beethoven's most interesting achievements in what was for him a secondary genre up until the writing of *An die ferne Geliebte,* which seems to have followed directly on the composition of this song. *Sehnsucht* was written in 1815 and was first published in June 1816. It was based on a poem by C. L. Reissig, a professional military man and dilettante poet of idiosyncratic character, whose works were used by Beethoven for as many as seven songs written between 1809 and 1815; this is the last of the group.[5] In the familiar jargon of lieder categories, as used by Hans Boettcher in his useful survey of the Beethoven songs, *Sehnsucht* stands halfway between the extremes of the purely strophic and the thoroughly through-composed.[6] Boettcher labels it, appropriately enough, "variierte Strophenlied" (strophic song with variations) of the type in which variation is most prominent in the successive patterns of figuration with which the instrumental component accompanies repetitions of the melody. As Boettcher observes, this type is represented by only a few of Beethoven's vocal compositions, all relatively late works: the present song; the *Abendlied,* WoO 150, of 1820; and the *Opferlied,* Op. 121b, of 1824 (a work that also goes back to early antecedents).

The text of *Sehnsucht* is laid out in three double stanzas of eight lines each: 4 + 4 lines regularly alternating seven and six syllables with three main stresses per line (iambic trimeter) and an alternating rhyme-scheme: *a b a b, c d c d,* and so forth. The image evoked is that of a sleepless lover whose inner torment contrasts with the calm peace of night:

1a   Die stille Nacht umdunkelt
     erquickend Thal und Höh',
     der Stern der Liebe funkelt,
     sanft wallend in dem See.

1b   Verstummt sind in den Zwei-
     gen
     die Sänger der Natur;
     geheimnissvolles Schweigen
     ruht auf der Blumenflur.

2a   Ach, mir nur schliesst kein Schlummer
     die müden Augen zu:
     Komm, lindre meinen Kummer,
     du stiller Gott der Ruh'!

2b   Sanft trockne mir die Thränen,
     gib' süsser Freude Raum,
     komm, täusche hold mein
     Sehnen
     mit einem Wonnetraum!

3a   O zaub're meinen Blicken
     die Holde, die mich flieht,
     lass mich an's Herz sie drücken,
     dass edle Lieb' entglüht!

3b   Du Holde, die ich meine,
     wie sehn' ich mich nach dir;
     erscheine, ach erscheine
     und lächle Hoffnung mir!

This type of four-line stanza is less frequent in earlier Beethoven songs than a pattern alternating eight and seven syllables (for example, Op. 52 No. 1, the very early song *Urians Reise um die Welt*) or eight and six (Op. 52 No. 8, *Es blüht ein Blümchen irgendwo*),[7] but he had set this pattern at least twice before. One example is his equally early setting of Goethe's *Flohlied* from *Faust* (Op. 75 No. 3); another, perhaps significantly, is an earlier setting of another text by Reissig, *Der Zufriedene*, Op. 75 No. 6, of 1809.[8] In both earlier settings of 7 + 6–syllable verse, Beethoven had used the conventional $\frac{2}{4}$ meter in a moderate to fast tempo, thus contributing to what we now see as the larger background for Schubert's masterpieces in this verse pattern, such as *Die Forelle* and *Wohin*. The declamation of the earlier examples furnishes a basis for comparison with *Sehnsucht;* see Example 3.1.

Example 3.1   Declamation in Op. 75 No. 3 and Op. 75 No. 6

(a) Op. 75 No. 3

Poco Allegretto

Es war ein-mal ein Kö-nig der hatt' ei-nen gros-sen Floh etc.

(b) Op. 75 No. 6

Froh und heiter, etwas lebhaft

Zwar schuf das Glück her-nie-der, mich we-der reich noch gross etc.

From the relative simplicity of Op. 75 it is a long step to the unhackneyed choice of triple meter in *Sehnsucht,* with its concomitant effect of enjambment for paired lines, its subtle differentiation of accent for parallel words and syllables, and the many delicate rhythmic features by which Beethoven elaborates not only the pianoforte figurations but selected bars in the vocal strophes themselves (compare the vocal part in mm. 11 and 22, mm. 6 and 27, mm. 9 and 30). Essential to the conception of the song is its completely syllabic textsetting and its larger organization in parallel phrases of four bars each (eight bars each strophe), with introductory units of two bars each preceding the main strophes (except at m. 23, where it is one bar long) and with one bar between half strophes (mm. 7, 18, and 28). Both the upper line and its harmonic underpinning are so tightly confined to the functional domain of E major that the piece lacks scope for all but the lightest suggestion of a tonicization of the dominant (mm. 8, 19, and 29); the only other chromatic inflection anywhere is the passing A♯ at mm. 10, 21, and 31.

Boettcher is surely right in associating a strophic variation song of this type and period with Beethoven's continued use of variation procedures in such works as the *Archduke Trio,* Op. 97, and the Piano Sonata, Op. 109.[9] Not only in key and meter but also in initial thematic contour, this song has come to be seen as foreshadowing the variation movement of Op. 109.[10] Apart from its variation form and unusual meter, the basic layout of the song is simple enough, and its strophic design is an essential background condition for the sketches. For when we find that Beethoven doggedly explores a wide variety of linear, metrical, and rhythmic formulations for the opening of the song, we need to keep in mind that he was, in effect, testing a formulation that would decisively determine the form of the entire piece. This is a substantially different situation from those in which he reworks a single subject that can form only a fractional segment of a diversified musical continuum. The point needs emphasis precisely because the many reshapings of this material—and even these sketches themselves, as incompletely presented by Nottebohm—have been taken as typical examples of Beethoven's sketch process as a whole, while in fact it would be safer and saner, in the light of present knowledge of the vast source material, to take them as sketches definitely linked only to the working out of this single strophic song, thirty-four measures in total duration.

III

In his essay in *Zweite Beethoveniana* entitled "Ein Skizzenbuch aus den Jahren 1815 und 1816," Nottebohm published a series of melodic entries for *Sehnsucht* that have since remained the exclusive basis for comments on the sketches for the piece.[11] The sketchbook from which they are drawn was one that Nottebohm had studied in Vienna, since in the mid-nineteenth century it was the property of a private collector, Eugen von Miller. Later it passed into the collection of Louis Koch, and recently it has been acquired by William Scheide.[12] It is Beethoven's major sketchbook for 1815 and at least the early part of 1816, to judge from the completed works for which it contains preparatory studies; these include not only *An die ferne Geliebte,* Op. 98, on which Joseph Kerman has written, but also the Piano Sonata, Op. 101, and the last of Beethoven's violoncello sonatas, Op. 102 No. 2. It also contains material for a number of projects that remained incomplete, among them a D-major piano concerto and an F-minor trio.[13] On pages 60–65, directly following ten pages of sketches for Op. 102 No. 2, and preceding six pages of sketches for Op. 98, it contains six pages devoted solely to material for this song.

From these sketches for *Sehnsucht,* Nottebohm printed some sixteen entries. His transcriptions exhibit the high degree of musical insight we learn to expect from Nottebohm, but they are presented with the limitations characteristic of his methods. First, the material is by no means complete, and it lacks all indication of the basis for selecting some items and omitting others. Second, there is no hint of the basis on which the order of the transcriptions was decided, beyond a tacit commonsense inference that they probably occur on the sketchbook pages in a top-to-bottom, left-to-right order, corresponding to what Nottebohm gives us (as will be seen, this is a most difficult and crucial point). Here, as elsewhere in Nottebohm, there is no mention of the entire problem of spatial grouping in the source material or of the possibility of devising various possible genetic orderings in the light of spatial arrangements. Third, the entries are not given in diplomatic transcription: stems are reversed, clefs are tacitly entered without indication of whether they were in the original or not, there are no footnotes indicating doubtful readings (this may be the fault of Nottebohm's editor, Mandyczewski), and words of text are regularly included whether or not they appear in the original.[14]

If one defines as an "entry" any intelligible unit that is not the continuation of preceding material, there are not sixteen but thirty-one entries for the song spread over five pages of the sketchbook (pages 60–64), plus jottings on a sixth page (page 65). Even after subtracting from these what might be considered truly minor variants, we can distinguish twenty-three entries on pages 60–64 (see Examples 3.5–3.9 at the end of this chapter), all but three of which include portions of the vocal line. As a first means of establishing the scope of the material, I have tried to codify the entries as shown in Table 3.1, in which the capital letters at the left represent what I take to be the major units that can be distinguished as individual entries.

The crudity of such a table is all too obvious once one has made it, yet it nevertheless supplies a tabulation that makes possible direct reference to particular entries and their possible interrelations. I am well aware that one cate-

Table 3.1   Sketch entries for *Sehnsucht*

Entry	Sketchbook Page	Sketchbook Staff	Nottebohm (N II) Page and item no.	Corresponding bars in WoO 146	Comments
A	60	1 left	332 (no. 1)	3–4	
B	60	2 left	332 (no. 2)	3–4	
C	60	1 right + 2 right	332 (no. 3)	3–4	
D	60	3 right	—	3–4	
E	60	4 right	—	3–4	
F	60	5 right	332 (no. 4)	3–4	
G	60	6 left	332 (no. 5)	3–4	
H	60	7 right	332 (no. 6)	3–4	
	60	8 left	—	4?	= alternative for H?
I	60	9 right	333 (no. 1)	3–6	
		10			
		11			
J	60	12–13 + 14	333 (no. 2) incomplete	3–6	
	60	15	—	5–6?	= alternative for J, mm. 5–6?
K	61	1 center	333 (no. 3)	3–4	
L	61	3 center	—	3–4	
M	61	4 center	333 (no. 4)	3–4	
N	61	6 center	—	3–4	
O	61	8 center	—	3–4	"oder C" [$\frac{4}{4}$]
P	61	9 center	333 (no. 5)	3 (4 implied)	related to O
Q	61	10–11	—	3–4?	
R	61	12–13	—	3–6	
S	62	1–2 left	333 (no. 6)	3–6	in E♭
	62	2 right + 3	—	5–6 (twice?)	= alternative for S?
T	62	5–8	333 (no. 7) incomplete	3–11	
U	62	11	333 (no. 8)	3–4	
	63	1 (fragment)	—	pfte., m. 2?	
V	63	3–4, 5–6, 7	333 (no. 9)	3–11	
	63	10	—	10–11?	variant of mm. 10–11 for V?
	63	12	—	10–11?	variant of 10–11 for V?
	63	13	—	14 (pfte.)	fragment of pfte. part
W	64	1–2–3–4–	333 (no. 10) incomplete	3–11	
	64	5 (two fragments)		11?	
	64	10, 12, 13, 14, 15, 16 (all right side)	—	16ff., pfte?	
X	65	1–2, 3–4, 5–6 plus other fragments	—	3–4 (plus others)	fragments of pfte. part

gory in the table is particularly gross: the terms "right," "left," and "center" as indications of location of entries on individual staffs. Perhaps open to question, too, in a few cases is the assignment of an entry to particular bars of the finished version, though here I think the attribution of most of the entries to the opening bars of the vocal line (mm. 3–4) is unequivocal once one has seen the larger organization of the song. Much more arbitrary, and inevitably so, is the precise basis for setting up the alphabetical order in the way I have done. A close look at the page, staff, and "Nottebohm" columns, however, should indicate that the primary ordering follows the material across and down each page, while also holding to Nottebohm's ordering of his examples, to facilitate comparison. What cannot be grasped from the table at all are the spatial relations and graphic character of pairs and groups of entries (for example, the proximity of A and B, or the close similarity in size and writing style of C, D, E, and F), as well as many more subtle nuances. For this my defense is that these can hardly be grasped from any transcription, even an exact diplomatic one, without close comparison with the original, as recent publications of sketchbooks have shown; effective judgments in such matters can only be made on the basis of access to good-quality facsimiles.[15] The table and the transcriptions given here and in Nottebohm should be compared with Figures 3.1 and 3.2 (reproducing pages 60 and 61).

Grouping on paleographic criteria. In broad terms there is a basic distinction between pages 60–61 and 62–64. The first two pages present numerous elaborations of segments of the basic theme, as well as some full statements of it, while pages 63–64 present, essentially, only complete versions of the subject, one to a page. If we attempt beyond this to group the entries by some sort of paleographic criteria, the first observation to be made is that pages 60–61, with the sketches, and pages 62–63, with the complete subject, are all in ink; while page 64, again presenting the full theme in a broad and central position on the page, is entirely in pencil. Pages 64 and 65 are the only pages in pencil in this part of the sketchbook, and they are two of only five in the entire sketchbook that are wholly in pencil.[16] The importance of this point is purely negative: it establishes that we have no reason to think that pages 60–63 were done at different times, times when quite different implements and ink could have been at hand and could have created quite different appearances for certain entries on these pages. Quite the contrary: the whole appearance of these pages suggests much more strongly that they were written rapidly and consecutively. Since they evidently represent a highly concentrated effort to explore various possibilities for the organization of the opening phrase (and its declamation), they could, indeed, be plausibly interpreted as the product of a very short span of time—and would thus represent not long and tedious labor, but the rapid tumbling out of ideas, one after another.[17]

Perhaps the principal paleographic problem in these entries is the spatial layout of page 60. Here I propose to classify the material into "primary" and

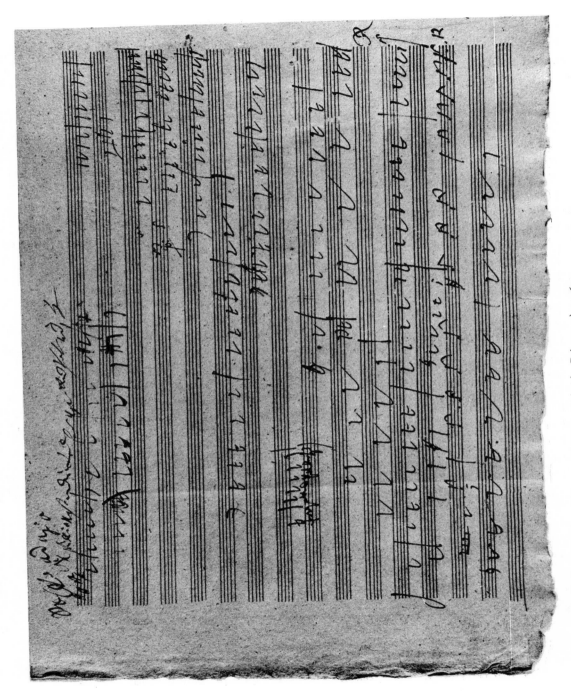

Figure 3.1 Scheide sketchbook (library of William Scheide, Princeton), p. 60

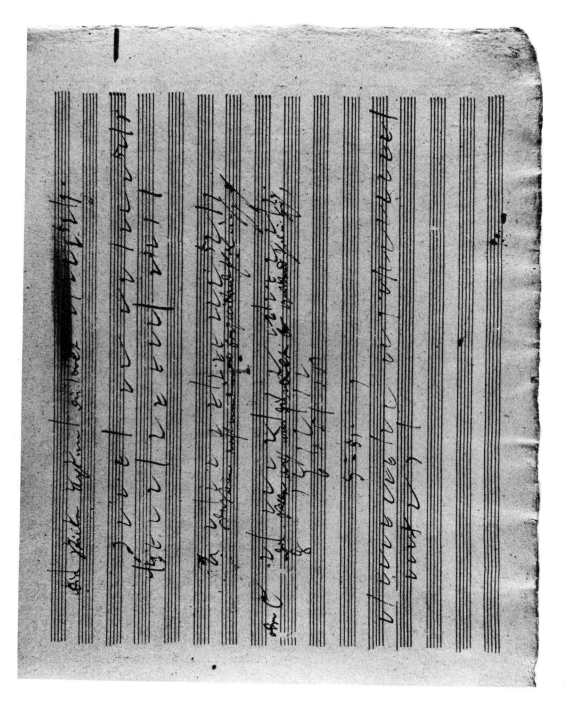

Figure 3.2 Scheide sketchbook (library of William Scheide, Princeton), p. 61

"secondary" groups, both with regard to location and with regard to possible order of writing. For page 60 Nottebohm's ordering moves across the first two staffs, so that his A and B are followed by the four short entries in the upper-right-hand area that I am calling C–F, even though these units are quite different in manner of writing (they are smaller and more crowded in comparison to everything else on the page). Starting at staff 6, the writing once again becomes bold and centrally spaced, resuming the character of A and B. It seems at least plausible to imagine that the entire group in the upper-right-hand area of page 60 could have been quite literally a secondary group, and that it could have been inserted into an available space after the remainder of page 60 had been filled out. Against this is the coincidence that the "primary" group resumes directly after it on staff 6. Yet even if one holds fast to Nottebohm's inference that the group C–F follows directly from A–B, it is well to realize that there would have been room for entry A to go on into the remainder of the main theme, if Beethoven had not then begun to experiment with just the first two measures of that theme; entries C–F represent, on the other hand, small-scale jottings that rework the same two bars (3–4) of the theme but lack the bold spacings of the other entries and, located at the margin, lack even the possibility of continuing on with the theme. These entries, then, are "subsketches," and in that sense, too, seem to be "secondary" items. On the remaining pages no such anomalous group appears. On page 61 everything is in the same broad style of writing as the primary group of page 60; the only secondary units here—secondary on internal, not paleographic, grounds—are P and Q, which may possibly be immediate alternatives to O. On page 62 everything is primary; on page 63 all the material from staff 3 to staff 7 is primary, the remaining staffs having local variants. I should repeat here that page 65 contains a set of jottings for the pianoforte part alone, and may be thought of as leading on to the autograph, where extensive revisions of the accompaniment are also found but in which the vocal line is fully established in its final form.

Metrical and rhythmic variants. With the spatial groupings in view we are prepared to look more closely at the material itself, particularly the variants of mm. 3–4 that are spread through pages 60 and 61—the "sketch pages." Although the separation of metrical and rhythmic features from those of contour is inevitably arbitrary, it will simplify the discussion and make possible a synthesis of details at a later point. Again, it must be kept sharply in view that the piece for which these variants are proposed is a short strophic setting of a 7 + 6–syllable verse pattern, for which the choice of meter determines not merely the autonomous musical shape of the line but the declamation of the text. If we tabulate once more, a more comprehensive view is possible, and these entries should be examined with the words of lines 1 and 2 in mind (see Example 3.2).

Example 3.2 Rhythm in the sketches for *Sehnsucht* (entries A to R)

*Written as a quarter-note in the sketchbook.

Immediately striking in larger terms is a general parallel between the two pages of sketches: on page 60 the material begins with two units in $\frac{2}{4}$ and only reaches $\frac{3}{4}$ at entries H, I, and J; this is so whether or not the sketch group C–F is regarded as an interpolation. On page 61 the process is virtually the same: a series of $\frac{2}{4}$ elaborations leads to $\frac{6}{8}$ and finally to $\frac{3}{4}$. After this point in the material, the remaining pages contain only entries in $\frac{3}{4}$—the final metrical form has been decided.[18] The larger parallelism of the two sketch pages suggests, beyond this, that what I am calling A and K, both of which are boldly written entries at the tops of their respective pages and both of which have text, could have been written as deliberately conventional points of departure for the excursions which follow upon each one. If this is not so it is an astonishing coincidence that of the $\frac{2}{4}$ entries these two—and only these—are rhythmically identical to each other; the only major discrepancy is the "molto adagio" before A, while K has no tempo marking. One could even imagine that A and K could have been written first, for some reason, at the tops of the pages, and the remainders filled in. But while this can be imagined, it cannot be verified.

That Beethoven is systematically exploring a range of possibilities in meter and rhythm is further made clear when we separate the entries into $\frac{2}{4}$ and $\frac{3}{4}$ groups and their subdivisions. Entry A opens the $\frac{2}{4}$ series with a simple treatment of the text in which the first weak syllable is on the upbeat; this is followed in B, K (as we have seen), and then consecutively in M, N, and O. The alternative in $\frac{2}{4}$, beginning on the second eighth of the measure, turns up first in entry F, and is followed by G (with sixteenth-note offbeat), and then by L. On page 60, entry C shows a first trial of $\frac{6}{8}$, but this is not followed up until the next page in the fragmentary entries P and Q. The next major phase is the $\frac{3}{4}$ group, in which an interesting point is the arrival at the final rhythmic version of mm. 3–4 fairly early in the series. Entry E seems to apply in $\frac{3}{4}$ the opening with weak beat following the downbeat, as does H; but at I the final version is reached. On page 61, R is the only $\frac{3}{4}$ reading at all, and it has the complete rhythmic form of the final version. The metrical state of affairs between pages 60 and 61 strongly suggests the hypothesis that in writing out page 60 Beethoven worked his way through to the $\frac{3}{4}$ meter and then, on page 61, returned to an exploration of $\frac{2}{4}$ before settling once and for all on $\frac{3}{4}$.

The inner rhythmic intricacies of some of the entries are best considered in the light of their contours, but a few points can be made here. The difference between m. 2 of entries A and K and almost all the others (whether in $\frac{2}{4}$ or $\frac{3}{4}$) is very striking. A and K give a half-measure agogic accent to the first beat of m. 2 ("um-*dun*-kelt") that is more in the manner of Beethoven's earlier declamation than of the refinements he is seeking in this song. In all later entries this syllable is reduced in length and integrated into the rhythmic flow, propelling the motion forward without extension or pause on the accented syllable.

Contour variants. Although the variants of pages 60 and 61 cover as wide a span of possibilities in inner contour as in rhythmic design, they are more constrained in choice of their initial melodic point of departure and local melodic goal (equivalent to the first tone of m. 3 and the last of m. 4 in the final version). The ultimate decision, of course, in mm. 3–4 is to begin the upper line on scale step *3* and establish a motion to step *5* at the end of m. 4 (on the word "Höh' "), but a *5* of which the harmonic support is a weak position of the pre-established tonic triad, producing a quite different and far less active effect than *5* supported by even a passing dominant harmony in root position. (In this discussion italicized arabic numbers are used exclusively to refer to scale steps, while Roman numerals have their conventional meaning of tonal harmonic functions.) The result in the final version is to render the melodic *5* on "höh" essentially subordinate to the strong *3* from which it emerged. In a first reduction, the motion of mm. 3–6 of the final version can be represented as shown in Example 3.3.

Example 3.3   Reduction of *Sehnsucht*, mm. 3–6

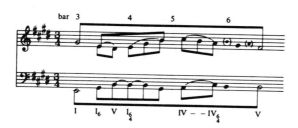

If we attempt to follow the sketches of pages 60 and 61 on the basis of choice of initial and final tone for mm. 3–4, some rather surprising results emerge. The first is that not just many but nearly all of the entries open on *3;* the only ones that do not do so are D, F, and J, which attempt fresh starts on *1* and move in rising direction to a first goal at the end of the next bar. Of these, J is the most developed. That there are no versions at all beginning on *5* is important. It seems clear that from the outset Beethoven had *3* in mind as the initial melodic tone, and that essentially he held fast to it through other transformations, giving only passing consideration to the alternative of an opening on *1*. The opening vertical relationship of upper-line *3* over the tonic triad in root position is, therefore, essentially a fixed point against which variants are played out over the remaining entries.

If we try to see the larger mapping-out of the various motions that evolve from initial *3,* another tabulation will help. In Table 3.2 a broad cyclic parallel emerges between the sketches of page 60 and those of 61, just as it did for metrical organization. Starting from A and progressing to I, we can see an almost pedantically systematic alteration of the closing step. In the first three entries (A, B, and C) Beethoven takes the line to *5;* in the next (E) to *4,* and in the next pair (G, H) to *3*. In entry I, closing the group on page 60, he leads it to *4* once more. On page 61 the situation is parallel. The first four entries (K–N) again revert to *5,* and then the next (O) employs *4;* although the next pair are incomplete (P, Q), R uses *4* once more. In both series the sketch page itself constitutes an apparent framework for the elaborative procedures used, and

Table 3.2 Sketch entries for *Sehnsucht:* Initial and closing scale steps

Page no.	Entry	Initial scale step (m. 3)	Closing scale step (m. 4)
p. 60	A	3	5
	B	3	5
	C	3	5
	E	3	4
	G	3	3
	H	3	3
	I	3	4
p. 61	K	3	5
	L	3	5
	M	3	5
	N	3	5
	O	3	4
	P	3	incomplete
	Q	3	incomplete
	R	3	4

the larger direction of the procedures on each page is, in this respect, substantially identical. Important, too, in the *3–5* group so far (A, B, C, K, L, M, N) is that *all* the entries at the top of page 60 and all those at the top of page 61 (K–N) move toward *5* by means of its leading tone (sharped *4*), implying a light tonicization of *5* at the end of m. 4. This brings up a crucial point about the notation of page 61 which contradicts Nottebohm but seems to me valid: in entries K, L, M, and N the penultimate note seems to have not a sharp sign but a natural sign, whereas on page 60 it had been a sharp; this would mean that the entries on the top of page 61 (K–N) are intended to be in E♭ major, not E major, and that they anticipate the explicit signature of E♭ major of the full melodic version at S (page 62). While the change of key has no effect on the linear details themselves, it helps to reinforce the sense of fresh beginning that is conveyed by entry K and what follows it.

If we look a step beyond pages 60 and 61 to the larger contours of the vocal line that were written out on pages 62 (S, T, and partly in U) and 63 (V), we can see the remaining step prior to the final choice of linear direction.

While S returns to *5* as closing goal, it seems regressive in its first measure, in which it reintroduces the passing-tone *2* between *3* and *1*, which had gradually been disappearing and would not re-emerge in the final version; also it implies a wholesale change of harmony at m. 2 that is retrospective in these sketches. In T the opening motion is reduced again to a minimum (the sustained repetition of the opening *3* before step motion to *1*) and recalls the simplicity of repetitive openings of the entries A, B, and C but is quite distinct from K, where the final opening motion is actually anticipated. The same line of direction is further pursued in m. 1 of entry V, which resembles T in having 4 as its goal and has just as little motion in m. 1. At last, in W, with the apparent exception only of the second note of m. 2 (still a passing-tone 2), the ultimate contour of the upper line is achieved.

Although I shall not attempt here to comment on the complexities of inner contour of each entry—which would require a vastly expanded discussion—a few points can be noted. One is that the course of events after the initial 3 can have many different forms and emphases, resulting in the attribution of different degrees of importance and melodic "weight" to the principal tones in the unit—3, 2, 1, and 5. For example, in A the motion from 3 to 1 is subordinated in two ways: by the repetition of 3 and by a strong motion to the dominant at m. 3 of the entry. In K, step 3 moves decisively and immediately to 1 (as in the final version), then ascends again to 5 through the dominant of the dominant. As was seen earlier, by the time Beethoven has come to the bottom of page 61 he has reached the final rhythmic formulation of the line but has yet to establish its definitive contour. When he does so, the total assembling of the details will produce a text setting that gives maximum attention to the vowel pitch-distinctions between the opening words "Die stille" and the following "Nacht"; the tone repetition of opening 3 (G♯) reflects the close similarity and high placement of the vowels of the first two words, while the drop to 1 (E) reinforces the lower vowel of "Nacht." A similar refinement in the next pair of lines is brought about by the tone repetition for "der Stern der," with motion then a step higher for the open vowel ie of "Liebe." This goes beyond anything in Beethoven's declamation in songs of an earlier period.

Finally, a passing glance at the autograph, which is preserved in Berlin (DStB, Grasnick 18).[19] As mentioned earlier, the only revisions of any real consequence are in the pianoforte part, and especially in the rhythmic location of the punctuating chords separated by rests, as in mm. 5 and 6 (see Example 3.4). But also one detail in the voice part is revised: the last beat in m. 4, on the first word of the group just mentioned, "der Stern der"; the B for the first "der" is changed from a sixteenth to an eighth note. Thus an exact parallel is made between upbeats (cf. m. 2, last beat), and the contrasting functions of dotted and even eighth-note pairs in mm. 3 and 4 are clarified and carried over also into mm. 5 and 6.

IV

In his remarks on the sixteen variant entries for *Sehnsucht* that he published, Nottebohm wrote:

The song *Sehnsucht* is not at all the product of a moment, but the result of assiduous, continuous labor. The melody is gathered together from portions of the whole, and is built up in a steady metamorphosis. Only gradually and by means of steady industry do the emerging fragments weld themselves together and group themselves, first into a smaller, then a larger entity.[20]

This is an entirely characteristic sample of what I called earlier the "prevailing view" of the composition process in Beethoven's sketchbooks. It not only reflects the traditional type of statement that grew out of the evidence first discovered by Nottebohm, but is obviously also designed to rebut an earlier nineteenth-century view of composition as being the spontaneous product of unpremeditated art. It is not so much that Nottebohm's paragraph is "incorrect" as a commentary on these entries, but that it stands at so lofty a level of abstraction above the particular compositional problems entailed by the material that it can hardly be more than a panoramic generality. To speak of a series of variants merely as being gradually "gathered together" to form a melodic totality means little without careful discrimination between those elements in the series that remain more or less constant and those that are decisively subjected to transformation. Nor does Nottebohm's comment suggest the possibility that there is a way of viewing these sketches other than as embodying a gradually emerging series of variants whose goal is only discovered en route. One might, for example, be persuaded that Beethoven had in mind

Example 3.4   Sehnsucht, mm. 1–6, from Beethoven's autograph manuscript (Berlin, DStB, MS Grasnick 18)

from the beginning one or more fixed points in the conceptual scheme, and that against these fixed points he proceeded to develop variant possibilities, emphasizing different dimensions of the final scheme, dimensions that are brought to realization not simultaneously but in consecutive phases and in the order displayed by the sketches.

One such fixed point, I would contend, is the text—not merely its sentimental content and imagery, though these are by no means negligible contributors to the genre of which the song is a mature example for Beethoven, but more essentially its stanza structure, its rhyme scheme, and its 7 + 6–syllable verse form. The poetic factors are directly and, I believe, crucially related to the metrical and syllabic organization of the setting. In determining the final choice of meter, Beethoven seems to have elaborated on these pages two sets of entries that begin with a fully conventional choice and develop toward the unconventional $\frac{3}{4}$; in the process he fixes the metrical, and even the inner rhythmic, aspects *before* determining finally the details of contour. This last point implies that the problem of syllable length and agogic stress is solved before the problem of vowel pitch. In turn, decisions about contour are also bound up with the linguistic characteristics of the song and serve to reinforce them; and our evaluation of the "better" or "worse" linear alternatives considered in the sketches inevitably entails declamatory correctness and refinement as criteria of value.

To the extent that this fragile reed—a single series of entries on five pages of a single sketchbook—will bear a thesis, it is that the traditional notion of Beethoven's simply "building up" a structure from fragmentary sketches remains inadequate without an attempt to uncover the direction and purpose of the building up along with consideration of the prior constraints from which the process has begun. To do less is to fall back upon what may now be regarded as merely a traditional pious acknowledgment of the importance of Beethoven's sketches—namely, that they show us how allegedly lacking in distinction his original ideas were, and how much hard work he needed to do to bring them to realization. The alternative is to come down to cases and to encourage serious and close-grained examination of particular problems that will focus instead on the variety of specific structural purposes the sketches seem to have been designed to fulfill.

Example 3.5　Scheide Sketchbook, page 60, transcription

　BEETHOVEN'S SKETCHES FOR *SEHNSUCHT*

Example 3.6 Scheide Sketchbook, page 61, transcription

Example 3.7 Scheide Sketchbook, page 62, transcription

Example 3.8 Scheide Sketchbook, page 63, transcription

Example 3.9   Scheide Sketchbook, page 64, transcription

Stern der Liebe funkelt sanft wallend in dem See Verstummt sind in den Zwei - gen die Sänger der Natur ge-
heim nis volles Schweigen
ruht auf der Blumen flur

NOTES TO TRANSCRIPTIONS

P. 60, st. 4, item E, notes 3–6.

The rhythmic values here are not fully clear but were probably intended to be ♪. ♪ ♪. ♪, as in entry D.

P. 60, st. 6, item G, bar 2, note 4.

The upper stroke above this note is not transcribed here as a separate notehead.

P. 60, st. 7, item H, first note after barline.

The note here can be read as A or G♯.

P. 60, st. 7, item H, second note after barline.

The note here can be read as F♯ or E.

P, 60, st. 10, item I, first note on staff.

An apparent dot after the first note is not transcribed here.

P. 60, st. 12, item J, bar 3, first note.

I follow Nottebohm in reading A–G♯ here, but it could be read as G♯–F♯.

P. 60, st. 14, item J, last noteheads of this entry.

It is unclear what note was intended here.

P. 61, st. 1, item K.

A large smear partly obscures bar 2, second beat.

P. 61, st. 1, item K, penultimate note.

The symbol here is doubtless ♮.

P. 61, st. 8, item O, second bar.

Beethoven evidently intended the rhythm ♪ ♪ ♪. ♪ in this bar.

P. 61, st. 12, item R, second bar, notes 5–6.

This is doubtless intended to be a ♪., not a ♩.

P. 62, st. 3, item S, seventh note before the last.

Beethoven doubtless intended a ♪, although it is written ♪

P. 62, st. 6, item T, seventh note.

This F♯ is only partly visible.

P. 62, st. 7, item T, notes 6–7.

These two notes were doubtless intended to be sixteenths.

FOUR

Eroica Perspectives: Strategy and Design in the First Movement

Surely no other Beethoven symphony, not even the Fifth or the Ninth, has evoked a wider flood of commentary—whether historical, analytical, or broadly interpretive—than the *Eroica*. In the vein of biography one could fill an anthology with variants on the thesis, by now the most obvious of commonplaces, that this symphony marks a decisive turning point in Beethoven's development. Wagner, whose published remarks on the *Eroica* are only outnumbered by his writings on the Ninth, regarded the *Eroica* as the first work in which Beethoven thrust forward in what was to be his own fully individual direction.[1] Equally canonic by now is the famous episode in which Beethoven abandoned the dedication of the symphony on receiving news of Napoleon's imperial ascendancy; the testimony for this effectively began with Ferdinand Ries, was picked up by Schindler and by Thayer, and in the wake of Thayer reappears in one book after another.[2] A valuable and dispassionate review of the matter was provided by Maynard Solomon, who persuasively demonstrates the ambivalence of Beethoven's attitude toward Napoleon.[3] Approaching from another direction, Alan Tyson suggests that the work forms part of a crucially important and definable segment of Beethoven's creative growth, from about 1801 (and his first accommodation to his growing deafness) to the completion of the first *Leonore* in 1805. In this "heroic phase," as Tyson calls it, Beethoven finds his way to the realization of heroic themes in oratorio and opera, with the *Eroica* as a monumental midpoint in this tremendous development. *Prometheus* and *Christus am Oelberge* lie before it; the explicit affirmation of personal redemption and political freedom in *Leonore* come directly after it.[4]

But my purpose here is not primarily to explore the personal or evolutionary significance of the symphony. It is, rather, to focus attention on certain well-known and long-established analytic perspectives upon it (restricted here to its first movement), to sum up current patterns of thought about the work, and to bring out some aspects that seem to me to have been neglected. This too is certainly not owing to any lack of published commentary; the literature is large and sprawls over many different avenues of approach. Inevitably it partly divides along lines of intellectual prejudice, partly along linguistic and national boundaries.

In the nineteenth century vast battles were waged over the programmatic interpretation of the *Eroica*, not without overtones of Franco-German rivalries in the post-Napoleonic and post-Beethovenian era. On the French side are the programs of Berlioz and Oulibicheff; on the German side, among others is the far less pictorial and more abstract program note by Wagner (1851).[5] In 1859 A. B. Marx reviewed the entire matter in a separate chapter in his book on Beethoven. He abruptly dismisses what he calls the "French hypothesis" but quotes Wagner and insists on a purely musical interpretation.[6] A late example of programmatic and hermeneutic exegesis is that of Paul Bekker (1911).[7] It was Bekker who made the truly remarkable suggestion that Beethoven's revelation of his heroic subject would have been improved if only the slow movement and Scherzo had been reversed in order. Bekker explains that Beethoven must really have intended such an ordering, but "did not dare" to use it, "having offered his contemporaries enough innovation for one occasion."

In a different and more responsible quarter stands Nottebohm's presentation of the sketches for the symphony in his monograph *Ein Skizzenbuch von Beethoven aus dem Jahre 1803*, issued in 1880.[8] However limited Nottebohm's transcriptions and commentary may be, they opened up a larger body of genetic material for the *Eroica* than anyone could have anticipated, and laid a basis that has yet to be seriously challenged or drastically modified—although the eventual publication of the full contents of the sketchbook may afford new perspectives. I shall return later to some issues posed by the sketches, or what is now known of them, but it should be said that the rich material presented by Nottebohm has still been only sparsely cultivated by his successors and is explicitly neglected by his normally enthusiastic supporter Heinrich Schenker, who usually spares Nottebohm the scorn with which he treats most other earlier writers.

To the turn of the century belongs the chapter by Grove in his book on the symphonies, a mild and gentle exegesis that was followed more brilliantly and incisively by Tovey in various writings.[9] Then from Germany in the 1920s and 1930s came a succession of *Eroica* commentaries, most of them analytical essays of one type or another. This series began with the highly portentous analysis by Fritz Cassirer in his book *Beethoven und die Gestalt* (1925), which employed what were then quite new approaches to the perception of formal structures, developed by the pioneers of Gestalt psychology.[10] In contrast is a pair of essays by the Wagnerian Alfred Lorenz, who found in the middle section of the *Eroica* first movement the same formal-periodic symmetries he was then seeking to reveal as the "secret of form" in Wagner's *Ring,* and which he would later claim to find as well in Wagner's other late major works. The second of Lorenz's essays is a sensitive discussion of the first-movement sketches as published by Nottebohm.[11] The same year saw the publication of a striking article by August Halm, on the so-called new episode in the middle section, which Halm was apparently the first (in print) to associate with the contour of the main motif of the opening of the movement.[12] And in 1930 there appeared the most detailed and far-reaching analytic study of the symphony yet published: Schenker's tract on the *Eroica* as issued in volume III of his yearbook *Das Meisterwerk in der Musik* (1930).[13] I shall come back to the Schenker essay shortly; for now it suffices to mention briefly a few later commentaries of different kinds: one is Walter Engelsmann's article of 1940 on the organic unity of the motivic material of all four movements of the symphony.[14] Another is the lengthy analysis of the first movement, primarily on motivic lines, by Walter Riezler, issued as an appendix to his book on Beethoven and thus the only one of these contributions available also in English.[15]

If the Lorenz and Schenker analyses are exempted, there emerges a by now familiar underlying concept, or *Grundgestalt,* which pervades these essays in one form or another. They embody the view that not only is the *Eroica* (and especially the first movement) a landmark in the entire development of the symphony, but its immensity of scope is correlative to its presentation of an unusually large number of musical ideas, and that it reveals an exceptionally high degree of interrelationship among these ideas—whether themes, motifs, or rhythmic units. For some writers this is especially true of the first movement; for others, of the whole work. Along with this expansion of the formal structure goes its transformation, in the first movement, into a vast four-section structure, with greatly extended coda and middle section balancing the exposition and recapitulation.

One could write a brief history of the idea of motivic interconnection from *Eroica* commentaries alone, so pervasive is the concept in writings on the symphony's first movement. An early exponent of the idea of motivic interconnection in a Beethoven symphony was E. T. A. Hoffmann in his essay on the Fifth Symphony (1810).[16] And its most relentless twentieth-century advocate, Walter Engelsmann, not only proposed the close motivic linking of all movements, but perhaps knowingly distorted for his own purposes a valuable anecdote that reveals something of the mature Richard Wagner's view of the material of the first movement. Since this anecdote does not seem to have been available hitherto in English, it is worth quoting here. It stems from a young and enthusiastic admirer of Wagner, the budding composer Felix Draeseke, who visited him at Lucerne in 1859 and later reported the following episode to a biographer:

Finally he gave me an explanation of melody that totally altered my musical out-look and has been more useful to me than the entire course of studies that I took at the Leipzig Conservatory. In a quite unexpected way—I am not sure how it came about—on a very hot August afternoon he began to sing the first movement of the 'Eroica.' He fell into a violent passion, sang on and on, became very over-heated, quite beside himself, and did not stop until he had come to the end of the exposition. "What is that?" he cried out to me. To which I naturally replied, "The 'Eroica.'" "Now then, isn't pure melody enough? Must you always have your crazy harmonies along with it?"—At first I didn't understand what he meant by that. When he later calmed down he explained to me that the melodic flow in the Beethoven symphonies streams forth inexhaustibly, and that by means of these melodies one can clearly recall to memory the whole symphony. This gave me a spur to later consideration that has had a deep effect on my own production.[17]

It is of the highest interest to realize that at Lucerne in 1859 Wagner had just finished the gigantic third act and thus the whole of *Tristan,* which is mani-festly the quintessence in his own work of wide-spanned and continually re-surgent melodic flow, as well as of complex developmental processes within the musico-dramatic scheme. Draeseke's report is also consistent with Wag-ner's program note for the *Eroica,* written eight years earlier, and his later dec-laration, in an essay of 1879, that the great achievement of his dramatic music lay in its attaining the unity of a symphonic composition: "The whole artwork is a thorough web of basic themes, which, as in a symphonic movement, relate to one another through contrast, mutual complementation, formation of new shapes, articulation, and connection."[18] In such discussions he often invokes the name of Beethoven: "If there had not been a Beethoven, I could never have composed as I have."[19]

This approach, which seems to me inescapable in some degree, finds its way into the most diverse *Eroica* writings; even Grove, who is scarcely a transcen-dental motif-hunter, writes as follows: "The Eroica first shows us the methods which were so completely to revolutionise that department of music—the continuous and organic mode of connecting the second subject with the first, the introduction of episodes into the working-out, the extraordinary impor-tance of the *Coda.* "[20] Fifty years later Walter Engelsmann was at pains to derive all four movements from the same basic *Werkthema,* which in turn can be re-duced to three basic *Urmotiven.* Engelsmann traces the transformation of this material through all four movements, and for him it collectively forms an "artistic law of the symphony."[21] This is said to be a musical equivalent of Goethe's concept, which Engelsmann quotes, that all organic life consists of transformations of a single basic substance (*Urstoff*) through procedures that can be called metamorphosis, evolution, variation, and osmosis. Goethe him-self had originally developed these views in connection with his early botanical studies on the growth of plants from seeds, and it comes as something of a shock to realize that his first publication on this subject appeared as early as 1790.[22] In 1940 Engelsmann not only explicitly quoted Goethe's "Gesetz des Lebens" but claimed to find musical counterparts for each of these means of transformation, including osmosis. The later approach of Rudolph Réti is fully prefigured in this study. And Engelsmann's invocation of Goethe shows that the quasi-biological cast of much thinking along these lines is, if I may use the expression, rooted in German traditions of science and aesthetics characteristic of the late eighteenth and early nineteenth centuries, in particular the fusion of scientific observation with German philosophical idealism, which Goethe proudly espoused and which found in him its most eloquent and, for later generations, its most authoritative spokesman.

In turning to the published analysis by Schenker, one enters a different world. By 1930 Schenker's views had totally departed from what then seemed to be firmly settled traditions of harmonic analysis as expounded by Riemann, and of motivic analysis as expounded by Engelsmann and others. Schenker's monograph on the Ninth Symphony had been published in 1912, before his analytic views had crystallized in the concept of the *Ursatz* (fundamental structure) and its ramifications; and his essay of 1925 on the Fifth Symphony had elucidated background features but had also included much discussion of motivic details, sketches, and other aspects of the foreground.[23] The *Eroica* analysis, on the other hand, is conceived uncompromisingly from the standpoint of his later concepts of tonal structure and syntax. Even though these views have spread, more through Schenkerians than through Schenker's own writings, at a rate that would be envied by an evangelical missionary, it may not be useless to review once more some aspects of the approach.

Although the Schenkerian method is popularly believed to consist in the search for a supposedly single *Urlinie* (fundamental line) and *Ursatz* that underlie each tonal composition, it appears that it is more adequately perceived as proceeding from the concept of levels or layers (*Schichten*), coexisting planes of organization of musical content in tonal music.[24] The layers are seen as being connected and related to one another as if they were closer and more distant perspectives upon the same phenomena; Schenker applies to the *Schichten* the familiar spatial terms foreground, middleground, and background (without claiming that there are only three), and uses them as analytic constructs or frameworks for the diverse types and forms of prolongation of musical units (linear, contrapuntal, and harmonic, of various durations and directions) which emerge as basic components of the tonal language. Again, to put something complex very simply, the so-called reduction procedure appears to consist in using the traditional concepts of tonal species counterpoint as analytic tools, in order to reformulate or reconceive a given passage according to voice-leading rules and to produce distinctions between its more essential and less essential members. The application of the rules of tonal species counterpoint makes the reduction procedure less arbitrary than it might seem otherwise, and has seemed to many of Schenker's critics. It also reinforces the sense that one of the strengths of Schenker's later theory of tonal music is not merely its comprehensive attempt to formulate a grammar of tonality, but its attachment to the traditions of tonal counterpoint as descended from Fux and as utilized in tonal music.

Closely related to the reduction procedure is Schenker's concept of diminution, which is explored at length in *Der freie Satz,* published five years after the *Eroica* analysis.[25] Here Schenker seems to reach a partial rapprochement with motivic analysis; "diminution" designates a complex of linear details visible at the foreground level, small-scale "figurations" that are susceptible of reduction to their basic decorative elements. Schenker accepted that such diminution techniques were connected historically to diminution and ornamentation procedures of late Renaissance and Baroque vocal music, which were later developed in instrumental as well as vocal music in the tonal era.[26]

In his *Eroica* analysis Schenker provides a massive foreground "picture" (*Bild*) of each movement of the symphony, and follows these with "figures" (*Figuren*) that represent closer and more distant perspectives upon segments of varying length, ranging from short passages to entire movements; they show the foreshortened and synthesized representations used to delineate the more background layers. His *Bild* no. 1 represents the first 399 measures of the first movement. Some essential features of the opening are these: the upper-line 3̂ (g″) of the very opening sonority is seen as the primary initial triad member of the upper line and is prolonged by various means in the first violin part through the passing-note 2̂ (f′) in m. 12 to 1̂ (e♭) in m. 15; all this forms a *Terzzug* (a prolongation of the interval of a third, with the two triad members connected by the passing-note) in the upper line; it is supported in a complex way by the bass, which grafts its chromatic motion of mm. 6–11 into a supporting bass for the upper-line motion. This bass support is displaced, however, at its beginning, through the chromatic descent to d and c♯, returning through d to e♭. Simultaneously *Bild* no. 1 shows many other prolongation-units of various lengths and registers, interlocking with one another, and all potentially to be subsumed into a larger and more sweeping structural motion in the upper line, consisting in a long-range rise through members of the tonic triad; this begins from g″ in m. 1, proceeds to b♭″ in m. 23, and to the still higher e♭‴ in m. 37; then in its turn it will move upward through the crucially important rising semitone motion to f‴ at the moment of achieving the first motion by step to the dominant key area, at m. 45. This larger motion forms part of another layer at a somewhat more background level, but not far behind the foreground; and this is essentially what Schenker shows in his *Figur* no. 6.

Despite the brevity of this glimpse of Schenker's treatment of one aspect of the first movement, I want to linger a moment more over some details of his *Bild* no. 1 to consider what sorts of detail Schenker's approach tends to bring out and what it tends to minimize or suppress. Let it be said first, however, that the collection of analytic tools at his disposal for conceptualizing the smaller- and larger-scale procedures of tonal music must be impressive to anyone, whether one is inclined to love or to leave it, whether one is prepared or not to follow him from foreground to more background layers, and whether or not his particular analyses seem convincing. My own respect for the scope of his achievement in this analysis, though I shall try to signal its limitations with regard to certain musical events, even suffices to excuse, in my mind, the title of his essay, "Beethoven's Third Symphony, presented for the first time in its true content." [27]

To return to Schenker's "picture" of the opening of the first movement: In addition to the larger framework he is at pains to establish several smaller segments as well: the upper-line g″ generates several prolongations of different lengths, while the bass e♭ in m. 3 expands to the g″ in the upper line in m. 7; then there is the chromatic motion in the bass (indicated by the arrow in m. 8), which he calls in the prose commentary the "first breath" of the piece. What is obliterated from view is at least one small-scale, but to my mind vital, harmonic implication that arises early in the piece: this is the momentary inflection of G minor that emerges in mm. 7–9, as the bass reaches its lower chromatic neighbor, c♯, and proceeds to d while the upper line holds g″; the second violin in m. 9 deftly converts its repeated g′ into a new figure that alternates g′ and b♭. Thus in m. 9 the entire texture lightly touches upon a I$^6_4$ of G minor before the immediate reassertion of E♭ major by means of the upper-line motion to a♭″. [28] But this implication of G minor has considerable importance for later aspects of the symphony: not merely those significant uses of G minor in the first three movements, but the striking use of a descending G-minor scale to open the Finale and the same choice of tonality for the powerful dance episode that stands at the center of the movement. Similarly, in Schenker's picture of the opening, his insistence in mm. 12–14 on small-scale prolongation-units of a third (*Terzzugen*) seems to me to involve rather arbitrary choices in the upper line, which may be interpreted quite differently and, to my mind, more convincingly.

One more instance will show even more strikingly Schenker's divergence from the viewpoint of motivic analysis: this is his treatment of the transition passage in mm. 23–36, which separates the second and third statements of the opening subject. In *Bild* no. 1 Schenker's analysis discloses the following features: in the bass the progression by step downward from the bass B♭ achieved in m. 23 through A♭ in m. 29 and G in m. 31; then the repetition of those pitches in quarter-note diminution in mm. 34–35, reaching the cadential F and B♭ in mm. 35 and 36 and aiming at resolution to the tonic E♭ in m. 37. In the upper line he presents in mm. 29–35 the continuation of a b♭" prolongation from m. 23, which is fundamentally maintained all the way to the rising cadence in mm. 36–37; in mm. 29–32 he sees small-scale realizations of the harmony V_2^4 moving to I_3^6, first in half notes, then in quarters. All this is conceptualized in such a way as to make the most of the large-scale prolongation of the pitch 5 (B♭) and the dominant harmony it expresses, from m. 23 to m. 36.

But another way of looking at the material of mm. 29–35 is hinted at darkly by Riezler, was later mentioned by Philip Downs, and is said by Charles Rosen to be obvious to everyone; I have noticed it myself and so, no doubt, have many others.[29] The point is that the means by which this transition is made not only prolongs the dominant but does so in such a way as to repeat the basic triadic interval succession established at the opening of the movement by the triadic subjects—now, however, with the pitches transferred to other registers. Thus the first violin in mm. 29–30 rises through members of the dominant triad in the same order in which the cellos at the opening rose through members of the tonic triad 1–3–1–5–1 (adding triad members to the root but returning to the root before moving to the next new triad member). The effect of the interval succession here is to infuse this transition passage with obvious motivic importance and give it a close (may I say "organic"?) connection to the primary thematic statements that stand before and after it. It is especially striking that in the recapitulation, in which the descending chromatic motion of the opening is entirely reinterpreted and leads to new elaborations, this transition passage is cut out. Its important uses lie elsewhere: it reappears in the middle section in mm. 250–271 as a component of the vast motion toward E minor that is to bring about the famous "new episode," beginning at m. 284. It then reappears at the end of the middle section, in mm. 338–364, in a new form, as the first segment of the extended retransition and dominant preparation for the return at m. 398. Later it makes two further appearances, both in the coda: in mm. 603–631, following the return of the "new episode," and finally in mm. 685–689, at the very end, to reinforce thematically the final assertion of the dominant harmony before the last chords. In each case it functions as a dominant transition or retransition, and typically in the role of prolonging an unstable phrase segment on its way toward resolution.

———

I want now to focus on the kinds of structural purpose indicated by the uses of the figure that I have just discussed—purposes that I believe are inadequately reflected by traditional motivic analysis on the one hand, and by the Schenker analysis on the other. The category that I have in mind can be characterized as "compositional strategy." By this I refer to Beethoven's deployment, as part of the design of this movement, of certain small-scale foreground units of musical structure in such a way as to shape the larger conformation of the movement, using them as widely separated points of connection and association that are outside the sequential norms of exposition and recapitulation. Thus the importance of a particular musical idea may be projected over long time-spans and over the boundaries of the familiar large-scale divisions of the movement.

I return to the age-old but essential observation that the first movement of the *Eroica* is of a length unprecedented in the symphonic tradition. A defensive-sounding note was included in the first edition of 1806, referring to the symphony's having been "deliberately written at greater length than is usual."[30] In certain early works Beethoven had written first movements of great length, by contemporary standards, even some in the less frequent $\frac{3}{4}$. Among these are the first movements of the E♭-major Piano Quintet, Op. 16, which runs to 395 bars, and the still longer opening Allegro of the G-minor Cello Sonata, Op. 5 No. 2, of 509 bars (not including the slow Introductions). These are still short of the immense 691 of the *Eroica,* but of course neither movement possesses the rich profusion of ideas, the complexity of content, or the capacity for integration that is found here.[31] To lead up to the main point I now need to focus attention particularly on the exposition of the *Eroica*.

Not only does the dominant section of the exposition consist of a long thematic chain, but it subdivides into six clearly formed segments, each possessing highly individual melodic, motivic, harmonic, and rhythmic features. Of these one of the most important, as Tovey points out, is the unit in mm. 57–64, which emerges *piano* from a *fortissimo* cadential figure. This passage brings in contrary motion a diatonic, ascending upper line and a partly chromatic, descending lower line. The upper line appears to have the particular function of transporting scale-degree 3 (now d in the key of B♭) from a middle-range octave to a higher one; then an elaborated repetition in the next two bars moves this scale-degree still another octave higher, while the bass expands to the lower octave. I shall designate this entire phrase, mm. 57–64, "Unit C" of the exposition.

Now another necessity for the coherence of this complex exposition is the use of decisive cadential passages to introduce each of the six thematic segments; and for this purpose Beethoven furnishes a chain of articulative figures, which are shown in short score in Example 4.1. The first one sets a pattern, in mm. 35–36, within the tonic section of the exposition, by preparing the arrival at E♭ for the final statement of the opening subject; it is characterized by eighth-note motion in all voices and contrary motion in the upper lines, arriving at the tonic through rising and falling scale patterns.

Example 4.1 Cadential figures in the exposition

With one exception, each of these strongly articulated cadential figures lands firmly on a downbeat and on a contextually stable harmony, normally the tonicized B♭ major. An apparent exception is the unit that arrives at m. 123 on a D-major chord, which is to function as local dominant of a G-minor harmony; but this D-major chord has at least the relative stability possessed by a major triad in root position. The only genuine exception, therefore strikingly anomalous, occurs in m. 65 (see part c of Example 4.1). Here the cadence arrives on a diminished-seventh chord with f♯ in the bass, which fortifies the chain of descending sequential figures in the upper line; these develop with increasing power over the next eighteen bars and lead to a new climax in m. 83 with a firm cadential motion to B♭ once more, introducing the next new segment.

The entire passage in mm. 57–64 recurs in the same form in the recapitulation as part of the full and literal return of all the material of the dominant section of the exposition. The *coup de théâtre* is reserved for much later, in the enormous coda of the movement. The coda encompasses five segments in all: first a restatement of the opening subject with new counterpoint, then the return of the "new episode" of the middle section; then in mm. 603–631 a return of that version of the syncopated transition figure, originally from mm. 25–36, in the form that had animated the immense retransition at the end of the middle section. The next, central, event in the coda is the climactic peroration on the opening triadic theme, now in a form that makes possible powerful and simple alternations of tonic and dominant harmonies, covering mm. 631–672. At m. 673 the last great cadence could end the movement, but there is one more stroke to be accomplished: there returns, in sudden *piano,* the contrary motion subject, Unit C, of the exposition and recapitulation, in virtually literal form, only slightly retouched in orchestration owing to the voice-leading in the violin parts. In both its earlier uses this passage led to a diminished seventh. Now as it moves to its destination in m. 681, the goal is converted to a *forte* attack on a full-range dominant seventh, and from here on the dominant is held steady for eight more measures, rising to a peak a♭‴ in the first violins at m. 684 and driving home the conclusion in the two final tonic chords. In this view, m. 681 is a "resolution" of the moment of instability established in m. 64 and reiterated in m. 468 in the recapitulation. That this point of resolution comes so late only serves to reinforce one's awareness of the magnitude of the span over which this connection is extended, by means of which Beethoven is able to hold the coiled spring of this passage at maximum tension before releasing it at the last possible moment. This event confers on the end of the coda a function parallel to, but different from, the transformation that takes place at the opening of the recapitulation; what is parallel is the dramatic change that coincides with the articulation of a major structural boundary.

The point of view espoused by motivic analysis has long since contributed to the characterization of the first movement as a congeries of intricately linked musical ideas. The point of view of reduction analysis has shown, or has the potential to show, a deeper skeletal structure that gives shape and foundation to the myriad of details of the movement. The kind of strategy operating here is of a type unlikely to be apprehended by purely motivic analysis, since what is important in the long term is not the complex derivation of one figure from another but the significant location of similar or associated events over long time-spans; and these events are more likely to consist in literal or nearly literal repetition than in subtle thematic transformations. Such strategies may also fail to emerge from reduction analysis (though this depends on the particulars of the analysis), for the elements are all units of the foreground, and their points of articulation may not coincide with those more background shapes of the basic prolongations which it is the purpose of the reduction procedure to elucidate. Schenker's analytic discussion of the coda contains a number of very subtle observations on voice-leading, as one might expect, and on motivic transformation, or "diminution" procedures as he prefers to call it; but according to his analysis the crucial events of the coda are the prolongations that bring the upper line down eventually from scale-degree 5 in m. 595 to its eventual resolution to E♭ in m. 631. He comments briefly on the choice of foreground upper-line pitches in measures 668 to the end, but has nothing at all to say on the recurrence of Unit C in m. 673. In Schenker's layered analysis the fundamental issue is the final achievement of tonal closure in m. 631 (and perhaps the further close in m. 673, though he does not say so).

Even more remarkable, in my view, is the discussion of this passage by Philip Downs, whose concern (which is similar to mine in this essay) is with motivic relationships within the formal structure of the movement. Downs recognizes the reappearance of Unit C in mm. 673–681, but for him the essential point is that "this material stands as representative of the second group in its unchangeability . . . that is, it stands for the necessary formality of the sonata principle."[32] In my view this is somewhat like noticing that the concluding lines of Keats's *Ode on a Grecian Urn,* " 'Beauty is truth, truth beauty . . . ,' " occur at the end of the poem and are therefore part of its culmination, but not noticing that they are given in quotation marks and are therefore qualitatively and rhetorically different from all other utterances in the poem.[33] The point is not merely that the coda bears a far-flung relationship to two earlier moments, but that the coda version differs in its kinetic force from the antecedents that give its recurrence associative meaning.

That analogies to such procedures may be found in other works by Beethoven, certainly of the great middle period and perhaps of other periods as well, seems to me rather more than likely. One, surely, is to be found in the first movement of the so-called Ghost Trio, Op. 70 No. 1, which employs near the beginning a chromatic motion that is drastically reinterpreted harmonically at the point of recapitulation, and in which, too, the strong implications of a harmonic motion to the subdominant, G major, are utilized early in the movement and receive their final confirmation in the motion to the subdominant at the beginning of the coda.[34] Another parallel of a different kind is the dramatic postponement of a crucial formal element in the first movement of the *Appassionata* Sonata, Op. 57. Here the first attempt at a cadence (mm. 3–4) stops unfulfilled on a weak dominant; this is left unresolved while the harmony moves to the distant Neapolitan G♭ that follows, and it is subsequently used again and again in the movement without resolution to the tonic. Then at the end of the movement the coda consists of nothing else than the powerful repetition of a full cadence in which the dominant is driven down to its tonic again and again.[35] I am certain that other similar cases of various types can be found.

———————

One more, larger, question remains to be dealt with. The kind of question that I am projecting into the foreground—that of long-range planning and compositional strategy—is manifestly the kind of issue that might be illuminated by the study of surviving sketches, above all, of course, those wide-spanning sketches that encompass entire large formal divisions of a movement, and which evidently have the function of laying out, in rapidly written one-line drafts, the basic direction of whole sections. From such "continuity drafts," notably those for the Second Symphony and other works of the same period, it appears that Beethoven's characteristic size of framework for a draft of this kind was the single large section—an exposition, a middle section, or a coda.

The sketches for the *Eroica* first movement follow this procedure through the first 41 pages of the *Eroica* Sketchbook (Krakow, Bibliotéka Jagiellońska, Landsberg 6). This sketchbook contains a large body of sketches covering all parts of the symphony, and for the first movement exposition there are four large continuity drafts, plus extensive supplementary drafts of portions.[36] For the moment I shall focus only on certain aspects of these exposition drafts, all of which were published by Nottebohm but which I have carefully and closely studied with a view to improving his readings if possible. Again, Tovey's view, based on Nottebohm, is striking: he sees them as evidence of Beethoven's working at top speed, putting down "any cliché that would mark the place where an idea ought to be . . . when he had advanced to sketching whole sections of a work . . . he often found it easier to begin again from the beginning and copy out the unaltered parts of the sketch, so that the act of writing had the same continuity as the flow of his thoughts, rather than tinker at isolated passages."[37]

The first three of these continuity drafts are on consecutive pages in the sketchbook, while the fourth, after some complications, begins five pages after the end of the third.[38] Taken in their order of redaction, as a working hypothesis, they show a substantial evolution of procedures and ideas, though not without puzzling elements. For example, three of them display a feature that was to become untenable in the final version: namely, the appearance of the main theme in literal form in the dominant directly after the opening statements of the main theme in the tonic. And the one draft that lacks this feature is not no. 4 but no. 2. But in numerous other ways these drafts show a steady tendency toward the sharpening of the rhythmic and linear profile of the individual motivic ideas, and a growing individualization of the successive motivic units. For present purposes one feature is particularly striking. The passage that I am calling "Unit C" in the exposition, the one that moves linearly up a sixth from *3* to *1* with contrary motion in the bass, is—apart from the triadic opening subject and its chromatic continuation—the only one that is present in essentially fixed form in all these drafts (Example 4.2). It maintains

Example 4.2   Sketches for the exposition, *Eroica* Sketchbook (Landsberg 6)

(a) Continuity draft 1, mm. 55–63 (p. 11)

★The repeat signs for these four measures are found in the sketchbook for this draft only.

(b) Continuity draft 1, variant version of mm. 59–71 (p. 10)

(c) Continuity draft 2, mm. 57–66 (p. 12)

basically the same contour that it is to have in the final version, undergoing some refinement in rhythmic continuation and in its registral position, but remaining fundamentally a fixed element in the web of transformations. Around it are shaped thematic units that have much further to go before they reach their final linear and harmonic form. Although the fourth continuity draft possesses a number of these units in shapes close to their final ones, it still would have required some important elaborative changes before it could have been used in a final version. In the absence of the autograph, and of any drafts in reduced-score form, one can only speculate about where this later phase may have taken place.

The fixed and significant position of Unit C vividly supports the presentiment that its role in the larger strategy may have emerged at a relatively early stage of planning. Yet there were steps to be taken: the drafts also show that the sequential figure that follows it (the material of mm. 65–66 of the final version) was not always intended to open in a G-minor context. In continuity draft (CD) 1 plus its variant, and in CD 2, these bars express either a B♭-major context or the dominant of B♭, with a conspicuous f♮. Thus there was no very early thought of arriving on an f♯ diminished seventh. But by CD 3 and CD 4 the final form of the upper line is given, allowing for at least the possibility of the diminished seventh as local harmonic framework for both measures (Example 4.3). And then later, in the sketches for the coda, for which Beetho-

Example 4.3   Sketches for the exposition, *Eroica* Sketchbook (Landsberg 6)

(a) Continuity draft 3 (p. 14)

(b) Continuity draft 4 (p. 20)

ven made at least one continuity draft and some preliminary patches, the flow of ideas is once again absolutely clear.[39] The coda continuity draft shows that certain problems in this final section could only be worked out, for obvious reasons, in conjunction with Beethoven's plans for the middle section. And this essential draft for the coda already contains a statement of Unit C as the closing thematic material in an upper line, implying its long-range "resolution" to a dominant harmony before the final tonic (Example 4.4). It is hardly surprising that even if Beethoven was putting down on paper as fast as possible his flow of thoughts for a given section, he should have been aware of the implications of certain ideas for another, partly analogous formal division of

Example 4.4 Sketch for the coda, *Eroica* Sketchbook (Landsberg 6, p. 37)

the same movement. And in fact this is exactly the feeling that he confesses in a famous letter to Treitschke (Anderson No. 479), in connection with the revision of *Fidelio,* in 1814: "I could compose something new far more quickly than patch up the old with something new, as I am now doing. For my custom when I am composing even instrumental music is always to keep the whole in view."

FIVE

The Earliest Sketches for the *Eroica* Symphony

For more than three generations after the appearance of Gustav Nottebohm's long essay on the *Eroica* sketchbook, published in 1880, it was generally believed that this source contained all the surviving precompositional material for the *Eroica* Symphony.[1] But in 1962 the appearance of the so-called Wielhorsky sketchbook, edited and transcribed by Nathan Fishman, opened up a new perspective on the source material for the origins of the symphony.[2] Dating from 1802–1803, it is the principal sketchbook used by Beethoven just before the *Eroica* sketchbook, and it contains extensive sketches for works composed in the period between the Second and Third Symphonies. These include the Piano Sonata, Op. 31 No. 3; the two crucial and unconventional sets of Piano Variations (the Six Variations in F Major, Op. 34, and the Fifteen Variations and Fugue in E-flat Major, Op. 35—the so-called *Eroica* Variations); as well as the oratorio *Christus am Oelberge,* other vocal works, and the first extended work on the *Kreutzer* Sonata, Op. 47. In Fishman's commentary and in a paper that he presented at the Bonn Beethoven Congress of 1970, he announced the discovery that two inner pages of the Wielhorsky sketchbook contain the earliest sketches that can be specifically identified with the *Eroica* Symphony.[3] Apart from the content of these earliest ideas for the symphony, this material has the further distinction that it was probably written not later than the autumn of 1802, whereas the main work on the more developed phases of composition is not thought to have gotten under way before the spring of 1803. The earlier portion of this draft for the *Eroica* in the Wielhorsky sketchbook is the central material to which this essay is addressed.

Beethoven scholarship is indebted to Fishman for being the first to reveal and describe these sketches, yet further commentary upon them by others is not only predictable but inevitable. By 1978 there had appeared a new monograph on the background of the symphony by Constantin Floros, entitled *Beethovens Eroica und Prometheus-Musik,* which dealt with Fishman's presentation from a quite different angle of approach.[4] Fishman's aim was to show that the Wielhorsky sketches indeed qualify as the earliest known for the *Eroica,* to determine their date, and to seek to relate the first-movement material in Wielhorsky to Beethoven's decisions about thematic content, made when the first movement had grown to its final size. Floros instead looks outward to what he takes to be the aesthetic and conceptual background of the idea of the "heroic" in this symphony. By this he means not its eventual connection to Napoleon but its links to certain categories or dramatic genres common in the period: namely, several scenic categories that Beethoven had used in his *Prometheus* ballet, including the "tragica scena," the "danza eroica," and the "giocosa scena." By a process of association, Floros claims to find analogues for each of these categories within each of the four movements of the symphony. His view of the *Eroica* finale is that Beethoven's resumption of material previously used in the contredanse, the final section of the *Prometheus* ballet, and in the Piano Variations, Opus 35, represents a symphonic usage of the category of the "danze festive" in which the hero Prometheus ascends to the company of the immortals. Floros thus claims to find a new implication in Beethoven's final wording of the title of the work when it was published in 1806—that is, "composta per festeggiare il sovvenire di un grand' Uomo" ("composed to celebrate the memory of a great man")—by associating the word *festeggiare* with the concept of the "danze festive" from the ballet.[5] In addition, Floros also devotes a short chapter to the compositional origins of the symphony, reviewing Fishman's primary points. Here he comes close to the issue that is at the basis of this essay, and for the sake of clarity I shall quote Floros briefly:

> The fact that in the Wielhorsky sketchbook the sketches for the *Eroica* movements immediately follow the sketches for Opus 35 permits the conclusion that it was during the summer of 1802, while Beethoven was working on the Piano Variations, that he first conceived the idea of composing the Third Symphony. Accordingly, he must have planned from the beginning to establish the *Eroica* finale in formal and thematic materials as a movement similar to the Piano Variations. It is particularly noteworthy that in this sketchbook there are no sketches for the *Eroica* finale. Beethoven must therefore, in a sense, have considered the Piano Variations as the first sketches for the *Eroica* finale.[6]

The thesis that the *Eroica* sketch in the Wielhorsky is directly related to the preceding work on the Opus 35 Piano Variations is in my view essentially correct. Floros goes beyond Fishman in observing that the symphonic sketch material directly follows the Opus 35 sketches; to which one may add that these sketches are evidently the last that Beethoven needed to complete that work. But neither Floros nor Fishman pursues the further implications of this physical proximity in analytic terms. Accordingly, I can briefly spell out the main contentions of this essay, and then develop the consequences and details in what follows.

(1) The purpose of the *Eroica* sketch material in Wielhorsky is to establish an abbreviated preliminary plan for an entire symphony. It presents in brief form a series of thematic incipits and structural elements that constitute a short plan for a slow introduction and an Allegro first movement, in E-flat major; a $\frac{6}{8}$ slow movement in C major; and a *Menuetto serioso* in E-flat with Trio in G minor. The absence of any thematic notation for a last movement is not owing to uncertainty about the finale, as might be immediately thought; rather, the content and location of the material invite the conclusion that the Opus 35 Variations were in some way to form the basis for the symphonic finale.

(2) This earliest *Eroica* sketch belongs to a type of preliminary compositional plan for works in several movements that is especially prominent in Beethoven's sketchbooks during these productive years. As Robert Winter observed, these plans have been little studied by Beethoven scholars; Winter calls them "tonal overviews," a neologism with which I differ on the ground that the word "tonal" here is not fully germane. I prefer to call them "movement-plans," emphasizing their focus on the sequence of movements or principal sections and above all on the concatenation of movements planned for the larger compositional totality.[7] Although samples of the same type of compositional model can be found down to Beethoven's last years, and for the last quartets as well as other works, they are more frequent between about 1800 and 1804 than in the years just before or later. Needless to say, it is hardly surprising to find Beethoven recording such plans for large works during these years of innovation and expansion of his compositional aims.

(3) The Wielhorsky movement-plan in fact suggests that from the beginning of Beethoven's planning of this symphony, its finale, in content if not in form, was the basic springboard, the essential invariant concept to which the remaining movements of the symphony were then adapted. Another way of putting this is to say that the symphony, at this incipient stage, was composed from its finale forward to the other movements. Furthermore, the finale, or its material, not only is the key to the shape and character of the symphony as a whole but also influences its thematic material as well, especially the opening theme of the first movement Allegro. For it is possible through these sketches to trace the derivation of the Allegro theme from the celebrated *Basso del Tema* that opens both Opus 35 and the main first section of the symphonic finale. And it is not too much to say that, if this can be shown, it has useful implications for analysis and biography, as well as suggesting some of the potential importance of the sketches for both domains.

II

Let us look closely and analytically at the earliest sketches for the symphony in Wielhorsky. The entire material occupies two adjacent pages in the sketchbook, the facing pages 44 and 45 in a book that now contains eighty-seven leaves but originally consisted of ninety-six leaves (192 pages). The Wielhorsky was among the sketchbooks of typical sixteen-stave oblong format which Beethoven obtained already made up, or ordered to be made for him, and which were assembled in uniform gatherings, of the same or nearly the same paper throughout. Alan Tyson, in his 1970 paper on the 1803 version of *Christus am Oelberge,* showed that the eighty-seven leaves now in the volume can be augmented by eight other detached leaves, now in Modena and in Bonn, which clearly fit into the later portions of the sketchbook and which belong to the sketches for the Oratorio, not the segment with which we are concerned.[8] For present purposes, then, it suffices to make clear that the portion of the sketchbook discussed here shows no sign whatever of having lost any leaves or suffered other tampering that affects its content. The only minor exception that must be mentioned is the harmless vandalism inflicted by Ludwig Nohl, who examined the sketchbook while it was still in the private collection of the Wielhorsky family and described it in a book of 1874; Nohl numbered the pages of the sketchbook and in several places wrote down marginal notes identifying works to which he thought the sketches belonged.[9]

The basic layout of the material is as follows. Page 44 opens with a brief initial sketch idea for the Bagatelle, Op. 33 No. 1, followed on staff 1 by an arpeggiated figure of unknown use; the *Eroica* sketches then begin on staff 3 and occupy the remainder of the page; then all of the next page (not given here) continues with a series of drafts for portions of the first movement. For present purposes we shall be concerned almost entirely with the first page, 44, and especially with staves 3 through 9, which present the slightly elaborated movement-plan as the first portion of the entire material. Let us briefly consider the components of this movement-plan (see Example 5.1 and Table 5.1).

(1) The Introduction (staff 3, all but the last two measures). Though not marked with a tempo indicator, this segment almost certainly implies a slow introduction to the first Allegro, which begins at the $\frac{3}{4}$ later on staff 3. This primitive representation of an introductory phrase divides into two subphrases, of six and four measures, of which the first is a triadic formula in E-flat major moving from tonic to a fermata close on the dominant; the first phrase, in bass register, is then followed by an upper-register continuation beginning identically and petering out at measure 10 with the perfunctory mark "etc." From here Beethoven moves to a simple sketch for the possible conclusion of the introduction, indicating as briefly as possible two elements: one is a dominant pedal in the bass, with triplet upbeat to a metrical strong point; the other is the chromatic rising upper line from c to d-flat to d-natural to e-flat (see Example 5.2). This foreshadows the approach to the tonic through a linear ascent from flat seven to leading tone and presages the eventual use of that motion at structurally important places in the final version of the work—not only in the famous chromatic motion of the opening of the

Example 5.1a   Wielhorsky Sketchbook, p. 44: transcription

Example 5.1b

Table 5.1 Outline of material by staff, page 44 of Wielhorsky sketchbook

		Keyboard figuration
1	Bagatelle, Op. 33 I, incipit	
2	(blank)	
3	*Eroica* movement-plan: Introd. ....3/4 (Allegro)	
4	1st mvt. opening, cont. // 1st mvt., trans. to V	
5	1st. mvt., cont.; from V area to double bar .... //	
6	2nd mvt., Adagio, C major 6/8	
7	2nd mvt. sk, cont. ...."fag[otto]"	
8	2nd mvt. sk, cont. "cresc. più forte sempre più voci" to provisional ending .... // "aus dem Adagio im M."	
9	'Menuetto serioso", incipit Trio, incipit .... "etc."	
10	1st mvt. sk resumed; 1st theme (8 mm.), "etc" // Exposition draft	
11	Exposition draft continued (56 mm.)	
12	" " " "	
13	" " " "	
14	" " " to double bar with repetition sign (provisional end of Exposition)	
15	(blank)	
16	(blank)	

Example 5.2 Wielhorsky Sketchbook, p. 44, st. 3: rising chromatic line to *1* at end of Introduction

first movement but just as strikingly in the coda of the Scherzo in the final form of the symphony.

In effect, this brief outline of an introduction provides simply the beginning and the ending of a potential introductory section, which would obviously have undergone major elaboration before it could have become acceptable. It is very similar to the initial idea for an introduction that Beethoven had sketched for the Second Symphony at a somewhat similar phase of work, in the sketchbook Landsberg 7 (see Example 5.3). Primitive though it is, it

Example 5.3 Early sketch for Second Symphony, first movement, Introduction (from Sketchbook Landsberg 7, p. 39)

nevertheless shows that Beethoven's earliest notated idea for the first movement did present its main Allegro material in triple meter but with a duple meter introduction to set it off and prepare it. For this, plausible models would not be difficult to find, among them Mozart's Symphony No. 39. Yet among Beethoven's ten published works up to Opus 55 that have slow introductions to first movements, only two match this plan in metrical sequence—the G-minor Cello Sonata, Op. 5 No. 2, and the Piano Quintet with Winds, Op. 16. The Cello Sonata, parenthetically, anticipates in the unusual length of its first movement and in some other features certain aspects of the formal layout of the *Eroica* first movement, although it is hardly comparable in power or density of expression. At all events, looking ahead to the more developed *Eroica* sketches of Landsberg 6, we see that the question of settling on the right choice of initial attack for the first Allegro remained open and variable until long after the basic theme itself had indeed been achieved and fixed in form. When the conventional slow introduction disappears, it is not immediately replaced by the two percussive chords; instead, other experiments are ventured first.

(2) With the last two measures of staff 3 we arrive at the earliest known version of the opening of the Allegro, which continues on staff 4, mm. 1–4, followed by a double bar to signify a temporary stop. The shape of the phrase, again, is crude enough: two measures of tonic followed by two of dominant and a suggested repetition of the dominant phrase an octave higher (see Example 5.4). The apparent naiveté of the phrase is only partly due to its rhyth-

Example 5.4

(a) Wielhorsky Sketchbook, p. 44, st. 3–4 (opening figure of Allegro)

(b) Piano Variations, Op. 35: *Basso del Tema* (in analytical reduction)

mic simplicity, in which the same rhythmic figure is repeated in every measure (in Beethoven, of all composers, this is hardly surprising even in works of the utmost subtlety). What is truly distinctive in this phrase is the choice of intervallic motion in its first two measures—the motion is that of a "turning figure" using the scale steps 1–5–5–1, and only in the second measure introducing 3. The direct and literal connection of this opening turning figure to the *Basso del Tema* could hardly be more obvious. And in light of the location of this movement-plan in the sketchbook, directly following twenty-three consecutive pages of sketches for the Opus 35 Variations, the basis for speaking of "derivation" of the theme is equally clear.

Yet if we now assume that the compositional aim in the first Allegro sketch was to associate the main subject directly and literally with the *Basso del Tema* (which in turn would then form the basis for the finale), we can also see that this purpose was quickly developed a step further within this same sketch-complex. For immediately following the movement-plan, on staff 10 of this page, Beethoven returns to work on the opening phrase of the Allegro and now modifies it as follows (see Example 5.5). The original motive of measure 2 is now shifted to measure 1; the basic motion of the turning figure starting on pitch 1 is stretched to occur on the downbeats of the first three measures (and remains harmonically on V rather than returning to I); the rhythmic repetition, however, is maintained. Between this version and the first-movement sketches in Landsberg 6, we have no further extant sketches; by the time of

Example 5.5   Wielhorsky Sketchbook, p. 44, st. 10

Example 5.6   Sketchbook Landsberg 6: first theme, as found in all continuity drafts

Landsberg 6, the final form of the opening triadic theme is established and remains a fixed point in the elaborative process (see Example 5.6). We may now observe that in its final form the triadic subject remains in primary linear form a "turning figure," so designed that it introduces the members of the tonic triad in order, returning to pitch 1 after each motion to other triadic pitches—first 3 and then 5. Thus it maintains the same absolute intervallic boundaries of 5 above and 5 below 1 which had been stated in direct form in the *Basso del Tema*.

The consequence of all this may be stated as follows: we are now in a position to claim, on verifiable evidence, that the triadic formation of the final version was not an original linear gestalt, but that it developed in visible stages from the intervallic content, the boundaries, and the linear order of the *Basso del Tema*, which will then itself resurface in the Finale. At this primitive stage of projecting the idea of the symphony, Beethoven temporarily considered the possibility of an exact motivic correspondence between the opening of the first-movement Allegro and the *Basso del Tema;* he then sought to elaborate and disguise this relationship for the sake of obtaining a thematic idea both more complex and more susceptible to elaboration (I have in mind the immediate juxtaposition in the final version of triadic and chromatic motions, in bass register). Yet despite his abandonment of the more literal connection, the outline of that connection remains intact. Accordingly we can see that, if we accept the sketch evidence as a basis for analytic insight, the host of commentators who have sought to find motivic correspondence between the first and last movements of the symphony—most prominently Engelsmann and Riezler—are both right and wrong: right in tracing the relationship between the two motivic complexes in certain particulars that have a degree of similarity; wrong in accepting as basic the literal connection between the linear cell 1–3–1 of the opening of the first movement and the *upper-line theme* in the Finale, with its 1–3–1 incipit. We now have reason to attach much greater importance to the *Basso del Tema* as the progenitor of both themes.

An additional dividend provided by the Wielhorsky sketches is that they should obliterate for all time any notion of a connection between the *Eroica* opening theme and Mozart's Overture to *Bastien und Bastienne,* of 1768; even now this myth dies hard in some quarters, but it can surely be laid to rest for good. The transformations in the first-theme idea in these sketches indicate one way in which sketches may show us connections in finished compositions that we would not have noticed otherwise, as Philip Gossett observed in his Pastoral Symphony study. Moreover, even if we had noticed them, abstractly, we would not have been able to substantiate them, in the absence of this kind of evidence, as having validity for the actual composition process.[10]

(3) We come now to the slow-movement sketch on page 44, staves 6–8. It is marked "2da, Adagio, C dur"; there is no doubt of its function. Again Beethoven sets down an opening idea, then moves to a sustained d-flat marked for a bassoon, in the middle of staff 7 (marked "fag[otto]"). He then sketches out a closing section which picks up the 1–3–1 figure in C major used earlier, now augmenting it (staff 8) through clear indications of the adding of voices in higher registers and the remark, "crescendo più forte, sempre più voci." Finally he suggests in a few measures at the end of staff 8 a quiet ending in C major.

From this incipient slow-movement plan, Beethoven maintains in later phases only the primary tonality, C, and, at some distance, the idea of a C-major section with triplet subdivisions of the basic metrical format. Of course the concept of a C major, $\frac{6}{8}$ movement is to be discarded in favor of the *Marcia funebre,* $\frac{2}{4}$, C minor, which is still to undergo all its larger planning and elaboration in the *Eroica* sketchbook. Among other things, this confirms that the Funeral March, with its well-known implications of celebration of the death of a hero, was not part of the earliest scheme of the symphony but emerged at a later phase.

We also note, with some astonishment, that the $\frac{6}{8}$ C-major theme in Adagio set down in this sketch (Example 5.7) directly anticipates the $\frac{6}{8}$ Lento slow

Example 5.7   Wielhorsky Sketchbook, p. 44, st. 6: opening of sketch for slow movement

movement of Opus 135 (Example 5.8)—serving there, of course, as the basis for a variations slow movement in a vastly different context. That this is not the purest coincidence is suggested by the parallel concept-sketch, or movement-plan, for the Violin Sonata, Op. 30 No. 1, in A major, in the Kessler sketchbook of 1801–1802, which had just preceded the Wielhorsky (Ex-

Example 5.8 from String Quartet, Op. 135: Lento Assai, Cantante e Tranquillo, first violin, opening

Example 5.9 Kessler Sketchbook, fol. 37v, st. 1: movement plan for Op. 30 No. 1

ample 5.9). In that plan the slow-movement idea was an Andante in F-sharp minor, *Alla breve,* which was then suppressed but emerged twenty years later as the Allegro subject of the first movement of the Piano Sonata, Opus 111; the example has been known since Nottebohm but now appears in a somewhat more complete context. That Beethoven not only looked back into his sketchbooks but at times made use of a recent sketchbook while working on another has recently been shown precisely in connection with the Opus 35 sketches in Kessler and Wielhorsky. It has been independently discovered by Christopher Reynolds and by Sieghard Brandenburg that a large number of the individual Opus 35 entries in Wielhorsky are copied directly from the same entries in Kessler, then utilized for further development.[11]

(4) The Menuetto and Trio sketch in Wielhorsky also deserves brief comment. Beethoven's marginal designation, "Menuetto serioso," is unusual. Kurt von Fischer observed that Beethoven used the term *serioso* only twice in finished works: for the title of the Quartet, Opus 95, which was labeled *Quartetto serioso* in the autograph, and in which the Scherzo is headed "Allegro assai vivace ma serioso"; and later in the Diabelli Variations, in which the sixth variation is called "Allegro ma non troppo e serioso."[12] Kurt von Fischer plausibly interprets the term as the antithesis of "scherzando"—its use is to prevent a light and playful approach to performance. In the *Eroica* sketch it seems to

signify a movement in *tempo di menuetto* but of serious and portentous character (so far as it had any at this stage), suitable to a symphony but not as rapid and dynamic as the third movements of Beethoven's two earlier symphonies. The brief four measures of the Trio suffice to show a strongly contrasting character and the key of G minor, which is to play an important role in the final version of the work, but not in this movement. Incidentally, in the later *Eroica* sketchbook Beethoven still calls the third movement "Menuetto" in its earlier sketches.

In retrospect, we can see that the processes of transformation that led from this primitive movement-plan to the later conception of the symphony, with all its ramifications, really only entail two vital shifts in the basic outline of the material. One is the suppression of the Introduction to the first movement already discussed. The other is the change from a $\frac{6}{8}$ Adagio slow movement to the $\frac{2}{4}$ *Marcia funebre*. We can hardly doubt that this change reflects a deepening sense of need for a slow movement that can hold its own with the powerful and immense first movement; but we can also see that what Beethoven obtains in the later choice is a slow movement that offers metrical contrast with the triple and twice-triple meters of the first movement and Scherzo. In this connection, the manifest and long-recognized pattern of $2 \times \frac{3}{4}$ measures (quasi $\frac{6}{4}$) in the first movement would have been especially striking. In fact, the combination of a $\frac{6}{8}$ slow movement with a $\frac{3}{4}$ Allegro first movement simply does not occur in Beethoven's early or middle-period works. The nearest approximation is to be found in the Quartet, Op. 18 No. 1, with its Allegro $\frac{3}{4}$ followed by its $\frac{9}{8}$ slow movement, which is marked, in the later version, "Adagio affettuoso ed appassionato," and which we know from the sketches in Grasnick 2 as well as a contemporary remark was associated in Beethoven's mind with the death scene in *Romeo and Juliet;* in Grasnick 2 he writes such entries as "il prend le tombeau" and "il se tue" followed by "les derniers soupirs."[13] The piece is therefore wholly exceptional in this period. To find later examples of a subdivided triplet motion as a basic slow-movement meter against a $\frac{3}{4}$ first movement, we must wait until the little G-major Piano Sonata, Opus 79 (a deceptively simple-looking piece), and the two late masterworks, Opus 110 and Opus 127. As for the alternative procedure—a $\frac{3}{4}$ first movement and a $\frac{2}{4}$ slow movement—it is fairly common across the years; witness the early Piano Quintet, Opus 16; later, the "Ghost" Trio; the Eighth Symphony; and the Violin Sonata, Opus 96, among others. Nothing can be more obvious than Beethoven's sensitivity to metrical relationships between adjacent movements; but if we are looking for relevant evidence in exactly this phase of his career, we can find it readily in the Variations, Opus 34, the companion piece to Opus 35. These Variations are equally innovative in that each variation is not only in a different key but also in a different meter. In the movement-plan for this work, in the Kessler, Beethoven indeed begins by writing out the incipit of

Example 5.10 Kessler Sketchbook, fol. 88v, st. 1: movement plan for Op. 34: "jede Variation in einer andern Taktart oder abwechselnd einmal in der l.h. passagen und dann fast die nemlichen oder andere in der rechten hand"

the theme, then the words, "jede Variation in einer andern Taktart . . ." (see Example 5.10), a plan that he then followed rigorously in developing the piece.

Now at last we come back to consideration of the *Eroica* Finale. Once again, to reiterate the premise, we see that the movement-plan in Wielhorsky contains no trace of a finale. But, as with the document in *The Purloined Letter,* the reason we cannot see the evidence is that it is right in front of our noses. As Floros observed, and I am seeking to confirm, the location of this entire movement-plan, directly after the final sketches for Opus 35, permits the inference that the idea of a symphony concluding with some use of that same material was a fixed point in the conceptual scheme from its beginnings. Looking ahead again to the *Eroica* sketchbook, we find this view supported again. Nowhere is there any trace of an alternative idea for a finale; and Beethoven elaborates the movements in the first ninety pages of the *Eroica* sketchbook essentially in their consecutive order in the symphony. For the finale, as Nottebohm observed, the amount of work needed for the basic material was considerably less than for the earlier movements.[14] Particularly significant is the internal movement-plan with which Beethoven begins this segment of the sketchbook (see Example 5.11). He begins with the *Basso del Tema;* then come

Example 5.11 Sketchbook Landsberg, 6, p. 70: plan for Op. 55 Finale (as given in N 1880, with some suggested accidentals)

a series of segments labeled "variations," in order, for solo clarinet and for solo horn; a running passage on the dominant of G minor that would eventually form the opening of the movement and is marked "principio"; then a fugue in E-flat; finally an Adagio, closing with the words "varié et deducé." [15] The very terminology of this movement-plan coincides with that of a similar plan he had put down for the Piano Sonata, Opus 26, in the sketchbook Landsberg 7, in the year 1800 (see Example 5.12). There he had written the heading "Sonate pour M," the entire variations theme for the first movement, with the comment "variée tutt' a fatto—"; then he verbally projects a "Minuet or some other characteristic piece, for example, a March in A-flat Minor—and then this—" and he writes a theme for a $\frac{2}{4}$ Allegro finale, evidently a Rondo. [16]

Although a sonata with variations first movement was not as innovative as a symphony with variations finale—witness the Mozart A-Major Piano Sonata—nevertheless it represents a new departure for Beethoven keyboard sonatas and signals a break with his earlier procedures. In the final form of the *Eroica* fourth movement, the variations-form with fugue of Opus 35 is transformed into a complex blend of variations and developmental form in a movement having no contemporary formal analogues. I see the movement as falling into three large segments, of which the first is a quasi-exposition involving the gradual creation of the *Basso del Tema* and the upper-line theme itself, all in E-flat; the second is a set of five variations, with the two fugato sections surrounding the G-minor March which is at the very center of the entire movement; the third is a closing peroration, again in E-flat but with inflections of G-minor, for which the Poco Andante is the formal equivalent of a recapitulation. [17] At the end the real climax occurs when the long-familiar upper-line theme descends to bass register for its last presentation, displacing in register the *Basso* from which it had originated. Clearly, Opus 35 had formed the culmination of more than twenty sets of variations that Beethoven had written along Classical lines, expanding the concept but not altering its formal boundaries. Now, in reconstructing the same material for the Finale of his greatest symphony to date, Beethoven held fast to the sequential order of basic events from Opus 35 but reshaped the middle and later portions of the movement, maintaining the variations in principle but closing up the formal breaks that would normally separate them, thus containing them in a special kind of sonata finale, "quasi una fantasia." It cannot be stressed too strongly that the very idea of an elaborated variations finale marks a breakthrough of grand proportions in the traditions of the symphony, and that Beethoven surely was aware of it as such. His essentially radical decision about the shape of the Finale for this work, however, fits in well with his tendency to experiment with new or unorthodox formal schemes from about 1800 to 1803; witness the Piano Sonatas, Op. 26, Op. 27, and all of Op. 31, which are innovative in this respect; also the Violin Sonatas of Op. 30 and the *Kreutzer* Sonata. Something

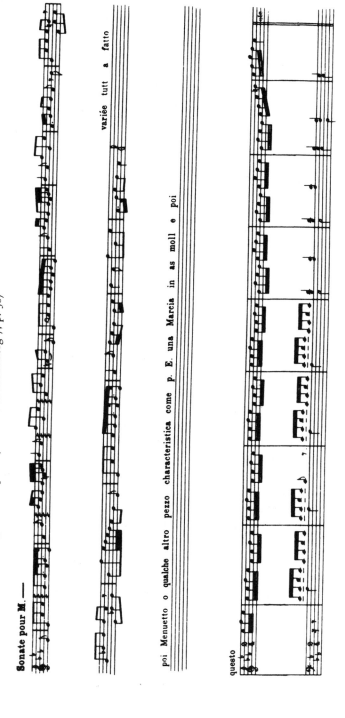

Example 5.12 Movement plan for Op. 26 (Sketchbook Landsberg 7, p. 56)

similar is afoot in the abandonment of the luxurious *Andante favori* as slow movement for the *Waldstein* Sonata in favor of the intensely concentrated short Adagio.

This period of innovation in formal schemes also fits in well with Beethoven's extensive use in the sketchbooks of concise but quite adequate movement-plans for several of these same works: as we have seen, these include Op. 26, Op. 30 No. 1, and Op. 34, as well as this "Ur-*Eroica*" movement-plan in Wielhorsky. In the *Eroica* sketchbook, once the further elaboration of the symphony was completed, other works were similarly planned—including an early movement-plan for what later became the Fifth Symphony; in that case it is the first-movement idea that becomes the invariant against which the other movements are developed.[18] For the Fifth, as for the *Eroica,* in setting up such a plan Beethoven was giving himself a synoptic idea of what the work as a whole might look like, and he was setting himself a goal that might be far off in realization but to which he could return, after taking care of other preoccupations. In all this there may have been not only a sense of artistic progress and direction, but also a practical sense of having more compositional tasks in hand than he could possibly work out at one time. On the one hand, the sketchbooks show us Beethoven dealing with his own development by advancing his creative powers in works that embrace every major contemporary genre—at this period even plunging into a major opera, almost before he was quite ready; yet, on the other hand, at the same time the sketchbook method helped to solve the practical need to develop his career by coming to terms with the demands of patrons, publishers, and the musical marketplace, and keeping up a steady stream of publications.

A final word about the Wielhorsky movement-plan: whatever else it shows us about the origins of the work, it also gives us a basis for asserting that the colossal size and length of the *Eroica,* in all its movements, which both Beethoven and later commentators have repeatedly emphasized as its greatest departure from earlier norms of symphonic composition, was probably not an integral aspect of the work in its earliest stage but grew as a consequence of later phases of elaboration. A more basic and earlier dimension of the work, chronologically and conceptually, was its point of origin in the specific material of Opus 35, and the key to its development now appears to have been the artistic decision to use that material, with all the necessary modifications, as the finale of a symphony. In the end was the beginning.

SIX

The Compositional Genesis of the *Eroica* Finale

No Beethoven movement presents more basic issues of aesthetic autonomy or
originality than does the *Eroica* finale. In the annals of Beethoven criticism it
has aroused its share of comment mainly for its unusual formal structure and
its derivation from the Piano Variations, Opus 35 (as well as from the *Prometheus* finale and the contradanse). Further, the common line of discussion
about the size, density, and organic structure of the symphony, as well as its
pathbreaking status among Beethoven's middle-period works, has always reserved certain questions for the finale in its role as summation and completion
of the work as a whole. Yet there is one little studied but important body of
evidence that has the potential to modify our critical perceptions of these questions at all levels, aesthetic, structural, and historical: the sketches for the finale
that are preserved in the "Eroica Sketchbook." This vitally important sketchbook, formerly MS Landsberg 6 of the Deutsche Staatsbibliothek in Berlin,
has since the Second World War been housed in Poland and is now at the
Bibliotéka Jagiellońska in Krakow, where I was able to study it firsthand in
1984.[1]

To some writers the formal structure of the finale is anomalous and controversial. Tovey proclaimed it as "a form which was unique when it appeared,
and has remained unique ever since," and he even felt it necessary to combat
what he called "a widespread notion that it is formless or incoherent."[2] Although Tovey sidestepped formal labels in his program note, elsewhere he
described this movement as a "compound of variations with fugal and other
episodes."[3] Others too have seen it as a movement which manifestly owes its
formal organization primarily to the genre of variations (the means by which
its basic material had been exploited in Op. 35). Of course, in Op. 35 the long-
established classical model had already been extended to new limits; yet despite its massive proportions and its *Introduzione* and *Finale,* that work is still a
variation set in strict formal terms. In the *Eroica* finale, the variation chain is

dismantled in most of its rigid features and is blended with fugal and other quasi-variation segments to form a new type of movement. In effect these new features invade and alter the overt associations of the movement with the variation concept, yet do not destroy it completely; the result is a blending, a hybrid form that may well be differently described by various commentators.

For Schenker, in the brief formal remarks he drops in his massive reduction analysis of 1930, the finale is so closely related to the Variations Op. 35 that he can use Beethoven's terminology from the Piano Variations in designating the segments of the *Eroica* finale.[4] Schenker observes that the first part of the movement is clearly an "Introduzione col Basso del Tema" followed by the theme itself in mm. 76–107; then in place of the fifteen variations of Op. 35 comes a fugato that, like the "Finale alla fuga" of Opus 35, has the function of supplying a new set of pitch relationships to the predominant E-flat sonority of the main section. Beyond this, Schenker's approach moves wholly into the analysis of the larger voice-leading of the movement and not its morphology, which for him remains, above all in this most massive of his published reduction analyses, merely the surface. In Schenker's view the principal motions are the rising fifth of the Basso del Tema and the complex 5th-descent of the upper-line theme that is its complement.

From another angle emerges the viewpoint of Kurt von Fischer, in an article comparing the formal structure of the finale with that of Op. 35.[5] For von Fischer the Variations form a large-scale structure that presents analogies to a three-movement composition—that is, the Introduction (so labeled by Beethoven) leads to the equivalent of a first movement (upper-line theme plus variations 1 through 13); a second movement follows (= Variations 14/15, the slow movement); then there is a fugue as finale with two additional melodic variations to close. As for the *Eroica* finale, von Fischer sees it as modifying this scheme in a way that is approximately comparable to a sonata-form finale: it consists of an Introduction; an Exposition (upper-line theme plus variations); a Development section (from Fugato 1 to the second Fugato and the episode that follows); a "Reprise" (signaled by the Andante return to the statement of the opening theme) and a coda, beginning with the A-flat major segment.

I shall not attempt to elucidate these large-scale formal overviews further, nor to sort out the types of morphological approaches they embody. Suffice it to say that all of them share the view that the *Eroica* finale owes not only its thematic material but in some way its formal origins to Op. 35. It is surprising, however, that neither Tovey, Schenker, nor von Fischer considered that the surviving sketches for the finale may contribute to our understanding of Beethoven's formal planning and aesthetic concept of the movement. They could have done so, at least tentatively, drawing upon Nottebohm's brief description of the finale sketches from Landsberg 6.[6] Similar neglect seems to have befallen a later discussion of the finale sketches from the same sketchbook that was included by Paul Mies in his article on Beethoven's "Werke über seinen Kontretanz in Es-Dur," in *Beethoven-Jahrbuch* (1953/54)[7]; moreover, Mies's article is not mentioned or listed in the recent and comprehensive Johnson-Tyson-Winter compendium, *The Beethoven Sketchbooks*, in the chapter on Landsberg 6.

That the sketches for the symphony can provide a fruitful basis for understanding both larger formal dimensions and details of organization is hardly surprising. I have tried to follow up this line of evidence, both for the first movement and for the earliest version of the entire symphony, in Chapters 4 and 5 above. In Chapter 5 I sought to show that if we look at the earliest idea for the symphony, found on two pages of the Wielhorsky Sketchbook of 1802, we can reconstruct its emergence from the Piano Variations, Op. 35, in a new way. This is evident from the following: (1) that this earliest known idea for a symphony in E-flat major follows directly upon the completion of Beethoven's compositional work on the Piano Variations, which had just been concluded; and (2) that the notion of a symphony in the same key includes initial ideas for three of its movements, lacking a finale. But I infer that this very fact allows us to hypothesize that the material of the Piano Variations was in some way to form a basis for the eventual finale, which is exactly what happened thereafter. (3) We also find that the Basso del Tema of the Piano Variations served as the original springboard for the intervallic form of the first theme of the first movement at this nascent stage, only later giving way to the triadic turning theme with chromatic continuation that became the basic opening material for the first movement in its final form.

By the time Beethoven returned to work on the Third Symphony, sometime in the winter of 1803–04, he had made the basic decisions about the formal structure of the work; comparison of the Landsberg 6 sketches with the brief movement-plan in Wielhorsky shows a substantial leap forward to a definitive idea of what the work was to be like.[8] The first movement is still in $\frac{3}{4}$ but now has no slow Introduction. The slow movement is no longer in C major, $\frac{6}{8}$, but is a *Marcia funebre* (retaining however in the Maggiore more than a few traces of the Wielhorsky attempt at a C-major Adagio). The third movement is no longer a *Menuetto serioso* but is in the process of becoming the powerful Scherzo we know from the finished work. Even though it is still called in Landsberg 6 a "Menuetto," we must realize that Beethoven interchanges the terms "Menuetto" and "Scherzo" throughout his early years. Finally, Landsberg 6 is the sole source of sketch material for the finale; in this manuscript the four movements of the symphony are sketched in their final order. Accordingly, Beethoven does not begin the finale sketch-work until page 70 of the sketchbook, and then continues it intensively for fifteen pages, up to page 85 (see Table 6.2); thereafter, leaving pages 86 and 87 blank, he completes this preliminary work on the movement on pages 88 through 90, picking up where he had just left off and continuing work on the Coda to the movement. Except for a fragmentary entry on page 3 (just the incipit of the fugato subject), these are all the surviving sketches that we are certain belong to the *Eroica* finale.

The sketches show us something of the process by which Beethoven now returned to the material of Opus 35 at the point of elaborating it into a symphonic finale. A century after Nottebohm, and more than thirty years after the article by Mies, they still have much to teach us. To clarify the discussion, I offer a formal overview of the finale as Table 6.1, with my overview of the main contents of the finale sketches as a companion (Table 6.2). From these we see that Beethoven opened the sketch material with a synoptic movement-plan for the finale and then worked out across these pages precisely those segments of the movement that he could not have elaborated readily from Opus 35. This may be no surprise, but it is also no speculation; the material is there to be interpreted. Thus, in Table 6.3 I show which portions of the finale receive differing degrees of elaboration in these sketches, and what types of elaboration they are given. Table 6.2 shows that after the movement-plan on page 70, Beethoven moved directly to work on the very ending of the movement, as if to frame it solidly and work out the main lines of its eventual completion; this tendency has been recently discussed by Peter Cahn in an article on Beethoven's formation of closings and codas.[9] Those parts of the movement that are worked out in continuity drafts are marked in Table 6.3 with the letters "Dr" (for Draft). The segments worked out with greatest care in these pages are as follows: the coda (for which we find the largest number of entries and at least five large drafts); the transition to the coda (mm. 397–430); the Andante; the second Fugato (mm. 277–348); and the first transition (mm. 107–116). The only portion not worked out in these pages is the short second Transition (mm. 206–210), and one of the biggest surprises is the absence of much elaboration of the Alla marcia episode in G minor that becomes the central element in the finale; for this episode only one draft is found, on page 71.

The first and most important item that claims our attention is the movement-plan that opens the entire sketch-package, as given on page 70 (see N 1880, p. 50, and Ex. 5.11 in Chapter 5). Though known since Nottebohm, this important synoptic overview of the movement has never been discussed in detail. It contains seven elements. The first is a statement of the Basso del Tema, first four bars only, as "concept sketch"; next is an early version of the opening Introduction, labeled "principio," on staves 2–3 (whether this was an afterthought or intended from the outset we cannot be sure). On staff 1 we see

Table 6.1   Overview of the *Eroica* Symphony Finale

Measures	Segment	Function					Tonal center
1–11	1	Introduction					g—E♭
12–43	2	["Basso del Tema" + 2 var. + "Tema"]					E♭
		(a) BdT	8	8 +	8	8	
			a	a¹	b	b¹	
			(s)	(s/w)	(s)	(s/w)	
44–59		(b) BdT ["A tre"] Bdt in mid-register; str. only; 8th motion					
60–75		(c) BdT ["A quattro"] BdT in upper register; str. only; triplet motion					
76–107		(d) ["Tema"] Upper-line theme emerges over BdT; repeats now written out and reorchestrated; winds first time, strings/tutti second time					
107–116		Transition					E♭—V/c
117–174	3	Fugato I (= *Variation 1*) on BdT incipit					c—f—b♭—g
175–206	4	*Variation 2:* T in Fl and Ob, then Fl diminution with portions of BdT in Bass register					b—D
206–210		Transition (= codetta to Var. 2)					D—g
211–256	5	[Alla marcia; Upper-line theme in dotted march rhythm plus BdT in bass] [= *Variation 3*]					g
257–276	6	[*Variation 4:* New development of T (Flute) and BdT; then T in lower strings, closing to Fugato II]					C—c—f—
277–348	7	Fugato II (= *Variation 5*). On two subjects: inversion of Bdt incipit plus diminution of T + extension					E♭
348–430	8	Poco Andante (= *Variation 6*). T reharmonized, reorchestrated (Oboes predominate), then builds to climactic statement of T in bass register; new elaboration in A♭ (mm. 404ff.) leads through rising chromatic bass motion to G minor (420–430)					E♭—g
431–473	9	Coda: Presto. Re-elaborates Introduction and brings fragments of T as closing figures					E♭

A further overview based on thematic, tonal, and textural features:

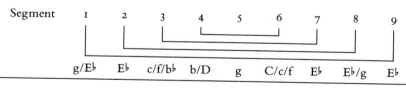

brief indications for the first two variations: the first is to be for solo clarinet; the second variation is for solo horn. There is then to be a fugato episode of some kind (note that only one is intended at this early stage); we now see the entry "Blas Instrumente, dopo in Es," which may refer to the ensuing Poco Andante, with its prominent winds, rather than to a secondary use of the woodwinds. That there is to be a slow-tempo variation is clear from the entry "un poco Adagio," and Beethoven explicitly indicates that it should have solo

Table 6.2 Overview of Landsberg 6 sketches for Opus 55/IV

Page		Page		Page	
70	(a) Movement-plan for mvt. (b)Skk for end of Andante + Coda	76	Andante (mm. 380ff.) varia	81	Coda draft
				82	Coda draft
		77	Transition to Coda + ending	83	Coda ending Andante (A♭ section)
71	Fugato II Introduction Alla marcia (G minor)		Fugato I + trans. Tema in D Trans. to Coda Andante Ending		
				84/5	Coda draft
72	Introduction + Exposition (cont. draft)			86–87	blank
		78	Tema in A major Andante transition	88	Coda draft
73	Fugato II Introduction Fugato I Fugato II fragments	78	Tema in A major Andante transition (396–413) Coda	89	Coda Trans. to Fugato I
				90	Coda draft; to end
74	Trans. to Fugato I (Coda? Fugato II?) Coda and ending	79	Tema in A Fugato II		
75	Ending Transition to Coda Tema in A major (unused) Ending	80	Fugato II Coda fragments		

wind passages. To finish this brief overview he merely suggests in one stroke of the pen that the rest of the movement is to be "varié et deducé"—that is, to consist of variations and developmental episodes, as yet to be worked out.

Scanty and embryonic as this overview may be, it nevertheless tells us a number of important things about Beethoven's idea for this movement. We see that it is indeed to be a special kind of variations movement; that it is to have a fugato episode somewhere in the middle and a slow episode later in the movement. We also see that he planned to make considerable use of wood-wind sonorities, with variations for both solo clarinet and solo horn near the beginning and with winds prominent in later portions of the Finale as well. Further, the movement is to use its Basso del Tema (and by implication its upper-line Tema) not in any strict variation procedure but in a structure in which both these elements are varied and elaborated—*varié et deducé*—thereby combining the sequential character of a variations movement with the developmental procedures familiar in a symphonic movement and in any kind of

Table 6.3 Sketches for Opus 55/IV in Landsberg 6 (by movement-segment)

Segment	Measures	Pages in Landsberg 6
Introduction	1–11	70, 71, 72–73 (frag.), 79/6
Exposition	12–107	71 (frag.), 72 (Dr)
Trans.	107–116	73, 74, 77, 89
Fugato I	117–174	73, 77 (end)
Var. 2	175–206	71 (frag.), 73 (in G)
Trans.	206–210	—
Alla marcia	211–256	71
Var. 4	257–276	76?
Fugato II	277–348	70, 71, 73, 74?, 79 (Dr), 80
Poco Andante	348–396	70, 76, 77
Trans. to Coda	397–430	70, 75, 76, 77, 78, 82 (frag.), 83
Coda	431–473	70, 74, 75, 77, 78, 80, 81 (Dr), 82 (Dr) 83, 84–85 (Dr), 88 (Dr), 89, 90 (Dr)

finale short of a conventional Rondo (which is excluded from consideration). Despite Beethoven's early intention to emphasize woodwinds, the plan for solo clarinet and solo horn display was abandoned, since neither here nor anywhere else in the symphony is there a truly extended and soloistic use of the clarinet. Similarly, although the finale makes important use of the horns, it does not match the solo horn passages of the first movement (for example, the famous "false entry" or the great horn solo that follows the Recapitulation); nor does it utilize the horn section as a structural aggregate, as in the Trio of the Scherzo. In fact, it is the oboe that emerges as the single most important wind instrument in the first and second movements, above all in the Marcia funebre; and both oboe and flute far outweigh the clarinet as solo wind sonorities in the Finale. Accordingly, the initial idea of differentiating the finale from the other movements through new use of woodwind color was later suppressed in favor of other priorities.

If we follow Beethoven's procedures through the rest of page 70 and the next few pages after this opening plan, the evidence is not systematic but neither is it unclear. Below the movement plan on page 70, he shifts at once to an idea for the end of the Andante and the coda of the movement, as we have seen. Then, on the page following (71), he works out in broad strokes some aspects of three other segments of the movement that are widely spread apart in the final version: the second fugato, the Introduction, and the G-minor Alla marcia from the middle of the movement. By doing so Beethoven has quickly established three passages, two of which (the Introduction and the March) could not have been derived from Opus 35. In short, he is blocking out the segments that are new and that must be worked out afresh from this point on, both as to content and location.

Beginning on page 72, we find a new point of departure for the whole movement. Now Beethoven goes to the trouble of once more writing out a full draft of mm. 1–107 of the finale, starting with the Basso del Tema and going through to the emergence of the upper-line Tema. Although he sprinkles the page with a few indications of instrumentation and dynamics, he nevertheless writes out completely in the sketchbook an entire exposition draft that could hardly have been anything but thrice familiar by now, since it almost entirely replicates the opening passages of Opus 35, including the successive shifts of the Basso del Tema up through three registers before the arrival of the Tema. And from here on, Beethoven's sketch sequence attends to working out myriad details of individual segments of the movement (see Table 6.2). His procedure at first goes partly in the order of these segments in the movement: thus page 73 deals with the fugatos (it now emerges that there can be two), and once again with the Introduction; page 74 takes up the transition to the first fugato, then skips to the coda; page 75 once more deals with the coda and experiments with a version of the upper-line Tema in A major that is not used in the final version. And page 76 deals with the Andante, now to be developed over the next three pages. In later pages of this sketch material it becomes clear, as Mies pointed out, that much of Beethoven's attention is given to working on transition passages; this suggests that the main outlines of the central episodes could be considered fixed, if not in all details, at least in basic function and role (thus, the two fugatos, the Andante, and the G minor episode). Then in the last pages of these sketches (pp. 81–90) Beethoven gives his attention unstintingly to the coda, for which we find here not fewer than five full drafts, not counting some other shorter entries. From all this we can see that the movement at this point was to have seven primary segments (see Table 6.4, Phase 2).

Table 6.4 provides a larger glimpse of three phases of Beethoven's elaboration of his basic ideas for this finale. Phase 1 (derived of course from Opus 35) is embodied in the movement-plan itself as it appears on page 70. It contains seven segments, including the Introduction and Exposition; the two solo variations that were to be cast aside; a single fugato; a slow section; and the presumed remainder. Phase 2 follows it immediately, and emerges from the work of elaboration over the remaining pages of this sketch material. Now the clarinet and horn variations are gone; there are two fugatos, an Alla marcia, an Andante, and a coda. The final version (Phase 3) then expands Phase 2 by adding segments 4 and 6 of the movement, by separating the Alla marcia from the two fugatos symmetrically, and by supplying parallel returns of the Tema

Table 6.4 Major phases of the genesis of the *Eroica* finale

Phase 1		(Opus 35)
		Movement-plan (Landsberg 6, p. 70)
	1	Introduction
	2	Exposition (BdT + T)
	3	Variation for Clarinet solo
	4	Variation for Horn solo
	5	Fugato
	6	Adagio
	7	Remainder, "varié et deducé" (Coda)
Phase 2		(visible in Landsberg 6 sketches)
	1	Introduction
	2	Exposition
	3	Fugato I
	4	Alla marcia [by p. 71]
	5	Fugato II [by p. 73]
	6	Andante
	7	Coda
Phase 3		(Final version)
	1	Introduction
	2	Exposition
	3	Fugato I [Var. 1]
	*4	Var. 2 [Winds]
	5	Alla marcia [Var. 3]
	*6	Var. 4 [W/S]
	7	Fugato II [Var. 5]
	8	Andante [Var. 6]
	9	Coda

*barely sketched in Landsberg 6

in upper register in literal form. Segments 4 and 6 fill out the scheme of the movement well, and at the same time allow for transitions to the more elaborated segments (above all the fugatos) that profit from being approached and left through gradual transition passages.

This final phase must have been achieved after the Landsberg 6 sketch material, which means that there could have been more work on the movement on leaves that are now unknown—certainly, I believe, before a final full score would have been settled upon. As often happens, too, what is presented in Phase 2 does anticipate almost all the primary segments of the movement, with a few of them worked out in great detail and the remainder left to a later stage of work. We also see Beethoven in these pages trying out a few versions of these ideas that would prove to be too far-reaching for the final form of the movement and thus had to be abandoned. This includes the A major version of the upper-line theme, which may have seemed for a while an attractive alternative to what became the D major episode of segment 4 of the final version (see Table 6.4, Phase 3, item 4).

It is important to note, finally, that the resulting large form of the movement possesses a remarkable degree of symmetry in its segmentation. In tonal centers, in thematic content, and in texture, the segments numbered 1 through 9 form a balanced series of nested pairs, from the G-minor/E-flat major motion of segments 1/2 and 8/9 to the two framing fugatos, and the two upper-line variations, nos. 4 and 6. All of these surround the vigorous G-minor Alla marcia that comes to stand as the focal midpoint and axial center of the movement. The largest symmetry of thematic action in the movement is that between segments 2 and 8 (the Introduction and the Poco Andante). In the Introduction, the Basso del Tema gradually rises in register, then gives way to the upper-line Tema that surpasses it as "theme"; in the Andante, the upper-line theme is first "recapitulated" in high register and then eventually passes downward in register to emerge as the basis for the last great rhetorical peroration in the movement. This in turn closes into the extraordinary A-flat major transition passage to G minor (mm. 404–420) that seems to evoke memories of the most distant wanderings of the first movement and its great development section, as well as evoking the Coda of the slow movement, with its own A-flat major extension (mm. 209–223).

⸻

For a brief sampling of what these sketches may provide by way of insight into a more detailed aspect of the movement, I turn to the group of entries brought together as Examples 6.1–6.7. These entries represent a series of ideas for the Introduction to the finale, along with just one (the only one) that represents the Alla marcia in G minor. Although the sketches for the Introduction were discussed by Mies, he did not connect them to the March segment, nor did he anticipate the conclusions that I should like to draw from them. If we look at the "principio" from the original movement-plan (Example 6.1), we

Example 6.1   Landsberg 6, p. 70: sketch for beginning of movement plan (modified from version in N 1880 and Ex. 5.11 above)

see that this primitive draft for a starting point for the movement established that the harmonic function of the opening was to move from the dominant of G minor to the dominant of E-flat major. At this early stage the dynamic gesture of rushing scalar sixteenth-note motion is established, thus providing a powerful rhythmic prologue to the abrupt and enigmatic chopped-off eighth notes of the Basso del Tema that immediately follows. At this stage too the "principio" is entirely in bass register and its motion lacks a sense of carefully profiled direction, in that the opening pitch, d, rises through the dominant 7th, becomes the goal after four measures, is reached again at m. 5, and then drops a major third to b-flat for the fermata. In Example 6.2 the register has been shifted up two octaves, making possible a fuller expansion of the harmonic material; now the motion is evidently in eighth notes (allowing for the possibility that these were thought of as each subdivided into sixteenths, however), but there is much internal repetition: the figure c–b-flat–a–g (4–3–2–1) of mm. 2 and 3 is stated in close adjacency three times without variant, only then rising an octave for the close. Although this pattern of A A A′ is certainly characteristic of much Beethovenian writing, its symmetries are evidently too literal for his purposes in this crucial opening phrase that serves as preparation for the Basso del Tema. Yet it also gives rise to another idea, right at this moment; it is the G-minor Alla marcia, which is sketched immediately below Example 6.2, on page 71, staves 6–9 (shown as Example 6.3). The connections of register, pitch-content, and linear motion are so clear between these

Example 6.2   Landsberg 6, p. 71: alternative sketch for beginning of finale

Example 6.3   Landsberg 6, p. 71: sketch for the G-minor Alla marcia in the finale

examples that even if they were not vertically adjacent on the same sketch-page, we would have no trouble in associating them. This unique sketch for the Alla marcia lacks the dotted rhythm (presumably a Hungarian twist) of the final version, but it clearly works out the idea of a G-minor descending line from 5 to 1 over the Basso del Tema that later characterizes the Alla marcia.

This case conveys a prime example of the principle, cogently discussed by Philip Gossett, that sketch material can disclose a connection between musical ideas that occur at far-flung points in a finished composition, the kind of connection for which evidence is, as a rule, easy to imagine but hard to find.[10] Here it emerges with a directness we can scarcely discredit, and even those skeptical of sketch studies might profitably consider an example as blatant as this. Of course, it can also be argued that one of the purposes of the Introduction is to stress further the G-minor region that has been important to this work since the fleeting appearance of G minor in the opening measures of the first movement. It is clear that part of the method of gaining harmonic breadth with organic unity in the finale is to establish the juxtaposition G minor/E-flat at the opening and G minor for the Alla marcia, which is to be the center of the arch of the movement while at the same time being stylistically the most eccentric moment in the finale. It may seem speculative to suggest that the Alla marcia, which was not yet in the movement on page 70, emerged precisely at the point where Beethoven turned over to page 71 and continued work on the G minor Introduction. But that is what these pages clearly suggest.

From this point it is not necessary to pursue all the ramifications of Examples 6.4–6.7. Briefly, Example 6.4 (page 72/1) brings the opening flourish up still another octave and gives it the double-octave grace-notes as impetus; but it is otherwise a repetition of the material of Example 6.2 for the first six

Example 6.4 Landsberg 6, p. 72: another sketch for beginning of finale

measures. It then moves decisively down through G minor to the sudden A-flat in its tenth measure; from here it attempts a brief prolongation of a II⁶ harmony in E-flat major, perhaps implying a shift to the dominant for the fermata; this sketch is given an alternative ending at page 73/3 and at 79/6 (Example 6.5) that surges back up to the registral starting point (the upward surge is to remain intact into the final version). Then Example 6.6 traverses the whole territory once more, but now introduces the important novelty that the phrase repetitions are suppressed in favor of scalar motions of four-note units, describing a downward chain of thirds from the uppermost d: thus d–b-flat–g–e-flat–c–a–f-sharp–d (see Examples 6.6 and 6.7). It thus moves through seven steps in a downward third-chain, replicating d as its first and last pitch, and arriving at the dominant pause in a new way. From here Beethoven was ready to go forward into the Basso del Tema, having found the form of the opening flourish that had enough directional impetus, intervallic integrity, and

Example 6.5　Landsberg 6, p. 79: alternative ending for sketch in Ex. 6.4

Example 6.6　Landsberg 6, p. 73: a further sketch for beginning of finale

Example 6.7　Analytical reduction of beginning of finale, expressed as descending intervallic chain

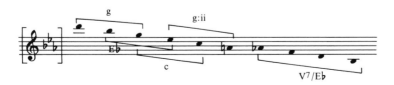

harmonic sense to support itself. We can also see (Example 6.7) that the downward third-chain contains a series of interlocking triads that go in the sequence g minor/E♭ major/c minor/ii of g, followed by a shift to the dominant seventh of E♭. In short, the succession g/E♭/c anticipates the principal tonal areas that will be utilized in the whole movement; and they are also the first tonal areas that the finale elaborates as it moves from the g-minor Introduction to the E♭-major Exposition, and then the C-minor Fugato. The feature of the final version that is still to be developed is only its total length; its eleven-measure phrase-length, in the final version, is of value as an asymmetrical opening that sharply contrasts with the rigid eight-measure phrase units that are to last through the entire Exposition of the Basso del Tema and the Tema.

Without suggesting that this brief survey of one set of variants is more than a sample, I will close with a few more remarks about the general character and importance of these sketches.

The study of Beethoven's sketches has the capacity to yield many different types of rewards, whether we focus on details or on the larger continuities of sections or movements. At the same time, the act of understanding an assemblage of sketches brings with it not simply an obligation to seek an analytical viewpoint for the musical entity, to which the sketches are then to be made relevant; but equally to attempt to reconstruct the process of musical shaping and ordering that eventually results in the realization of its compositional idea. However distant this goal may seem, it is the one toward which we strive, in my view correctly. Now in the case of the *Eroica* finale, the abiding question remains: once Beethoven had decided to fashion a symphonic finale (and, in my opinion, in its earliest stage, even the whole symphony) with the Op. 35 as starting point, what had to be done to convert this material from its use as a large-scale variation form to a symphonic finale?

In large part the answer is embodied in the central differences in genre, function, character, and length between the two entities—Op. 35 and this finale. These differences are broadly defined by the movement-plan and are then elaborated through the subsequent sketches on these pages of Landsberg 6. As the Third Symphony grew in Beethoven's hands to be the pathbreaking work that it is, the role of the finale in relation to the rest of the work must have changed as well. Accordingly, we should consider the Landsberg 6 sketches as attempts to meet the problem of remaking the Op. 35 material at a level adequate to the *Eroica* in its later phases of conception. From this vantage point, the finale fulfills certain conditions that enable it to stand up to the profundity of the other movements, with their scope, depth, and density. But it does something more as well. For, in fashioning the finale in the way that he did, Beethoven not only invented a new formal scheme that is wholly unprecedented in the symphonic literature but elaborated it by means that fit well with the earlier movements. One way is by means of thematic dualism. A contrast of thematic ideas is vital to this work from the very opening measures of the first movement, with its immediate juxtaposition of triadic turning theme with chromatic continuation. This dualism reappears in the slow movement, in the contrast between the *Marcia funebre* and the middle section in C major; and also in the Scherzo, between the rushing scalar passages of the Scherzo proper and the powerful horn triads of the Trio. In the finale, as we see, the Exposition dramatizes the dualism of the Basso del Tema and the upper-line theme as both successive and then simultaneous structural units. The theme emerges as the completion of the initial phase of the movement.

The second elaborative method is implicit in the choice of variation-like episodes that make up the bulk of the movement. By including, in the course of the movement, two fugato passages, an Alla marcia, a segment devoted to wind solos, and finally a long developed Andante (with more wind solos), Beethoven constructs a movement in which the familiar sequential logic of the variation form is distorted by the unexpected juxtaposition of texturally dissimilar segments, all of which in diverse ways can utilize the same basic material (either the Basso del Tema or the Tema) but not at all in the familiar order and symmetry of traditional variation schemes. The sequence brings extremes of genre into close contrast, thus elaborating the material in ways that challenge traditional concepts of both finale form and variation form. In this way the finale becomes a symbolic summation of the same juxtaposition of extreme movement-types that has characterized the entire symphony in its first three movements: the first a "heroic" movement on a vast scale; the second, a *Marcia funebre* (a "Charakterstück" within a symphony); the third, a dramatic Scherzo at the end of which Beethoven quotes the chromatic rising figure of the first movement (in Landsberg 6 Beethoven writes over an early Scherzo sketch, "M. am ende Coda eine fremde Stimme" ["Menuetto; at the end of the Coda a strange voice"]).[11] Now the finale becomes a movement embodying other "fremde Stimmen." It begins by incorporating the act of creation into the movement itself, building up the bass and then the theme before the ears of the listener. It then elaborates both elements in the episodes of the movement; and it closes with a powerful coda that forms a climax for the finale and for the work as a whole. The three phases of the finale, therefore, are these: thematic creation; elaboration; conclusion. Some similarity of conceptual ideal in the Opus 35 is undeniable; what counts for my argument, however, is that in the symphonic finale the entire larger rhythm of events is altered to fit a dynamic pattern in which the inner repetitions, the phrase symmetries, and the closed forms of even the most expanded strict variation set cannot find a place.

Thus the *Eroica* finale implicitly forms a statement not only about the material of this symphony but about the genre of the symphonic finale, which from now on can no longer be regarded as a predictable formal scheme but can take on any degree of innovation that suits the composer's purpose. The paradox is clear: for the finale Beethoven deliberately uses material he has used before, and in that sense it seems superficially the least "original" of the four movements.[12] In fact he shows that in hammering out this material in a new way, to fit the needs of a new kind of symphonic structure, the *Eroica* finale emerges as the most fully original symphonic finale that Beethoven had written up to this time.

SEVEN

Planning the Unexpected: Beethoven's Sketches for the Horn Entrance in the *Eroica* Symphony, First Movement

The horn entrance just before the Recapitulation in the first movement of the *Eroica* Symphony (mm. 394–395) is surely one of the most famous passages in the symphonic literature, yet in certain respects it remains surprisingly controversial. Controversy broke out as early as the first rehearsals of the work, shortly before its premiere on April 7, 1805. Ferdinand Ries tells that at the first rehearsal ("die entsetzlich war") the horn player made his entrance correctly but that Ries, thinking he was wrong, burst out with the remark, "Der verdammte Hornist! kann der nicht zählen?" ("The damned horn player! Can't he count?"). Ries then says that he was "sehr nah daran, eine Ohrfeige zu erhalten" ("very close to being slapped"); not that Beethoven actually slapped him, as often reported.[1]

That there were many later repetitions of Ries's misunderstanding throughout the nineteenth century is clear from anecdotes and reports. Much of this has widely circulated in the literature on the symphony and need not be repeated here; a sample is provided by Tovey's reference to "corrections" made by conductors in the later part of the century, among them von Bülow. One method of "correction" was undoubtedly to "normalize" the pitches of the horn part by shifting its pitches at mm. 394–395 from tonic triad members to those of the dominant to conform to the dyad b-flat/a-flat sustained in the violins; another, attributed to Wagner, was to shift the second violin part to g at these measures, to conform to the tonic pitches of the horn.[2]

This tradition of misunderstanding and disbelief persisted down into the twentieth century, as suggested by the recent claim that, as late as the 1940s, Arnold Schoenberg subscribed to the view that the celebrated clash of tonic and dominant at this crucial moment was some sort of error in notation and should not be taken literally. Dika Newlin describes an episode of 1944 in her memoirs of Schoenberg as teacher: "Uncle Arnold lived up to his promise to analyze in class today. He stuck mostly to the elaboration of the *Eroica* and especially to the so-called 'false entrance' of the horn, which, he claims, is a simple slip of the pen. Beethoven should have written 'B-flat Horn' over the passage, which would make things right with everybody. Maybe . . ."[3] Yet what for Schoenberg and other modern commentators is either a slip of the pen or a distinctive touch of subtlety at a dramatic point in this immense and powerful movement was for Ries a "wicked joke" ("eine böse Laune"), designed to surprise the naive listener and stimulate the imagination of the more experienced one. And Ries's characterization reminds us that in the context of Beethoven's development, this passage, in addition to its more serious implications and levels of meaning, could take its place in a long line of surprising strokes within tonal and formal designs, ranging from the well-known touches of delicate humor in Haydn to the abrupt and sudden reversals of expectation in middle-period and late Beethoven. Although my discussion of the horn entrance aims mainly at consideration of its genesis, authenticity, and structural role in the movement, I will begin with a brief review of its function as an element of surprise.

Even more than in other periods of music history, composers in the late eighteenth century, working within the confines of familiar classical tonal and formal schemata, could rely on listeners' expectations about the order, approximate length, character, and function of passages and events, based on conventions that had been solidly built up through the use of familiar methods of employing tonal syntax. The topic of "surprise" in instrumental music of this period is an old one in musicology, and no one needs to be reminded of its role in many works by Haydn.[4] The list of his "surprises" would be long and substantial; it includes abrupt and unexpected shifts in procedure at every phase of a typical movement, often entailing the engagement of attention to a significant formal event (for example, the moment of recapitulation) by playful anticipation of it through a "false reprise"; or the composing-out of a detail through a surprising variant in place of a direct repetition. The sudden pause; the double ending (as in the celebrated case of the finale of the quartet Op. 33 No. 2); the injection of an incongruous element into an established and patterned context—these are typical features of Haydn's way with surprise. Of course the most notorious case is the unprepared loud dominant chord at m. 17 of the slow movement of Symphony 94, for which we have numerous critical commentaries but also the personal dimension supplied by Haydn's gentle answer to the naive question asked by his biographer Griesinger. Griesinger wanted to know if Haydn had intended to "wake up the English audiences, who might have fallen asleep at this point"; to which Haydn replied (according to the biographer): "No, but I was interested in surprising the public with something new, so that my student Pleyel, who then had an orchestra in London, should not outdo me. The first Allegro of the symphony was received with great applause; but the enthusiasm reached its peak with the

Andante with the drum stroke; 'Encore, encore' sounded from every throat, and Pleyel himself complimented me on the idea."[5]

That Haydn's touches of incongruity operate on many levels has been well observed by Stephen Paul in a survey of these passages in the major instrumental works.[6] The same is certainly true for Beethoven as well, whether we trace his comparable passages in this category from early to late, or, as here, restrict our observations to a few key points. In early works Beethoven makes ample use of many of the same deviations from expectation that Haydn had perfected; witness Beethoven's use of surprising tonal shifts, especially in codas, in the Piano Trio, Op. 1 No. 1 (finale, mm. 337–360) and the similar effect in the First Piano Concerto, Op. 15, finale, mm. 462–477. If these deviations still seem within Haydn's aesthetic range, Beethoven's later excursions into the eccentric and grotesque go well beyond it. Examples occur as early as the Scherzo of the Violin Sonata, Op. 24, or the many instances cited by Longyear in his attempt to correlate surprises in Beethoven with the celebrated "romantic irony" developed consciously as a literary mode by Schlegel and Tieck.[7] However one attempts to distinguish Beethoven's use of "irony" from the other qualities of surprise and abrupt shift in affect that become thickly settled in his later works of certain types, and whatever the difficulty may be of establishing the precise tone and sense of these moments in verbal equivalents, there is still no doubt that they form part of his extension of the expressive range of the contemporary musical language. They also accord well with what we know from Beethoven's correspondence to have been his powerful wit, sarcasm, and irascibility in dealing with friends and acquaintances.[8] The fact that in his daily life this often masked almost inexpressible sensitivity and loneliness only further suggests the difficulty of correlating musical expression with direct and immediate life experience.

We now come to the horn entrance itself and its compositional background. In the many descriptions in the literature, some have stressed the anomalous qualities of this entrance as a harmonic event combining dominant and tonic properties. Others have emphasized the dramatic effect by which, after the vast dominant preparation has reached its final limits of intensity prior to resolution, the horn enters with the tonic motif, almost as if, in Tovey's words, "the suspense has become too much for it."[9] Still others have seen the horn entrance as a compact statement of an intervallic relationship that is closely associated with other important passages in the first movement.

Representative discussions are those by Riezler, Schenker, and Epstein.[10] In his general book on Beethoven, Riezler offered an extended descriptive analysis of the first movement of the *Eroica* and gave appropriate attention to the horn entrance. Among other instances in which Beethoven overlapped tonic and dominant harmonies, Riezler drew special attention to the coda of the Piano Sonata, "Les Adieux," Op. 81a, first movement; yet he noted that the dissonant character of the *Eroica* passage is more drastic in that here the pitch 3 is not only attacked simultaneously against 4, but is unprepared. Other examples are the transition from the third to the fourth movement in the Fifth Symphony, with its famous dominant preparation over a tonic pedal, and the passages in both Leonore Overtures Nos. 2 and 3, in which, soon after the opening of the Allegro, the bass continues with the tonic in the midst of the full harmony of the dominant seventh in the upper voices (Leonore Overture No. 2, mm. 69–88; Leonore Overture No. 3, mm. 49–58).[11]

Schenker in his *Harmonielehre* (1906) had discussed the passage as an extended instance of the anticipation of the tonic harmony during a statement of the dominant, pointing out that since the shape of the motif produces the effect of prolonging a I_4^6 harmony, the passage can be heard as a double suspension over the dominant, which then breaks into its resolution to the pure V_7 in the next bar. For Schenker this explanation seems to have carried lasting conviction, since in his massive analysis of the entire symphony, published many years later, he simply referred to his *Harmonielehre* discussion as still valid for him.[12] Crucial to his viewpoint is that the I_4^6 is heard as a background element of the progression; for in the foreground it is clear that the I_4^6 implied by the horn motif is not presented as a separate harmonic unit or as a member of a progression, but is introduced as a tonic component *striking against the prevailing dominant harmony;* it superimposes a temporary tonic element upon the surface of a dominant prolongation. Despite Riezler and even Schenker, this is quite unlike the effect of the echoing horn-fifths of the coda of *Les Adieux* (Op. 81a, first movement), with their romantic implications of a dreamlike farewell and distant echoing horns.

In Epstein's attempt to fuse the approaches of Schenker and Schoenberg (an enviable problem, not readily solved), we find the passage cited as an example of a structurally derived local dissonant event which exploits in a new context a relationship initially presented in the thematic material at the outset of the movement. Epstein rightly observes that there are other moments in the movement in which dominant is juxtaposed with tonic (for example, mm. 26–29 and 147) and that there are still more distant but palpable associations to be found, as in the massive clash of leading tone and tonic pitch at mm. 276–279 of the Middle Section (preceding the E-minor episode). He is also the first to note that in the horn entrance (mm. 394–395) this relationship is handled consecutively, not simultaneously, since the d of the V harmony is not present literally against the horn e♭ but arrives in the next measure (396).[13] To these remarks one may add that Beethoven's continuity drafts in Landsberg 6 for the whole exposition, as well as his final version of the first ending of the exposition, give a very good basis for perceiving his stress on the pitches 7—4 (and its inversion, 4—7) as primary interval for returning to the basic simultaneity, 3 over 1 (g over e♭), which is the primary element of tonic stability at the beginning of the movement. For a conveniently available transcription of the first continuity draft of the exposition from Landsberg 6, with its opening emphasis on 4 and 7, see N 1880, p. 6; for the first ending, see mm. 152–53 of the final score.

———————

To all this I should like to add some new observations on the horn entrance from the viewpoint of the strategic organization of the movement. My aim here, diverging from that of Epstein, is not to portray it primarily in its intervallic relationship to other distant elements in the movement, but to evaluate its location in the movement and reflect on the consequences of its special position in the stream of form-building events. The essential points are these:

(1) The horn entrance serves not simply to point toward a major formal event that is about to arrive, but also to signal the close of the great Middle Section, especially its last part, the retransition (mm. 366–397). In none of Beethoven's first movements is the retransition more clearly demarcated than in this one, with its long and persistent building up on the dominant as if to balance the broad span of key-relationships that has been traversed in the earlier space of the Middle Section. Table 7.1 shows in outline the division of the 32-bar retransition closing section into two 16-bar phrases, each in turn subdividing into 4-bar modules, then resubdividing, not symmetrically, into units of decreasing length. Thus the first phrase (mm. 366–381) subdivides into 4 + 4 and then 2 + 2 and 2 + 2; then the second large phrase (382–397) maintains the subdivision into 2-bar units all the way through the horn entrance at mm. 394–395. Table 7.1 also shows that this method of subdivision is articulated through dynamics, instrumentation, and gradual chromatic rising motion in the bass. The dynamic changes from *f* at mm. 366–369 to *p* at 370–373; then there is a decrescendo to *pp* at 378, with the *pp* level maintained all the way through the second large phrase until the further step downward is taken at 394 (however, this *ppp* is not found in the parts of the first edition!).[14] All this brings about a massive reduction in volume precisely as the harmonic and durational tension increases, thus dramatizing the quick return to the louder dynamic, which also takes places in two stages, but now telescoped—*f* at m. 396, *ff* at 397. The table also shows the initial use of winds and strings ("W" and "S" in the table), first at the distance of 3 bars plus 1, then at three beats' distance (mm. 374–377). Then the winds are sustained while the strings shift to pizzicato (mm. 378–381). In the second phrase there is an alternation of S with W/S pizzicato for two bars, and then the winds are liquidated at

Table 7.1   The *Eroica* first movement retransition: Outline of the last segment, mm. 366–397

Phrase 1	④	④	②	②	②	②
No. of bars	366–369	370–373	374–375	376–377	378–379	380–381
Dynamic	*f*	*p*	*decresc.*		*pp*	
Instruments	W + S 3 + 1	W + S 3 + 1	W$_S$ /	/ /	W$_S$ sustained pizz.	
Bass pitch or harmonic function	C♭	C	D	E♭	B♭ 4—3 V$_7$———	

Phrase 2	②	②	②	②	②	②	②	②	
No. of bars	382–383	384–385	386–387	388–389	390–391	392–393	394–395	396–397	398
Dynamic Instruments	*pp* S /	*pp* W$_S$ pizz.	*pp* S /	*pp* W$_S$ pizz.	*pp* S /	 S /	*pp* S / *Horn* (tonic)	*ff* Tutti	*fp* Tutti
Bass pitch or harmonic function	V$_7$———I								

Note: This segment consists of two 16-bar phrases. Phrase 1: mm. 366–381; Phrase 2: mm. 382–397.

W = winds; S = strings; W$_S$ shows winds and strings at different pitch levels. Diagonal slashes show repetition of the instruments used.

mm. 390–393, paving the way for the horn entrance against only the remaining upper strings. The whole procedure is one of graduated liquidation of sonorities from normal existence to nonexistence: complete disappearance for the winds, virtual for the strings.

(2) The registral technique of handling the horn entrance is another aspect of Beethoven's strategy. The horn enters, after all, not merely with a presentation of the opening motif of the movement, but at the same register at which the violoncellos had first presented the motif and at which they are about to return with it at the Recapitulation. This signals for the listener not merely the return of the opening material but the dramatization of register with which it had operated, recalling and foreshadowing this aspect of its structure along with its contour and rhythm. The vertical span at mm. 394–395, that is, at the horn entrance itself, is reduced to a totality of two octaves (from the low B-flat of the horn to the b-flat of the Violin I); then the outburst of the *tutti* in m. 396 brings back the wide span of more than three octaves and fills in all gaps with members of the dominant seventh harmony.

(3) The dynamics, registers, and sonorities of the passage force into atten-

tion a strong sense of immediate contrast between blocklike elements as the horn entrance gives way to the tutti. This is associated with other passages in the movement at which similar juxtapositions occur, and thus the horn entrance seems less isolated in its dimensions of contrast (as we have already seen for its pitch and harmonic implications, as shown by Epstein). Some of the principal places at which parallel juxtapositions take place occur in the Exposition at mm. 55–56 (two sudden ff bars, immediately preceded and followed by passages in p, with a parallel place in the Recapitulation), and at mm. 128–131, where the hammering syncopated chords abruptly give way to a bass p figure in rising triadic form (again with its parallel in the Recapitulation). In the Middle Section the same happens at mm. 276–279, in the great dissonant passage with the strident semitone dissonance f/e in high register, reinforced in ff and then succeeded by an abrupt shift in dynamics, register, and instrumentation, to low and mid-range strings on V of E minor. Here the clash is in ff and the resolution is in $pp;$ this is the precise opposite of what is to happen later at mm. 394–395, at the horn entrance—just as the two points are also at opposed points in the structural space (one at the midpoint of the Middle Section, the other at its very end). Similar events and contrasts occur in the coda, at mm. 551–562, with its fp steps from E♭ to D♭ to C; also at mm. 680–681, a place I have pointed out elsewhere as being part of the grand design of the movement as a whole, in which the previously unstable outcome of a transition figure is now finally resolved by reaching the relatively stable V_7 rather than its previous arrival on vii°.[15]

Although Nottebohm had included most of the sketches for this passage in his monograph of 1880, no one since has gone back to the source material to reinvestigate it or to determine with greater accuracy what the sketches show. The recent reemergence of the *Eroica* sketchbook itself now makes this possible.[16] From close study of the surviving sketches we see that there are not, as Nottebohm indicated, ten distinct ideas for the passage, but rather twelve. Some of them form part of larger continuity drafts for this part of the movement, but many are independent ideas. Most of them are clustered together in pages 30–35 of the sketchbook, that is, in close proximity to one another and to the central body of Beethoven's work on this part of the first movement. Accordingly, it seems likely that they were written over a short span of time in the course of his intensive work on the first movement, at the stage represented by this sketchbook—in other words, they were not afterthoughts. A summation of the facts about each entry is given in Table 7.2; the sketches are arranged in the order of their occurrence in the sketchbook. The only exception to this clustering is No. 1, which appears on page 4 of the sketchbook as

Table 7.2 Sketches for the *Eroica* first movement retransition (equivalent to mm. 382–397) in the *Eroica* sketchbook

No.	Page/stave	N1880 (page)	Length of sketch (bars)	Comments
1	4/6–8	28	24	The earlier part of this entry couples rising chromatic motion from g♭ to b♭ with the same motion from e♭ to f; then descends stepwise to the sustained dominant and horn entry.
2	30/6–7	29	17	This entry explores a remarkable deviant, namely the tonicization of the pitch-step 7 (D major) in place of the clash of V and I in E♭ Major; this elaboration of D major just before a V–I cadence in E♭ is a radical experiment that newly elaborates the chromatic descent motif of the opening of the movement.
3	30/8–9	29	11	An immediate variant to No. 2, restoring E♭ Major in place of the experimental motion to D major just before the cadence; it restores the horn entry on I against V in E♭.
4	31/13–14	34	13	The diminished seventh including the pitch-cluster d♭ and a♭ shows the origin of mm. 382–383 in the final version; although N 1880 reads a possible f at the second bar of the horn entry, I continue to read it as e♭.
5	32/2–3	29	31	N 1880 gives only the last 12 bars of the entry. Here, as a parallel to No. 2, Beethoven explores the notion of tonicizing the chromatic step above the tonic, E major, with an abrupt shift back to E♭ Major at the horn entry; this is then balanced by a substantial extension of the further preparation for the cadence to the tonic and the Reprise.
6	32/7–8, 10–11	—	14	This is close to the final version, and lacks only d♭—a♭ at the equivalent of mm. 390–391.
7	33/5–6	29	8	The last eight bars only; here Beethoven reaffirms the basic material of the final portion of the retransition, with horn entry again in the tonic and without any hint of the d♭—a♭ interval before the b♭—a♭ "cumulus."
8	33/9–10	—	17	While the earlier part of the retransition is now stabilized, and the horn entry against the "cumulus" is a fixed item, he experiments with another extension of the further V preparation for the cadence to I, thus separating the horn entry from the Reprise by an additional two bars.

Table 7.2 (cont.)

No.	Page/stave	N1880 (page)	Length of sketch (bars)	Comments
9	35/1–2	30	13	In a total departure from preceding versions, Beethoven reverts here to a scalar passage with syncopated repetitions in $\frac{3}{4}$ reminiscent of the *Egmont* Overture and other works, and considers building up to the Reprise without any of the procedures painstakingly worked out in the other versions.
10	35/8–9	32	15	A return to the idea worked out in No. 8 above, with four-bar extension after the horn entry, prolonging the dominant before the Reprise.
11	39/9–10	35	14	A partial combination of disparate features of earlier attempts, including the scalar motion from No. 9 and the "cumulus"-horn entry from all other versions; the extension of the segment after the horn entry is now to six bars, building up the V_7 through apparent orchestral incrementation once more.
12	39/12	36	16	As in No. 6, this entry has all essential features of the final version except the c♭—a♭ at mm. 390–391.

an isolated entry; this could have been entered by Beethoven at any point by going back to an early and then blank or little-used page in the book; but conceptually this segment does seem to belong to a fairly early stage of the sketch process. Since Table 7.2 contains a brief commentary on each of the entries, it should be read in the closest possible conjunction with the transcriptions of the sketch entries, which are presented in Examples 7.1–7.12.

What conclusions, however provisional, can we draw from this body of precompositional material, in terms somewhat broader than the comments given for the individual entries? Whatever the supposed hazards of doing so, it is undoubtedly the task of Beethoven scholarship to come to grips with sketch material of this type and of all other types, despite an effort some years ago to denigrate and underplay the potential importance of sketches to our understanding of the final version.[17] Our job is to interpret these entries as evidence of a process of intensive compositional activity, and the premise of this is that such study can never be wholly irrelevant to an understanding of the work itself. One way of looking at such a series of entries for a single passage is as a quasi-evolutionary continuum of ideas, which lead from "simple" to "complex" and from "primitive conception" to final version. Although this view is widespread, familiar, and to some degree plausible as a generality, I have argued elsewhere that there are other ways of conceiving the

Example 7.1   Landsberg 6, p. 4, st. 6–8

Example 7.2   Landsberg 6, p. 30, st. 6–7

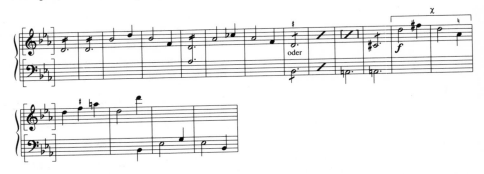

Example 7.3   Landsberg 6, p. 30, st. 8–9

Example 7.4   Landsberg 6, p. 31, st. 13–14

Example 7.5   Landsberg 6, p. 32, st. 2–3

Example 7.6   Landsberg 6, p. 32, st. 10–11

Example 7.7   Landsberg 6, p. 33, st. 5–6

Example 7.8   Landsberg 6, p. 33, st. 9–12

Example 7.9   Landsberg 6, p. 35, st. 1–2

Example 7.10   Landsberg 6, p. 35, st. 8–9

Example 7.11   Landsberg 6, p. 39, st. 9–11

Example 7.12   Landsberg 6, p. 39, st. 12

connection of such entries to one another—namely that of distinguishing within them the fixed points from the variable, the "invariants" from the "variants," to see what alternatives Beethoven considered as he proceeded and what those alternatives implied.[18]

For this series the primary invariants seem to be these:

(1) The basic harmonic organization of the passage as a whole, its primary function being that of prolonging a dominant and intensifying it before reaching the massive cadence to the tonic that will initiate the Recapitulation.

(2) The harmonic clash of tonic against dominant as a means of effecting this intensification near the end of the passage.

(3) The use of the triadic motif from the opening of the movement to give this clash associative significance.

The use of the horn for the motif is probably also an invariant, though the sketches do not specify instruments; the point is admittedly speculative but worth consideration, despite the absence of other sources such as a composing score or the autograph of the final version.

In conclusion, I shall briefly expand these points.

(1) That the larger harmonic basis is clear enough needs no further emphasis. But since Beethoven in two of these sketches actually considered tonicizations of other chromatic scale degrees (D major in No. 2 and E major in No. 5), it is clear that at least provisionally he conceived the possibility of intermingling additional chromatic motions into the larger framework of the passage as a way of enriching its harmonic color. The D major idea is radical enough, and yet it curiously harks back to that excursion into the key of the seventh at a comparable passage of "surprise" that I mentioned earlier—the move to D in the Coda of the E-flat Major Piano Trio, Op. 1 No. 1, bars 337–360, in which exactly the same harmonic motion is worked out in a final version. As for the E major variant in No. 5, its key is of course enharmonically identical to F-flat (the Neapolitan scale degree), and this scale step in the context of this movement is associated with other uses of the flat supertonic that occur from time to time in the movement, but especially with the powerful stress on the pitch and tonality E (principally E minor) in the Middle Section as one of the goal tonalities of the entire section. It is also noteworthy that this E minor is reached through a downward spiral motion from A♭ Major in the Middle Section, which shows that the major third above the pitch *e* is important for the larger harmonic structure of the section. The sketches show, in effect, both conservative and radical proposals for the way of prolonging the basic dominant function of this entire passage.

(2) The tonic/dominant clash has been well discussed by Epstein and is dealt with above as well.

(3) The use of the opening motif itself can now be seen as vital to the very idea of this passage and as being integral to it from the earliest known stages of Beethoven's planning of the entire segment. The sketches show that this was not a last-minute idea, but was fixed in one form or another—almost always in its final form, in the tonic, and in its basic register—at an early phase of the compositional work.

Against this brief list of invariants we can compare a few of the most obvious elements that are altered and shifted from entry to entry. Most important is the alteration of the phrase-length of the sketches, and especially of the individual segments of the passage in their relative proportions. The sketches will show this without detailed commentary here; the important point is that they resemble many other Beethoven sketches in series, in that they entail a search not merely for final adjustments of detail but for the absolute and correct proportions of the passage altogether. Sometimes Beethoven extends the phrase before the horn entry, sometimes after it, to further intensify the arrival at the great cadence. The horn entry as such thus emerges in the movement, in its finished form, as both a singular event and a contingent one—singular in its thematic and harmonic content; contingent in its associations with other elements in the far-flung web of ideas that are linked to it by structural or functional association. For the origins of both aspects, the sketches provide the best and most authentic testimony that is available to us.

EIGHT

The Problem of Closure: Some Examples from the Middle-Period Chamber Music

"Closure" is not synonymous with "coda." My title here does not refer to the large-scale dimensions of structure and function that are embodied in Beethoven's entire closing sections of movements and of works. Some aspects of his codas have been discussed in different ways by Joseph Kerman and by Peter Cahn, and this remains an area of interest for analytical criticism.[1] Instead, my focus in this discussion is on two smaller and more detailed aspects of closure: first, on the delicately shaped and psychologically crucial way in which Beethoven finishes an inner movement of a several-movement work, especially a slow movement, and by the nature of this conclusion prepares the resumption of activity at the start of the next movement; second, on a significant example from Beethoven's middle-period chamber music in which we see, from evidence in an autograph manuscript, his transformation and revision of the ending of a slow movement, showing once again some drastic changes and choices at a very late stage of composition.

Perhaps no composer before Beethoven strove so consistently to control the aesthetic and psychological effect formed by the moment when an inner movement ends and the next movement begins. This is most obvious when there is a strong change in tempo and character, and especially in the shift from a slow movement to the next movement, whether the latter is a minuet, a scherzo, or a finale. Even in early works, especially keyboard sonatas, Beethoven finds ways to create a special effect at this point. Sometimes he does this through a pedal marking at the end of the slow movement or through a striking contrast between a soft and tapering-off ending of a slow movement and a sudden eruption that wrenches the listener's attention into the new tempo and back to the primary tonality. One famous example of this is the ending of the E-major Largo of the Third Piano Concerto, in which the closing chord in the first violin part stresses the pitches g♯ over b, followed by the sudden Rondo

Allegro opening in which the g♯ is reinterpreted as a♭ over b♮ (that is, flat 6 over 7 in the key of C minor; see Example 8.1).[2]

But in the later middle period, with Beethoven's vastly greater flexibility in shaping larger formal relationships, his innovations at these points of closure appear in greater numbers and with greater variety of means. We can distinguish three broad categories of inner movements that display special sensitivity to these points of connection.

Category I. This includes full-length movements that are entirely complete within themselves and end conclusively with a cadence that closes each movement within its own formal and registral framework; but then the end of the movement is marked "attacca" and moves at once to begin the following movement. Examples:

Op. 27 No. 2: the first movement moves to the second movement with the same harmony (transformed from minor to major), but with a shift of register (see Example 8.2).

Op. 59 No. 3: the Menuetto is formally closed, but has a detached Coda (18 mm.) that leads to a V pause, and on to the fugato Finale.

Op. 74: the Scherzo has a lengthy coda (45 mm.) that leads to a close on V$^6_5$ and then on to the Finale.

Op. 96: the slow movement (Adagio espressivo, $\frac{2}{4}$, 67 mm.) is formally closed, but then has an augmented sixth with fermata that leads at once to the Scherzo (see Example 8.3).[3]

Category II. This includes full-length slow movements that are not completely closed; that is, they do not end with a full cadence in the key of the movement, but proceed by a short transition into the next movement, usually the Finale. Examples:

Op. 57: the slow movement (Andante, $\frac{2}{4}$, variations, 97 mm.) pauses with a diminished seventh fermata and then moves directly into the Finale.

Op. 59 No. 1: the Adagio molto ($\frac{2}{4}$, 132 mm.), instead of completing its coda with a cadence into the tonic, does not have any harmonic closure at this point and after the first violin cadenza holds a trill on 5. Under this the Finale begins with the *Thème russe*, like the first movement beginning without a firm tonic harmony in root position; there is no firmly settled tonic harmony until m. 18 of the Finale (see Example 8.4).

Op. 95: the slow movement, after its own final cadence, moves to a diminished 7th (with fermata) and then is marked "attacca il Scherzo."

Category III. This consists of short slow movements which not only lack their own tonal closure but also give the impression that they are left incomplete, are "interrupted" by the break in their material and elaboration, and that they serve, in retrospect, as introductions to the movements that follow— always the Finale. Again the examples are from middle-period chamber music, and none is found earlier than Op. 27 No. 1 (1801). Examples:

Example 8.1 Piano Concerto No. 3 in C Minor, Op. 37: end of slow movement and beginning of Finale

Example 8.2   Piano Sonata in C♯ Minor, Op. 27 No. 2: end of first movement and beginning of second movement

Attacca subito il seguente

Attacca subito

Op. 27 No. 1: the Adagio (3rd movement, Adagio, $\frac{2}{4}$, 26 mm.) leads directly into the Finale (Allegro vivace, $\frac{2}{4}$; see Example 8.5).

Op. 53: the second movement ("Introduzione," $\frac{6}{8}$, 28 mm.), which replaced the discarded *Andante favori*, WoO 57, is left harmonically incomplete on a V and then is resolved by the opening of the C-major Rondo on its tonic; see Example 8.6.

Op. 69: the lyrical slow movement (Adagio cantabile) breaks off on a V after 18 bars and the Finale begins.

Op. 81a: the slow movement ("Abwesenheit," Andante espressivo, $\frac{2}{4}$, 42 mm.) builds up a rising arpeggiation on its own VII harmony, which is then transformed into an intensified V_7 prolonged for the first ten bars of the Finale

Example 8.3 Sonata for Violin and Piano in G Major, Op. 96: end of slow movement and beginning of Scherzo

Example 8.4 Quartet in F Major, Op. 59 No. 1: end of slow movement and beginning of Finale

Example 8.4 *(continued)*

Thème russe.

Allegro

sempre p

sempre p

("Wiedersehen") before the arrival of the tonic resolution at m. 11. (The entire procedure is parallel to that of Op. 59 No. 1, third movement to fourth movement.)

Op. 101: the slow movement (Langsam, etc., $\frac{2}{4}$, 20 mm.), plus its codetta Andante ($\frac{6}{8}$, 8 mm., recurring from the first movement), moves directly into the Finale.

Op. 102 No. 1: exactly parallel to Op. 101, the slow movement (Adagio, $\frac{4}{4}$, 9 mm.) has as Coda the return of the opening $\frac{6}{8}$ Andante from the first move-

Example 8.5 Piano Sonata in E-flat Major, Op. 27 No. 1: end of slow movement and beginning of Finale

Example 8.6 Piano Sonata in C Major, Op. 53: end of *Introduzione* and beginning of Finale

ment, now only 8 bars long; then there is a V pause, and the Finale commences.

―――――――

If we evaluate these examples in their chronology and genre, we grasp something of Beethoven's middle-period approaches to the problem. First, the starting-point for the idea of the fermata closure, followed by an explicit "attacca" to show the immediate start of the next movement, stems essentially from the two Sonatas Op. 27 Nos. 1 and 2—"quasi una fantasia." Thanks to an essay by Paul Mies on Beethoven's use of the term "fantasia," we see that one basic meaning of "quasi una fantasia" for Op. 27 is its reference to a consistent use of *attacca* connections to bind the movements to each other, exactly as in the genre of the fantasia, in which just this kind of connection is a historically consistent feature.[4] These works also borrow from the fantasia its strong contrast of texture and key, but this is also true of other early works that do not use the *attacca* principle and do not intensify their endings and beginnings to quite this degree. That the *attacca* in Op. 27 No. 1 was noticed by contemporaries is suggested by Czerny's remark about No. 1 that it is "noch mehr fantasie als Opus 27 II" ("even more a fantasy than Op. 27 II"), and that in No. 1 "alle Sätze bilden nur ein zusammenhängendes Tonstück" ("all the movements form a single unified composition"). After these works of 1801 the way is clear to further uses of the *attacca* principle, or the more delicate shaping of the ending-beginning connection in the same or related genres. A crucially important stage is represented by the *Introduzione* movement of the Waldstein Sonata, Op. 53, which displaced the long, fully closed, emotionally placid *Andante favori*. After 1804 and 1805, Beethoven continued to find ways to develop this ending-beginning connection in other chamber works that I have already mentioned, but also in almost all of his concerti (the Triple Concerto, the Violin Concerto, and the "Emperor" Concerto). We might notice also that in works having a short slow movement that is left unfinished and moves directly into a full-length finale, there is now no true sense of closure in the slow movement at all; the Finale supplies the closure needed for the slow movement (quasi-Introduzione) as well as for the entire work.[5]

It cannot be denied, either, that in other "normal" middle-period works that do not have incomplete slow movements or *attacca* connections, there is often careful planning in the relationships between the slow movement and the following movement. This is visible through the closing dynamic (often *pp*) and a following *forte* or strongly accented opening; through timbral and registral shift, as well as the normal change of key; in keyboard works, through the pedal effects mentioned earlier; and through the time-honored use of pizzicato for the last chords of works for strings, to end a slow movement. For a further and much later example of the same principle, we need only look at the ending of the slow movement of the Ninth Symphony, where Beethoven invents, just for the ending, the idea of tympani double-stops, *pp,* for the first time in the literature; see Example 8.7.[6]

Example 8.7   Ninth Symphony, end of slow movement

II

I turn now to my example from the middle-period chamber music—the slow movement of the "Ghost" Trio, Op. 70 No. 1. The autograph manuscript was acquired by the Morgan Library in New York some years ago. That the autograph contains several massive revisions of material was shown briefly by Alan Tyson in his essay on the manuscript, and the revisions of the first movement at the autograph stage were discussed by Robert Taub in a doctoral essay of 1981.[7] But except for one example shown by Tyson in 1971, Beethoven's revisions for the ending of the slow movement have never been published or discussed in the literature. They furnish an instructive example of Beethoven's grappling with the problem of closure.

A brief look at the opening of this celebrated slow movement, Largo assai ed espressivo, will remind us of its structural organization and expressive character; see Example 8.8. It is the centerpiece of a work that is generally accepted as a major step in Beethoven's middle-period development. As much as the Op. 59 Quartets, this Trio made a deep and lasting impression on his contemporaries for bringing to keyboard chamber music the depth of Romantic sensibility that Beethoven had opened up in orchestral works between the Second Symphony and the Pastoral Symphony, completed just before this.[8] The powerful contrasts, the complexities of the keyboard writing, the innovative sonorities combining pianoforte and strings—all these and more serve to justify the reactions expressed by E. T. A. Hoffmann in his classic review of both Op. 70 Trios. Hoffmann compares the experience of listening to these works to that of a man who "wanders in the mazes of a fantastic park, woven about with all manner of exotic trees and plants and marvellous flowers, and who is drawn further and further in . . . powerless to find [his] way amid the marvellous turns and windings of [these] trios."[9] And Czerny in 1842 characterized this slow movement as being "geisterhaft schauerlich, gleich eine Erscheinung aus der Unterwelt. Nicht unpassend könnte man sich

Example 8.8   Piano Trio in D Major, Op. 70 No. 1, beginning of slow movement

dabei die erste Erscheinung des Geist's im *Hamlet* denken"[10] ("ghostly and terrifying, a very apparition from the underworld. One can think here, not inappropriately, of the first appearance of the ghost in Hamlet").

The central features of the opening of the Largo are apparent in Example 8.8. It presents two basic figures, both *piano sotto voce,* which I have labeled A and B in the brief analytical diagram given below the example. Figure A, for strings in octaves, brings a turning triadic figure encompassing all three pitches of the D minor tonic triad, in the pitch-order 1, 5, 3. Then the elaborated answering figure, B, in the pianoforte creates a figure that is in part an answer to A, in part a continuation: it forms in outline another triadic turning figure, now beginning on the pitch a and outlining the same triad members, then returning to a. The interrelationship of pitch-content in the two figures is spelled out below Example 8.8 by means of the lowercase letters x, y, and z, and below the literal version I have shown that these turning figures can also be interpreted as "folded" arpeggios; when "unfolded," they can be construed as directly descending members of a pure D minor arpeggio: first coming down from d through a to f; then, starting once more on a, descending to the a an octave below.

All this is important because Beethoven utilizes the two figures throughout the movement, for developmental purposes, as he constructs a three-part form consisting of a large first part (mm. 1–45); a greatly elaborated second part serving as varied reprise (mm. 46–86); and a 10-bar Coda (mm. 87–96) that serves to liquidate both figures, A and B, and once more defines the vast tonal space of the movement through the sweeping pianoforte arpeggios that rush down through four and a half octaves (see Example 8.9). Meanwhile, the strings in m. 89, for the first time in the movement, adopt the 64th-note tremolo motion that till now has been the province of the keyboard part only. This climactic rhythmic action is reduced to virtual immobility in the last five bars, bringing Figure A for the last time as the left hand of the keyboard and violoncello at mm. 93–94 against slowly rising chromatic motion, with the final cadence at mm. 95–96 punctuated by sudden *forte* and *piano* accents that epitomize, in the small, the entire series of sudden, powerfully contrasted dynamic juxtapositions that have been integral to the movement since its first section.[11]

Examples 8.10 through 8.14 show the alternative strategies that Beethoven considered for the ending of this movement. First, as regards physical placement, all of these versions are found in the autograph manuscript itself, not on supplementary sketch leaves, and they appear in the order in which they are presented here.[12] Thus, Example 8.14 presents the final version, the one that Beethoven accepted; in this case he arrived at a final choice as the last of his efforts at a solution. If we now look briefly at each attempted version of the ending, the central problems that this ending posed for him will be clear at once.

Example 8.10. This ending, like all others except the final one, leads from m. 92 to m. 98; that is, these original endings were all two bars longer than the final one. The basic idea of the quiet chromatic rising motion in the violin and pianoforte right hand is maintained, and instead of pausing on the b♭ crest, the motion continues on in mm. 95–96 to form the cadential progression ♭II$_6$—I$_4^6$—V$_7$—I. The crux of this progression is the move to ♭II$_6$ (the Neapolitan). This re-emphasizes the pitches E♭ and B♭ which had risen to prominence early in the movement, at m. 7, to form the cadence that closed the first phrase; see Example 8.8, m. 7. In short, the last phrase, with its inclusion of

Example 8.9 Piano Trio in D Major, Op. 70 No. 1, end of slow movement

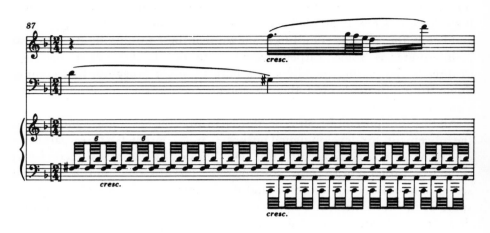

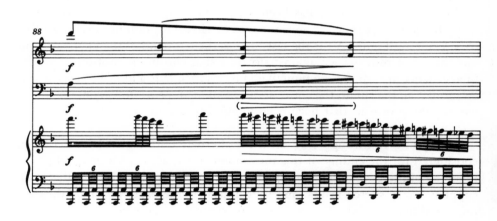

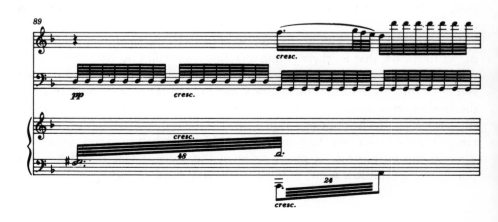

THE PROBLEM OF CLOSURE

Example 8.9   (*continued*)

Example 8.10 Piano Trio in D Major, Op. 70 No. 1, autograph manuscript, p. 15, st. 6–10 (end of slow movement)

★) Right hand illegible
★★) This staff replaces right hand in mm. 93–97

the Neapolitan, forms a slightly modified repetition of the first cadence of the movement, and thus rounds off the entire structure of the movement with a backward reference to its opening gestures. Looking once more at Example 8.10, we also see that in the last two bars Beethoven was considering a final statement of Figure B in the strings, and that the last note was to be a long-held fermata D in octaves, sustained in all instruments.

Example 8.11. Here Beethoven breaks completely with what he had just worked out, and tries out a totally different way of ending. The pianoforte was once more, in m. 97, to resume the expanding upward and downward arpeggios of its earlier action in the movement, while the strings sustained the tonic; but to our surprise the closing tonic is now D major. This would of course have given the ending a wholly different and affirmative quality, anticipating the D major opening of the Finale; it would have dissipated the tension rather than hold it to the very end, and it would have reshaped the quality of closure quite completely.

Example 8.12. Like Example 8.11, this is a brief and fragmentary attempt to form a different type of ending; only the violin part is notated, but it is enough. Starting at m. 95 the violin was to utilize once again the rhythmic figure which had played an important role in early thematic material of the movement, and was to use this figure as a bridge to the final detached eighth notes of the penultimate bar. Moreover, the last two strokes were to be *forte,* not *piano.*

Example 8.11 Op. 70 No. 1, slow movement, autograph manuscript, p. 15, st. 11–13 (left side)

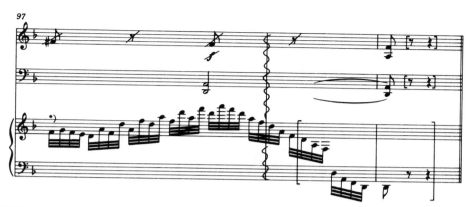

★) In pianoforte part, all beams, and also noteheads in brackets, are editorial additions

Example 8.12 Op. 70 No. 1, slow movement, autograph manuscript, p. 15, st. 11–13 (right side)

★) A marking before the f, which might be taken to be a sharp, is probably a canceled rest

Example 8.13. Here Beethoven returns to the extended cadential progression of Example 8.10, now redistributing and clarifying the voicing of the upward chromatic motion so that the strings and keyboard duplicate their functions; the new feature here is the full statement of Figure B in all instruments in m. 97, first in the pianoforte, then in the strings; and the powerful close with a *forte* cadence is taken over from the dynamic of Example 8.12.

Example 8.14. Here Beethoven arrives at the final version by cutting off the cadential progression at m. 95 without the motion to the Neapolitan; he introduces the sudden and final contrast of *forte* and *piano,* and shifts the string tone-color of the last bar to pizzicato. Crucial to this change, beyond what has already been said, is the shift from a phrase-length of eight measures to one of six measures. By the cutting off of the last phrase as a six-measure unit, the sense of symmetry is broken. The sudden effects of interruption, of shift from major to minor; of *forte* versus *piano* accents; of the final pizzicato—all these are projected in a phrase that can no longer be heard as a complex form of a classically symmetrical eight-measure unity, but rather as a series of two-measure modules that break off into silence after six measures.

Example 8.13 p. 16, st. 9–12; p. 17, st. 1–4

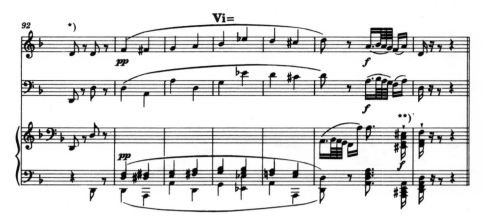

*) This example was published earlier by A. Tyson, "Stages in the Composition of Bee-thoven's Piano Trio Op. 70 No. 1," in *Proceedings of the Royal Musical Association* 97 (1970–71), p. 14.
**) A sixteenth-note rest after the chord in the right hand is canceled.

Example 8.14 p. 17, st. 5–8

The links between movements outlined here exemplify Beethoven's mature way of dramatizing the relationship between vitally important structural events—in this case, the ending of a slow movement and the beginning of the movement that follows. And in the Largo of the "Ghost" Trio, as in other major works of the middle years, there is evident an intensive concern to find solutions to the way of ending a movement. In this instance we find as large a variety of possibilities explored as I know to exist for any other single movement-ending in Beethoven. And in this Largo the search is evidently for an ending that will maintain the extraordinary tension until the double bar, that will complete the complex history of the movement, and that will provide the proper psychological point of departure for the opening of the Finale, with its energetic release of tension. The ghost of Hamlet's father is heard from below; he speaks his lines and delivers his message with masterful effect; now we see that Beethoven searches intently for the right dramatic means by which to let him depart.

NINE

Process versus Limits: A View of the Quartet in F Major, Opus 59 No. 1

No critical remark on the Opus 59 quartets is more timeworn than the observation that they break decisively with the classical quartet tradition and establish a new point of departure for the later development of the genre. That this is not just a modern view but an early one is attested by the reactions of Beethoven's contemporaries to these works. Among many famous anecdotes we recall the one about the violinist Felix Radicati, who was called in to finger the first violin parts. It was Radicati who is said to have suggested to Beethoven that these works "are not music," and that Beethoven in writing them was clearly a "musical madman." If he did, he was lucky to get off with the temperate reply, "They are not for you but for a later age."[1]

Commentators from Beethoven's time to our own have stressed the length, scope, and proportions of the first movement of Opus 59 No. 1, and of the quartet as a whole, beyond almost any other.[2] And indeed this work, with its four ample movements, its broad range of expression and of design, is the longest string quartet written up to its time. Familiar comparisons to the *Eroica* Symphony typically mention in the quartet a comparable immensity of scope and degree of formal innovation—and further, if the commentators are perceptive, a similarly high degree of motivic elaboration in every movement. One can even claim that the F Major quartet goes beyond any of Beethoven's earlier instrumental works—not excluding the *Waldstein* and *Appassionata* sonatas—in its fullness of development in every movement. Prime evidence for this is the Scherzo, by far the most innovative of Beethoven's scherzos up to this time: it is a full-scale scherzo all in one movement, with no binary repeats and no formal trio, as concentrated and as highly profiled as the other three movements. Every textbook tells us that Beethoven crosses a boundary in formal innovation in this work by using "sonata form" in every movement; I would modify this truism to stress instead that, while he maintains the sequence of movement-types typical of the classical four-movement plan, he enlarges every movement to an unprecedented degree. The four movements stand adjacent to one another like enormous pillars that uphold a vast structure—vaster than had ever been explored in the quartet literature up to this time.

Because of the great length of the F Major quartet, comparison to the *Eroica* and to some other middle-period works seems reasonable, but other connections to the *Eroica* are also worth mentioning. Certainly it is striking that in both works Beethoven's compositional blueprint called for the use of finale material as the primary invariant of the entire work—the starting point against which the other movements were developed and shaped. In the *Eroica* it is universally known that the basis for the finale was the celebrated bass and upper-line "Prometheus" theme that Beethoven had used three times earlier, most expansively in the great Variations and Fugue for Piano, Op. 35. And, as I have shown elsewhere, this basic material was in fact the starting point for the first sketch-work on the symphony as a whole, as we find it in the "Wielhorsky" Sketchbook of 1802.[3] Now in Op. 59 No. 1, first movement, we also have a finale based on a deliberately chosen "simple theme," in this case the *Thème russe* used for the finale and thus marked in the score. Everyone knows that this is an homage to the Russian patron for the quartets, Count Razumovsky; and also that Beethoven derived the Russian theme from a large printed collection of Russian tunes, the Prach collection, which had been published in Saint Petersburg in 1790.[4] We have very few sketches for the first movement, and only some for the middle two; so we can only conjecture about Beethoven's possible starting point for the quartet. But surely it makes sense to assume that the *Thème russe* in the Prach collection could well have been this starting point, and that Beethoven's decision to use it in the finale fits with the traditional classical preference for placing a popular and recognizable tune in a finale rather than a first movement (in a serious genre like the quartet). I am thus inclined to believe that the work was generated from this finale-choice back to the other movements, as in the *Eroica*. If so, this would help to justify the familiar perception that there are motivic and intervallic connections between the *Thème russe* and the famous opening theme of the first movement; the familiar opening with the rising fourth from pitch 5 to 1, from c to f, is only the most obvious of these connections.

I turn now to the first movement—its size, formal planning, and strategy—and some of the ways in which the special features of its famous opening theme and continuation establish conditions that make possible the larger development of the whole movement. The theme presents certain larger symmetries of phrase-structure (mm. 1–4, 5–8), yet with the subtle inner shifts and motivic interplay that we learn to expect in middle-period Beethoven (see Example 9.1). Thus the first four bars present at least three elements that he

Example 9.1   Op. 59 No. 1, first movement, opening theme, motivic segmentation

can detach for motivic use later on, and also provide a linear stream in which the pitch c (5 in F major) functions as the fulcrum or pivotal tone for the first two motives ("m" and "n"), then remains the pitch-goal for the third motive ("o") and for the phrase as a whole. The first motive rises from 5 to 1; the second is a characteristic Beethovenian "turning figure" that descends to the tonic after the turning around c. Then motive "o" projects the strong profile of the upward major sixth leap from F to d. As in the *Thème russe* of the finale, there is an immediate stress on the pitches c and d at the very outset. And nothing confirms the prominence of c and d more securely than the decision to start the answering phrase not on g, which would have led at once to the dominant, but rather on d (m. 5), replicating the rhythmic content of the first phrase exactly but adjusting its pitch content to clarify the tonal progression. In fact we have here two simultaneous procedures: (1) a thematic unfolding, providing the motivic material for the exposition and for the movement as a whole; (2) a broadly rising and registrally expanding statement which begins on the low c of m. 1 and extends upward gradually from one octave to four octaves, over the first 19 bars of the movement (Example 9.2). At m. 19 it climaxes formally on the F major tonic harmony, heard for the first time in root position as a clear point of arrival. The root position tonic at m. 19 in fact reminds us that the opening had been in the tonic but had also been poised on a relatively unstable form of the tonic harmony; the opening c–d–e–f linear tetrachord has an implied sonority of I⁶₄ that remains in the ear despite the momentary arrivals on the pitch f, all of which are other than definitive and cadential until m. 19. In mm. 16–19, concluding the passage, Beethoven compels us to make this association by presenting the rising tetrachord in the Violin I, one whole note per bar. As an interesting sidelight, we may note that Beethoven had carried out almost the same procedure, in the same key, in the opening of the first movement of his earlier F major quartet, Opus 18 No. 1; there too he moves from an initial single-octave f to the four-octave span of F up to f within the first 29 bars of the movement (see Examples 9.3, 9.4).

In Opus 59 No. 1, this initial registral expansion sets the stage for the larger compositional strategy of the movement, for which this opening large phrase

Example 9.2 Op. 59 No. 1, first movement, mm. 1–21

is a paradigm. Each phase of this strategy is articulated by the same basic thematic material—the opening theme in the cello in low register. The second phase occurs at the opening of the development section, where we find that the theme is precisely designed to sound as if it were returning to the opening of the exposition and starting over again—that is, as if the familiar exposition

Example 9.3   Op. 59 No. 1, first movement, mm. 1–19, registral expansion from one to four octaves

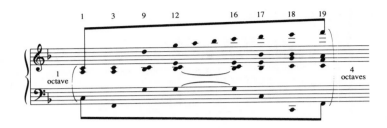

Example 9.4   Op. 18 No. 1, first movement, mm. 1–29, registral expansion from one to four octaves

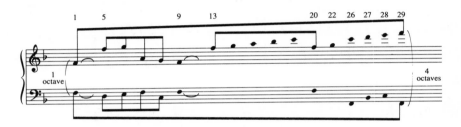

repeat had been observed. But within a few bars the cello theme now takes a sudden turn to g-flat at m. 108, thus shifting direction to move the harmony into B-flat major (m. 112) to start the long development section.

Important subsidiary stages in this strategy occur in the great modulatory development section itself. Here, as Steven Lubin has shown, we find an elaborately mapped-out series of modulatory motions, within which Beethoven three times prepares the listener for a return to the tonic and the main theme—and each time, in Lubin's words, "delays the satisfaction of these expectations by means of a surprise deflection."[5] That is, Beethoven twice prepares for the arrival of F major and then shifts course at the last moment. His first resolution is into F minor (mm. 158ff.). At the next one, at m. 222, Beethoven arrives at the long-awaited dominant that should usher in the tonic, but again deflects the return by delaying and extending the dominant through its own subsidiary harmonic motions. Tovey compares passages like these to a train that is approaching a station at which a passenger was expecting to change, "and then the passenger realizes that the train is quietly and inexorably passing through."[6] After this the next essential stroke occurs at the moment of recapitulation itself (mm. 242ff.), which in several ways confirms some of the ambiguity of the opening of the exposition and of the development. At this point the Violin I soars into its highest register and reaches the pitch c in the stratosphere. It is then dramatically left hanging at this great height while the exposition figure from mm. 20–29 returns as the first item in the recapitulation. It has long been obvious that Beethoven has thus reversed the order of primary elements in the recapitulation. What has hardly been noticed is that this first formal tonic return to an exposition figure brings an arrival at F major but in another weak form of the tonic harmony: the harmony at m. 242 is not I in root position but its first inversion. And there will be no root-position tonic for some time to come. When the main theme returns at m. 254, partly disguised by the continuing descent of the Violin I, it is again presented as before, not only lacking a firm f in the bass but running a course toward D-flat major.

All this paves the way for the triumphant return of the first theme at the beginning of the coda, mm. 348–354 (Example 9.5). Here at last the theme appears in its final and fully expanded form—with the melodic line for the first time in upper register, in Violin I and in *fortissimo*, with powerful *sforzato* accents on weak beats, to intensify the individuality of this version of the theme. Most important of all, it now receives bass support in unambiguous root position. This is the culminating statement of the main theme in the first movement. Parallels can certainly be found in other Beethoven movements, since the powerful restatement of an opening theme as the starting point of a coda is a trademark of several major works of these years. The coda, much more than the recapitulation, has been foreshadowed from the very beginning of the movement and has been artfully left unresolved at the crucial structural junctures at which the main theme has been presented along the way. The rest of the coda takes care of a few remaining thematic obligations: it resumes and liquidates the arpeggiated triplets that had first appeared in the development section; at mm. 373–387 it resumes the opening c—f tetrachord and expands it, reaching a high point in the Violin I in a way that is reminiscent of the last bars of the development, which had led to the recapitulation (mm. 238–239)—almost as if, to the listener's astonishment, the first theme were going to appear still another time.

———————

Having seen this much of the thematic and dynamic strategy of the movement, we can turn to the autograph score of the work, where we find enlightening clues to Beethoven's compositional purposes.[7] On page 1 of the autograph Beethoven went to special pains to make sure that the exposition of the movement should not be repeated in the usual way; he wrote across the top of the score, "la prima parte solamente una volta" ("the first part only once"). That this was not a casual thought but a mark of concern for the larger shape and proportions of the movement becomes clear when we look at the close of the exposition, where Beethoven went on to insert a large-scale recapitulation,

Example 9.5   Op. 59 No. 1, first movement, mm. 344–368 (Coda)

from m. 112 to m. 342 of the movement. At m. 112 there is a forward repeat sign, which was later erased with red pencil but is still perfectly legible; and in the margin he also wrote the instruction "la seconda parte due volte" ("the second part twice"), which was also later canceled when he changed his mind about this vast repeat. The end of this immense repeat of the "seconda parte" was to fall at the end of the recapitulation but before the coda. Accordingly, Beethoven also wrote into the autograph a six-bar transition passage that prepared the return to the opening of the development; then he deleted this transition when he decided to cancel the repeat altogether. A diagram of the entire repeat plan is given in Figure 9.1.

Why did Beethoven first intend to require this enormous repeat of the sec-

Example 9.5 *(continued)*

ond part, after having omitted the repeat of the first part? And why did he then change his mind? His reasons for omitting the exposition repeat seem clear: it is primarily to create a thematic strategy by which the return of the opening theme at the beginning of the development sounds like a return to the opening of the movement; and also to establish a new formal shape for this first movement that can accommodate the dynamic effect of the successive low-register statements of the main theme along the way, preparing for the eventual climax. We can also see that by planning to repeat the entire development and recapitulation of the movement, his aim was to intensify this strategy considerably. For, by means of the repetition of the "seconda parte," he was able to repeat the original, low-register version of the opening theme not three times prior to the "stable" statement of it at the coda, but rather five times prior to it. The purpose was to establish a set of expectations through the special character and structure of the opening statement which imply an expected "resolution" of its unstable features; then to postpone that "resolution" until a late point in the design. The repeat of the "seconda parte" thus was planned to stress and articulate the thematic strategy of the movement by means altogether outside the conventional repeat system of the classical first movement, just as the entire work and its formal and dimensional features are beyond classical norms. The two aspects of the work interlock.

But then why did Beethoven change his mind and delete the immense re-

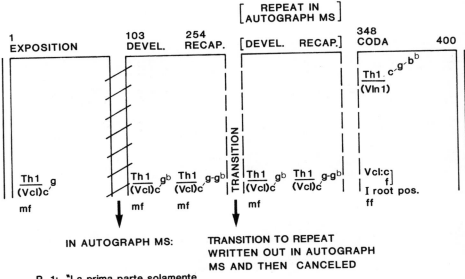

Figure 9.1 Outline of the first movement of Op. 59 No. 1 in the autograph version, before cancellation of repeats

peat after all, thus reducing the number of statements of the opening theme before the coda to three rather than five? My answer, to put it as squarely as possible, is that he may have realized that if he did so he would pay too high a price in distorting the proportions of the movement—not simply by making it "too long," as has been suggested, but by altering the interior balance of the sections and sacrificing in one dimension what he gained in another. This leads us into the issue of proportions, especially the proportions of the interior sections of this very long sonata-form movement. It also leads us into considerations of length, size, and scaling that go beyond this single work and even beyond music to the other arts and to their partial analogues in the life sciences.

In using for this essay terms such as "process" and "limits" I am deliberately borrowing language for musical description from the field of biology, and especially from the sector of biology that studies the relationship of organisms to their environments. The type of question that biologists ask about such matters is, "How large or how small can an organism be and still maintain a healthy and harmonious adjustment to the conditions of its life?" These words are in fact a quotation from a shrewd and striking article by the biologist Florence Moog, published in *Scientific American* in 1948.[8] Moog enlivened her discussion by using as her fanciful model Jonathan Swift's Gulliver, whose size keeps on changing in relation to changing surroundings. By Swift's calculations, Gulliver is 6 feet tall. He is twelve times taller than the 6-inch Lilliputians, but the 60-foot Brobdingnagians are ten times taller than he is. Now, to a biologist, Swift's fantasy about the Brobdingnagians is a hopeless absurdity; as Moog shows, a critic need only invoke a principle as old as Galileo, namely, that the weight of a system increases as the cube of its linear dimensions. Accordingly, if the men of Brobdingnag were 60 feet tall but built on the human model, they would each have to weigh 180,000 pounds, equal to 90 tons! But the upper limit of what the human frame will bear is generally estimated at about 500 pounds, no matter how tall the individual may be.

Some artistic analogues for Moog's observations were offered two years later by Bertram Jessup in an article entitled "Aesthetic Size" in the *Journal of Aesthetics and Art Criticism*.[9] While Jessup dissociates aesthetic requirements from the existential criteria of biology—that is, he allows that things impossible in nature may indeed survive and flourish in works of art—he nevertheless argues, to my mind cogently, that there is an approximate correlation between the size of a work of art and the "amount of aesthetic experience" that it conveys. Here "aesthetic experience" means something like the inner quality and coherence of the work—its structural and expressive cogency, its correlation of inner material with outer framework, its rightness of scale for the material that it conveys.

This brings us back to Opus 59 No. 1 with the same kind of question—how long or short should a Beethoven movement be, and what should be the normal dimensions of its formal sections? In the autograph of the first movement of this work we find evidence that Beethoven himself was asking the same question, and that he answered it at different times in different ways. His problem was to find the right framework for the material of this movement—not simply its themes, motives, and harmonic material, but the dynamic process that is formed by their relationship to the durational structure of the whole. The problem was how to reconcile this process with the necessary limits of duration imposed by contemporary aesthetic norms. Although in a number of his middle-period works Beethoven was expanding all the traditional resources of tonal music to new lengths, he evidently found that the added intensification of the process by means of the repeat of the "seconda parte" would make the movement too long for its "environment." The living space or "environment" of the movement can include the other movements of the entire composition; the range of expectations and attention spans of its listeners; and Beethoven's own highly developed sense of formal balance and goodness of fit.

There is also the question of the inner proportions of the first movement. In the final form of the movement, as normally played, the relative lengths of the exposition, development, recapitulation, and coda are in these proportions:

1/1.5/0.9/0.5. That is, the coda is about one-half the length of the exposition, and a little more than half as long as the recapitulation. But in the version with repeat of the entire development and recapitulation, the coda shrinks to a length of less than one-tenth of the movement as a whole; furthermore, the Brobdingnagian development and recapitulation, taken together, grow to be almost five times as long as the exposition, and more than nine times longer than the coda. The structural weight of the movement thus falls heavily upon the vast development and recapitulation—upon the "seconda parte"—with inevitable reduction of the structural prominence given to the first and last sections of the movement.

To look at the matter in another way, we can say that by inserting the repeat, Beethoven was aiming to heighten the dramatic effect of the climactic statement of the first theme by postponing its arrival until more than nine-tenths of the movement had passed by. By removing the repeat, he sacrificed something of this dynamic aspect of the movement, but brought the sections of the movement into a more balanced equilibrium. The exposition and development are now in balanced proportion, and the coda is correspondingly longer and more significant because its closure of the structure is given a length commensurate with its importance. I shall not go into any details here about the other movements of the quartet, except to say that the autograph gives evidence of similar thinking about repeats and proportions in two other movements—the Scherzo and the Finale; in both movements, lengthy repeats are first inserted into the autograph manuscript and then deleted.[10]

The question raised by this essay turns on the point at which two principles come into irreconcilable conflict. One is the dynamic tension created by the thematic, harmonic, and registral strategy for the entire movement, achieved by postponing a root-supported tonic statement of the first theme until the coda. The other concerns the formation of a balanced structure that can contain this process within a harmonious formal plan in which the four principal sections relate well to one another. Essential here is that each section should have sufficient size to fulfill its functions, yet not distort the equilibrium of the whole. Finding at the autograph stage that his gigantic repeat of the "seconda parte" had leaned too far in favor of one of these principles at the expense of the other, Beethoven changed his mind before it was too late. In the final form of the movement, the dynamic tension is sufficient and the formal balance is secure. The fortunate survival of the autograph manuscript, the most important document that can yield firsthand information about the final stages of composition, thus enables us to reconstruct substantially the decisions that led to this change. It reinforces our confidence that the study of a masterwork with cognizance of its authentic sources is no mere act of piety but a way to see the work as a product of craft and imagination tempered by relentless self-criticism.

TEN

On the Cavatina of Beethoven's String Quartet in B-flat Major, Opus 130

Recent discussions of Beethoven's work from about 1815 to 1827 have sought to identify a "turn toward lyricism" as a distinctive feature of his later style. As portrayed by Joseph Kerman in his extended biographical article on Beethoven in *The New Grove Dictionary,* this resurgence of lyrical expression emerges clearly in the song cycle *An die ferne Geliebte* of 1815 and in later works, whether vocal compositions or instrumental works in which vocal forms are utilized.[1] The latter type includes such famous examples as the Arioso of Opus 110 or the Arietta of Opus 111, along with the instrumental recitatives of the later piano sonatas and string quartets. In the Ninth Symphony, of course, both types of recitative are used, and the issue of contrast and conflict between vocal and instrumental expression gradually becomes the focal point of the entire work. Kerman and others recognize as a supreme instance the Cavatina of Opus 130—commonly regarded as the most concentrated example of Beethoven's lyricism in the instrumental domain, whether in his last period or indeed at any phase of his career. So poignant is this movement that we are scarcely surprised by Holz's testimony that Beethoven himself was deeply moved by it and could never recollect it without deep melancholy. Perhaps something of the same effect can be read from a revealing remark in the *Konversationshefte* made in early January of 1826, when the work was in its first rehearsals by the Schuppanzigh quartet: " 'Mylord' [Schuppanzigh] asks that you change nothing in the Cavatina."[2]

Yet although Beethoven's tendency to incorporate *cantabile* elements into instrumental works is evident in the years after 1815, it is insufficient to account for this movement even in its broadest and most generic features. In his excellent study of the cavatina tradition up to Mozart, Wolfgang Osthoff comments on this Beethoven movement and helps to put it into a new and historically revealing framework. Osthoff traces the central development of the cavatina as an operatic genre in the later eighteenth century, and identifies as well what he calls an "esoteric" subtradition that seems to have arisen from about 1750 onward.[3] This subtradition encompasses cavatinas that occur particularly in "ombra" scenes in opera seria, often with textual and dramatic reference to suffering and death. Osthoff suggests that the "Beklemmt" middle section of the Opus 130 Cavatina may refer to this tradition. Yet perhaps we may take this point a step further, in the light of Osthoff's findings. When Beethoven determined to make use of an E-flat major Adagio movement of songlike character in the context of this innovative work, he was doing more than assimilating a vocal genre into the string quartet. By heading the movement "Cavatina," he seemingly implied a reference to the operatic context and function of a movement of this type.[4] We are of course accustomed to the juxtaposition of strongly dissimilar movement-types in the last quartets—including sonata form movements, dance movements, scherzos, fugues, and slow movements of all types, including the *Heilige Dankgesang*. But this is the only case in which a specifically operatic title appears in a Beethoven quartet.

I suggest, accordingly, that the location of the Cavatina as the fifth movement of the quartet implies that the larger movement-plan of the whole work in some way reflects the shape of an operatic structure. At least this may be true to this degree: that the cavatina in many contemporary German operas often provides a serious, deeply felt lyrical utterance by a major character, who comments introspectively upon a dilemma of the plot and thus deepens the emotional seriousness of the dramatic action as it moves toward crisis and resolution. Sometimes this coincides with the first appearance of a new and serious character, as in the Countess's cavatina in *Figaro* at the beginning of Act II; or in the great aria of Florestan that opens Act II of *Fidelio* and directly reveals the dark world of Florestan's imprisonment and despair, tempered by hope of redemption. Although Florestan's aria is not labeled "Cavatina," a recent survey of German Romantic opera cites it as a perfect example of the genre in its text, key, periodic structure, and lightly ornamented elegiac melody.[5] A parallel exists in Opus 130 to this extent—the Cavatina is an intense melodic Adagio that just precedes the monumental fugue as the original finale. In this it is a parallel to the Arioso that precedes the fugal finale of Opus 110, but without the sonata's cyclic reappearance of the slow movement within the fugue. Despite the profundity of philosophical content that Opus 130 conveys from its very beginning, there is no doubt that this Cavatina strikes a deeper level of expression than had been reached in the earlier movements and that its original function was to prepare the way for the gigantic finale that followed. Even in the later version with the substitute finale, the Cavatina carries out the same function, after which the "lighter" finale restores balance and grace. The finale returns the work to the world of daylight and sanity, though not without hints of the depths that the Cavatina had revealed.

There is another aspect of the movement that arises from its operatic character and texture. Like any "cantabile" movement, it must have a quasi-vocal *Hauptstimme* that carries the primary melodic content, and clearly the first violin part fulfills this role throughout. Yet the basic line is constantly interspersed with striking moments in which the other voices penetrate the surface with lyrical and motivic impulses. Here and there they even take over the momentary role of leading voice; this is certainly true for the second violin part at certain key points, such as m. 19 and in the Coda at m. 61. The other voices are clearly more than mere accompaniment, not just because of their strong melodic role but also because it is characteristic of the late quartets that all voices share motivic importance in approximately equal proportions. Beethoven is reported to have said that in these last quartets he had achieved what he called "a new type of voice-leading."[6] I take this remark to mean just this— that in these works all four parts are designed to be as fully motive-bearing as possible, consistent with the registral necessities of tonal harmonic progressions. Wherever possible Beethoven shows an avoidance of traditional voice-leading methods. He intensifies the interactive role of the voices by unexpected shifts in register, both within instrumental parts and between instruments; by the resolution of dissonances in registers other than those in which they are introduced; and by the avoidance of traditional step and leap motions in the bass part. The bass achieves a participatory role in the motivic content and operates as little as possible in the role of harmonic support; in the Cavatina the avoidance of direct V—I motions in the bass at intermediate points of closure is one of the most striking features of the movement.

Accordingly, the movement presents a paradox. On the one hand, it "stands for" an aria within an instrumental context, and thus its top line must dominate as in a vocal work; it is the quasi-"speaking" voice. On the other hand, the "accompaniment" parts are so designed that they supply the upper line with a rich web of motivic content. Attention shifts constantly from the *Hauptstimme* to the other voices, and vice versa, sometimes without our being able to tell which is which. From the tension of these two aspects of texture— dominating "singing voice" and accompaniment, on the one hand, and the approximately "equal" distribution of motivic content, on the other—arises the remarkable textural richness of this movement. And in this we can discern a further consequence. By taking such an intensely operatic aria-type into the string quartet, Beethoven shows in the most palpable way that this late quartet is itself a transcendent composition of a new type (and the same is true in other ways for the other late quartets). It can not only encompass the most complex instrumental movement-types yet attempted in string chamber music, but can reach out to embrace genres from song and opera as well. The extension of expression that is often ascribed to Opus 130 and its neighboring quartets thus arises in part from the annexation of normally independent genres.[7]

To what extent do Beethoven's earlier works or sketch-plans show an engagement with this genre, or with movement-types that are close to it in character and format? The latter group is not easy to define closely, for the idea of a profoundly expressive Adagio as slow movement is a stable element across Beethoven's career, from the early piano sonatas to the late quartets. If we restrict ourselves for the moment only to his uses of the term "cavatina" itself, we find two examples already cited by Osthoff. One is the brief and partial sketch for an "Andante cavatinato" in the sketchbook Landsberg 7 of 1800.[8] The other example cited by Osthoff is the hymn-like "Cavatina," "Dem die erste Zähre," from the cantata *Der Glorreiche Augenblick,* Op. 136.[9] To these one can now add a third, although again a sketch: it is the hitherto little-known sketch for a "Cavatina" setting of the Goethe text, "Wonne der Wehmut" ("Rapture of Sorrow"), in a sketch leaf in the Library of Congress (SV 387).[10] Dated by Douglas Johnson to the years 1794–1795, on the basis of its watermark and its material for an early stage of the Piano Concerto No. 1, it also contains a fairly extended draft for a setting of the Goethe text. Although Johnson and others have called this, in effect, a sketch for an "early setting of Opus 83 No. 1" (Beethoven's complete setting of the same text), it would be better simply to designate it as a separate attempt altogether, since it has nothing in common with the Opus 83 setting of 1810.[11] The opening phrase of the sketch is shown in Example 10.1. The draft also shows a restatement in B-flat

Example 10.1   Sketch for "Cavatina" on Goethe's "Wonne der Wehmut" (opening measures)

major of its first theme and a chromatic rising sequence in the middle segment, after which it returns to a restatement of the first phrase and a closing phrase. Although this piece awaits full transcription and study, it suggests that the idea of the cavatina was associated with the theme of unrequited love and Goethean rapture even in Beethoven's early years.

II

I return now to certain aspects of the Op. 130 Cavatina itself: its sectional organization and proportions; its internal points of juncture between sections; and its motivic content across the first section and beyond. Although this essay will not deal with the numerous sketches that survive for the Cavatina, it will make brief use of the final autograph manuscript, which is preserved as MS Artaria 208 of the Stiftung Preussischer Kulturbesitz, Berlin.[12]

As an *Adagio molto espressivo* of 66 bars, the Cavatina exhibits in broad terms the familiar formal characteristics of a three-part reprise form with short coda (that is, A B A¹ Coda), but with important modifications of the generalized traditional formal scheme and of course a wholly achieved individuality of content. Against the formal background we see that the proportions of this movement are organized in the service of a clear-cut dynamic principle. Flowing lyrical expansion is the characteristic feature of the first large section, which in fact divides into two subsections (mm. 1–23 and 23–39) and has a full cadence in the tonic at m. 39 to terminate the entire section. Then comes an extremely compressed middle section in C♭ major, of only nine bars (the famous "Beklemmt" passage); this is less than a quarter of the length of the first section, yet must serve as the entire middle section for the movement. The reprise (mm. 49–57) takes on the concentrated brevity of the middle section, fulfilling its role in only nine bars. Then the movement closes with an equally short coda, again of only nine bars, to complete the motivic obligations established early in the movement and close the linear and harmonic motion—somewhat, in a distant yet imaginable sense, as if a short orchestral ritornello, alternating with closing phrases in a vocal part, were ending an aria. A brief outline of the sections makes clear in what way the scheme conforms to established models for slow movements and in what ways it is individualized:

Section	Form	Measures	
First section	A¹ᵃ	1–9	
	A¹ᵇ	10–23	(elided with next phrase)
	A²ᵃ	23–31	
	A²ᵇ	32–39	
Middle section ("Beklemmt")	B	40–48	
Reprise	A³	49–57	
Coda	C	58–66	

These unusual proportions (39:9:9:9) reflect the fact that the Cavatina is a type of lyrical Adagio in which the broad expanded style of the first section sharply contrasts with the extreme compression of the three segments that follow, all of which taken together make up only 27 bars, almost two-thirds the length of the first section. Of course, even ancestral operatic aria-forms had shown a strong tendency toward avoidance of a purely literal and static reprise with exact da capo. But a severely abbreviated reprise of these proportions is only possible in the abstract and malleable world of instrumental music, where no text need be accommodated. This extreme compression of the middle section, reprise, and coda into equal small units after the long first section gives the movement a sense of increasing tension as the lyrical material of the first part is progressively shortened, not literally repeated in leisurely fashion. The effect is that of containing the formal functions of the middle section, reprise, and coda within minuscule segments—producing a sense of the quickening of time across the spatial dimensions of the movement.

The formal scheme in the abstract is not new in Beethoven's works. Although Schenker accurately described a four-section slow-movement form that he encountered especially in Beethoven's piano sonatas (A B A¹ B¹), with or without coda, there is also a persistent strain in Beethoven's slow movements toward retaining the movement-type having the formal shape A B A¹ coda.[13] This form appears in a number of earlier works and is then developed in later slow movements, including those of Opus 7, Opus 10 No. 3, Opus 26 (Marcia funebre), Opus 28, and other works apart from piano sonatas. Whether this is to be construed as a three-section form plus coda, or as a four-section form that includes the coda, depends on the degree to which the coda functionally participates in the developmental aspects of the movement and thus balances the middle section by using its material; or whether it furnishes a necessary but nondevelopmental balance to the B section. In the Cavatina, the coda (mm. 58–66) seems superficially to be in the latter category, until one realizes not only that it completes and culminates the restatement of the motive from measure 1 of the movement, but also that its "new thematic idea" (Violin I, mm. 57/3–59 and Vcl, mm. 60/3–62/1) is a lyrical transformation of the agonized "Beklemmt" segment (Violin I, mm. 41/2–42; see Example 10.2a, b). The coda also makes use of closing figures from the end of the first section (mm. 38–39 and mm. 63–64, 64–65 show this clearly).

Example 10.2a   Violin I, mm. 41–42

Example 10.2b   Violin I, mm. 57/3–59/1

Violoncello, mm. 60/3–62/1

While the proportions show the dynamic balance of sections of unequal length, the points of closure and connection between sections in this movement form one of its most striking features. Significant among these are the ends of the subsections and moments of transition between them, as follows:

Section	Measure	
First section	8	Cadence to I
	9	Immediate repetition of cadence of m. 8
	10	Preparatory bar for return of Violin I theme (expanded repetition of preparatory material in m. 1)
First section	30	Arrival at I from full V–I cadence (mm. 29–30)
	31	Immediate repetition of cadence of mm. 29–30
End of first section	39	Cadence to I (full V–I cadence in root position, as at mm. 29–30, but with upper line moving 2–1, not 4–3; thus melodic closure is more complete at m. 39)
Reprise/Coda	56	Cadence (= m. 8)
	57	Immediate repetition of cadence of m. 56 (= m. 9)

It is very striking that, of these four instances, three are double statements in which a cadential figure is immediately followed by a repetition, or "echo," and in each case there is a shift of leading voice from Violin I to Violin II. This too evokes the spirit of an aria in which closing phrases in the voice part are echoed at once in the orchestra.[14] Beethoven uses the same device in the slow movement of the Ninth Symphony for the principal statements of the opening theme. The only exception is at m. 39 of the Cavatina, where the cadence to the tonic immediately moves into the new portamento triplets at m. 40 that form the "curtain" to the middle section, somewhat in the same way that m. 1 opens the way to the first theme. However, this discrepancy turns out to be a compositional afterthought, for we find in the autograph manuscript that Beethoven initially intended that at this point too there should be a double cadence, as at each of the other points of connection; this measure, which once stood in the autograph but was then crossed out, would have been the original measure 40 of the movement (see Figure 10.1). By deleting it, Beethoven continues the motion more directly from the first section into the preparatory triplets that begin the middle section; the removal of this measure is in the service of greater economy, moving the action forward more decisively into the new section rather than pausing in a more leisurely and symmetrical fashion at this juncture.[15]

The last point that I wish to consider, however briefly, is the complex thematic content of the movement. That the central thematic ideas are all present in the first section is clear enough from careful scrutiny, and even though the

Figure 10.1   String Quartet in B♭ Major, Op. 130, Cavatina: autograph manuscript, showing canceled measure after m. 39

connection between coda and middle-section thematic material emerges from a close look, it requires a bit more care beyond this to determine in what way the first section in turn foreshadows the material of the "Beklemmt" itself. Yet it is possible: such is the complexity of the sinuous thematic material of the first section that certain connections can readily be heard if we look for them. Thus, the basic rising major-sixth interval of the central opening theme (upbeat, b-flat to g, mm. 1–2) anticipates the basic rising contour of the Violin I theme that opens the middle section (mm. 41–42, g-flat up to e-flat); also fragments in the Violin I part in mm. 42–45 (Example 10.3) pick up stray bits of the contour of the opening theme.

The other feature that dominates is the opening figure in Violin II of m. 1 itself. This becomes a kind of countersubject to the principal theme in the first

Example 10.3a Violin I, mm. 42–45

Example 10.3b Violin I, mm. 1–3

section, and following its recurrences throughout the movement is another key to the structure. Consider, for instance, its appearances in the first section at m. 3 (with b-natural emphasized); at m. 10, to reintroduce the main theme; at mm. 17–21, alternating in register and instrument from bar to bar as the first subsection draws toward its subtle close, and its cadence at m. 23 turns out to begin a new subsection; also at m. 49, to introduce the reprise; and finally at mm. 58–59 and 61–62, with the figure achieving in m. 61 in the second violin its appearance in highest register, higher even than that of the main theme anywhere in the movement (the apex of the Violin I part is the a-flat at m. 44 of the middle section). In some way the very shape of this figure [3–5–6–5–4–2–(1)] encapsulates a central intervallic concept for this movement, anticipating the downward motion from 5 at mm. 2–3, 11–12, 23, 25, 34, and beyond, culminating at the very end in the upper line that closes the movement at mm. 65–66. Thus, the surface rounds off the opening pitches g (of m. 1 and m. 2) by closing with the same g's strongly stressed at the very end. The pitch g in mid-range in the quiet ending of this contemplative "aria" prepares the way for the g that follows—either the powerful opening unison g of the monumental fugue or the playful *pianissimo* octaves with which the viola begins the substitute finale.[16]

ELEVEN

Beethoven's Autograph Manuscripts
and the Modern Performer

In his autobiography Artur Schnabel describes his early training in Vienna in the 1890s. Amid recollections of life in the slowly decaying center of the Austro-Hungarian empire, Schnabel gives us glimpses of a musical world that is now legendary. As a young child he became the pupil of the famous pedagogue Theodor Leschetizky. At twelve or thirteen he became initiated into the circle around the aging Brahms, who often came to evenings of chamber music at which Schnabel performed. He also describes his early and formative impressions of the rich collection of music manuscripts possessed by the famous archive of the Gesellschaft der Musikfreunde. The curator, Eusebius Mandyczewski, was a friend of Brahms and successor of Gustav Nottebohm, the great Beethoven scholar. A few years later, in Frankfurt, Schnabel visited the home of Louis Koch, a collector of manuscripts. As he recalls: "Each time I went to Frankfurt he invited me to spend hours in his house, alone. His housekeeper had instructions to open to me whatever I was interested in. So in that house, quite by myself, I read, or played from manuscript, works like some of the last Beethoven sonatas and the last Schubert sonatas. It was an inestimable experience."[1]

From such exposure Schnabel acquired a deep and abiding interest in the autograph sources of the works he played, and in later life he sought to incorporate some of his knowledge and performing experience in his well-known edition of the Beethoven Piano Sonatas. Although this edition is a highly personal and interpretive one, it shows his effort "to get hold of as much original material as possible—manuscripts, copies corrected or seen by Beethoven, first and second editions of which Beethoven had seen the proofs."[2]

Schnabel died in 1951. A direct pedagogical line had descended from Beethoven to him: Carl Czerny, himself a pupil of Beethoven, had been the teacher of Leschetizky. Later Schnabel, preserving the tradition, in turn be-

came an influential teacher as well as a performer. Now, almost two generations later, when we look out at the divided musical world of our time, it is
not at all clear that the critical awareness that Schnabel brought to the original
sources of the classics of tonal music is being successfully transmitted to performers of today. Nor is there much evidence that the instructional processes
available to even our best performers include much if any informed exposure
to the potential value of such sources.[3] For this situation there are many reasons, and to explore them would take us far afield. But my main purpose here
is to suggest some of the kinds of insight into Beethoven's musical thought
that can be found through study of his autograph manuscripts—features that
may seem remarkable, peculiar, or idiosyncratic, but are in every case authentic. Since I also suspect that my thesis is tacitly accepted by many performers,
who are likely to agree as an article of untested faith that Beethoven's autographs are valuable potential sources of knowledge, I will also try to show that
the autographs have their own traps and snares, and at times pose problems of
interpretation. This suggests further considerations that will lead to a moral at
the end of the tale.

When we talk about the Beethoven autographs, what do we mean? A typical
but superficial answer is the "original manuscripts" of his works—therefore
seemingly the "authentic sources," as opposed to contemporary manuscript
copies made by others, or early editions of indeterminate origin. But this definition is far too broad to indicate the true status of many of the manuscripts
lumped together under this heading. Everyone knows that the process by
which many Beethoven works emerged from first conception to final realization was often long and laborious. The sketchbook method, which he adopted
early and maintained all his working life, is the most obvious evidence of this
aspect of his development. Yet despite widespread awareness of the existence
of the sketchbooks, and despite a century and more of scholarship on them,
only in recent years have serious efforts been made to identify, securely reconstruct, and publish the musical contents of the thousands of sketches that are
preserved in sketchbooks, in separate bundles, and in single leaves.[4]

Further, a close look at a number of Beethoven autographs shows that they
stand at various points along the creative paths that led to the realization of his
works. Some can be reasonably described as "fair copies"; others document
the creative process at a phase still short of the final stage. Although they were
probably intended when begun to be final versions, in many cases they under-
went complex changes of the type that we often associate with the sketchbooks.[5] As I have indicated elsewhere, in some cases it makes good sense to

interpret certain entries that we find in sketches and sketchbooks not necessarily as representing pre-autograph stages of development but as entries made in order to solve special problems that Beethoven encountered at the autograph stage.[6] Examples include the Fifth Symphony, in which the third movement was still in the process of elaboration when the rest of the work was substantially finished; and other examples can easily be cited, though they have yet to be closely or systematically studied in the Beethoven literature.

I begin this brief survey with an example of an autograph that provides evidence of an important compositional change at the autograph stage—a passage near the end of the Finale of the Eighth Symphony, Op. 93 (Example 11.1).[7] Not the least of many wonderful moments in the Finale of the Eighth Symphony is the climactic passage near the end at which Beethoven unleashes the full orchestra on the tonic F-major triad, in two successive eight-bar phrases each dividing four plus four, and with each phrase consisting of nothing but the tonic harmony in repetition—first in whole notes, then in half notes (see Example 11.1b). In the first phrase (mm. 450–457) the main features are the wide registral leaps in contrary motion from bar to bar in all important instrumental choirs. Especially important are the winds, with the high major third, a over f, in the flutes and clarinets; this major third, 3 over 1, is a primary generative interval for this entire movement, having dominated it from the very opening (mm. 1ff., first and second violins). Now at the apotheosis of the movement, in these two balanced phrases, the second phrase (mm. 458–469) answers and echoes the first, shifting to a *piano* dynamic, sustaining the low F in the basses and the middle-register a over f in the violins (as at the opening of the movement). This second phrase caps the climax by presenting another special effect of register and sonority in the winds. Now each third, a/f, descending and then rising through successive octaves, is assigned to a different orchestral sonority:[8]

Falling:						
(whole	458	Flutes	↓			↑
notes)	459	Oboes				
	460	Clarinets		465	Oboes	
	461	Horns		464	Clarinets	
	462	Bassoons		*Rising:* 463	Horns	

Falling:						
(half	466/1	Flutes	↓			↑
notes)	466/2	Oboes				
	467/1	Clarinets		469/2	Oboes + Flutes	
	467/2	Bassoons		469/1	Clar. + Oboes	
	468/1	Bassoons		*Rising:* 468/2	Horns + Bassoons	

Example 11.1a Symphony No. 8, Finale, mm. 450–469

Example 11.1a   (continued)

Example 11.1a (*continued*)

Example 11.1b Symphony No. 8, Finale, mm. 458–463 (autograph manuscript reading)

① Obliterated by palette knife; all other cancellations crossed out.

The identification of each octave register with a new sonority presages certain twentieth-century approaches to orchestration, and the falling and then rising parabola of the final version is in every respect a masterstroke within this marvelously subtle finale. But what the autograph shows us is that the whole idea of the falling and then rising curves, from mm. 458 to 469, came about at the last minute (see Example 11.1b). The autograph version originally contained a full-blown orchestral tutti fanfare, with all instruments maintaining the same registral levels throughout! Then Beethoven saw a way of reinforcing the effect with successive instrumental colors for each octave-register, and he simply crossed out the instruments not needed to produce the effect of the descent and rise through the wind choir. The improvement is incalculable.

***

From this example of an autograph with compositional changes we move on to autographs as witnesses for textual problems that performers must confront and attempt to solve. This is necessary because the text-critical evidence for almost all works by Beethoven is either poorly conveyed to performers by current scholarship or is hard for performers to find without doing their own spadework. A sample of an important textual pitch problem is found in the first movement of the "Waldstein" Sonata, Op. 53.[9] Early in the development section Beethoven spins out a sequential passage based on a short motive drawn from m. 3 of the movement (see Example 11.2). As his sequence turns

Example 11.2   Piano Sonata in C Major, Op. 53, first movement, mm. 104–105

to the temporary tonicization of F minor and to a light motion to C-flat major, m. 105 moves to C-flat major by means of a second-inversion dominant resolving to the C-flat major triad in first inversion; so much is clear from Example 11.2. But while the autograph contains a clear flat before the f at the beginning of the measure, in the left hand, this flat does not appear in the first edition, although that edition was engraved from the autograph itself. On close inspection it is further clear that in the first edition the engraver *did* originally insert the flat but later effaced it; the space for it is still visible in the earliest editions. In this case it seems quite likely that the publisher made the change at Beethoven's request, even though we have no documentary evidence to prove it; as a consequence of removing the flat, the motion to C-flat major is weakened in force and takes on a different and less firm harmonic connotation. This example shows that in certain instances we may have to favor an early edition over the autograph, but it shows even more strongly that in order to understand a textual problem a performer needs to amass all the surviving evidence, not just the autograph or the corrected copy or the first edition.[10]

For problems of pitch content, readings in the autograph manuscripts are always interesting and important but may not always be decisive. But for other features, especially those of articulation and dynamics, they are irreplaceable. I refer now to elements of articulation and spatial connection—dynamic markings, articulation signs, dots and strokes, spacings of notes and groups of notes, stems and beams. Beethoven's notation is often highly personal and idiosyncratic, and at times it violates traditional rules of notation; it seems to be a graphic representation of the way he heard musically. Paul Mies has referred to this as Beethoven's "auditory manner of notation." [11] By far the strongest claims for the autographs as bearers of insight on this aspect of Beethoven's music were made by Schenker in his analytical edition of Op. 101:

> Beethoven's powerful and direct thought produces a style of writing that is immediately perceived by the reader—the rise and fall of the individual lines . . . the deep meaning of the connecting beams, which convey to the eye what belongs together and what stands apart; the subtle eloquence of the slurs—sometimes they unite what belongs together . . . at other times they break a continuity in order to increase the sense of desire for it; the upward and downward motion of the stems, indicating the role and interplay of tones. [12]

Dynamics, on the other hand, provide more fertile ground for variation from one performance to another, since only relative values can be indicated and perceived. [13] Studies of Beethoven's original notation have revealed certain patterns of usage, though these have not yet been studied comprehensively across the whole of his working life. It seems clear that Beethoven's notation becomes more refined in this respect from early works to late ones; thus, beginning in the middle period his indication of "crescendo" markings (or his use of the word itself) takes on more and more the exact function of a spatial indicator over entire passages: he either spreads out the word itself or adds horizontal lines to make its field of application clear. Of course he also used hairpin markings throughout his life, but apparently these too increased in precision of applicability as he grew older, and certainly his attention to this feature in his autograph manuscripts is abundantly clear. Because this aspect of his notation was not always taken over literally by even the better copyists, let alone the engravers, the autographs yield insights beyond those of the early editions.

It seems to have been Beethoven's habit not to write down dynamics at once, as he was working on his autograph scores, but to set down the pitch content and articulation first and then make a separate pass through the manuscript for the dynamics and some other signs, such as pedal markings in piano music. Accordingly, the dynamics result from a concentrated effort to adjust this aspect of the notation to the pitch and rhythmic content. At times the indication of dynamics may seem haphazard or insignificant but on later reflection may furnish clues to performance intentions that should be followed. One such case, cited by Schenker, is in the first movement of the

Example 11.3   Piano Sonata in C♯ Minor, Op. 27 No. 2, first movement, mm. 60–68

"Moonlight" Sonata, Op. 27 No. 2 (see Example 11.3).[14] Toward the end of the first movement, Beethoven writes two groups of two measures with the same pitch content—a rising tonic arpeggiation in m. 61 leading to a dominant falling arpeggiation in m. 62; then the same in mm. 63–64. In mm. 61–62 the long crescendo-decrescendo marking, stretched across both measures, is found below the right hand, but in the next two measures it is placed below the left hand. This might seem simply inadvertent or a matter of graphic convenience, but as Schenker suggests, it is much more likely that it reflects an intentional difference in performance for the two phrases. In the first phrase the upper lines of the right hand are presumably to be brought out more intensively through a rise and fall in volume; whereas in the repetition the crescendo-decrescendo should be applied as nearly as possible to the left hand, while the right hand is kept more neutral, remaining an echo of the preceding phrase. This exact placement of the dynamics is found in the Schenker edition of the sonata—not, so far as I know, in any other editions.

Other articulation signs present more controversial problems, above all Beethoven's use of dots and vertical strokes. At times we need more original source material to make a judgment, as shown by Example 11.4. Here, in an example brought forward by Nottebohm, we see a change that Beethoven made in the original orchestral parts to the Seventh Symphony.[15] Nottebohm showed that in this case the hapless copyist misunderstood Beethoven's original distinction between a dot and a vertical stroke in the slow movement. The copyist rendered the sign consistently as a dot, whether it consists of two detached notes or two notes in portamento. Beethoven then went through the orchestral parts and changed the articulation as indicated in part b of Example 11.4, making a clear difference between dots, which remain in the portamento units, and strokes, which clearly apply to the separate notes. That Beethoven

Example 11.4 Symphony No. 7, second movement

(a) Articulation entered by copyist

(b) Articulation as corrected by Beethoven

laid stress on this matter is well known from a letter of 1825 to the violinist Karl Holz, concerning a copy of the A minor Quartet, Op. 132; he writes as follows:[16]

> Most Excellent Second Violin! The passage in the first violin part of the first Allegro is as follows [Beethoven writes out the passage] . . . so write it exactly that way. [Beethoven then writes out another passage in which dynamics must be inserted.] The marks *piano, crescendo, decrescendo* have been horribly neglected, and very frequently inserted in the wrong place. No doubt haste is responsible for this. For God's sake, impress on Rampl to copy everything exactly as it stands. Where there is a dot above the note, a vertical stroke must not be put instead, and vice versa . . . pay attention to what you are told by those who know better—why, I have spent no less than the whole of this morning and all afternoon of the day before yesterday correcting these two movements and I am quite hoarse from cursing and stamping my feet—In great haste, your
>
> > Beethoven

We move now to a pair of examples that reflect what Mies called the "structural properties" of Beethoven's notation; they deviate from the schoolbook rules of notation in ways that reveal groupings, phrasings, connections, and potential unities of musical shape that might well not occur to the performer and are most unlikely to be found in published editions, of whatever period.

Example 11.5, cited earlier by Mies, comes from the slow movement of the Ninth Symphony.[17] In this passage the first violins, in steady sixteenth notes, weave a figuration pattern around the basic melody, which is heard in slower

Example 11.5 Symphony No. 9, third movement, mm. 57–58 (Violin I)

note-values in the winds. Beethoven's instinctive use of beams and separate notes, as seen in the autograph, signals to the eye how the sixteenth-note groups should be phrased, joined, subjoined, and probably how they should be bowed. Here Beethoven's use of beams as well as slurs accomplishes an articulative purpose and breaks the normal and neutral patterns of evenly distributed sixteenth-note beams to make the grouping stand out.

In another example Beethoven's use of beams is normal but the direction of stems is unusual (see Example 11.6). It is the famous opening of the Pastoral

Example 11.6 Symphony No. 6, first movement, Violin I, mm. 1–4 (as in autograph)

Symphony, first violin part.[18] This passage in low register swings back and forth across the middle line of the staff, the accepted dividing line for stem-direction. But in the autograph Beethoven writes the entire passage with downward stems, right up through m. 4, with its fermata. It is harder to say why this is correct and effective than it is to realize it, as one does at once on seeing the original notation with its centrality of spacing, its noncalligraphic style, and its sizes of note-heads as well as depth of stems. The main point perhaps is that the procession of downward stems frames the entire phrase as a single unit, conveying as one long phrase its succession of inner motives that will later be separated out from one another. Beethoven writes it as he hears it, and the writing shows us clearly how it flows from its initial a (3 in F major) through the complex motivic motions of mm. 1–3, reaching a again by scale motion from f up to the same a in m. 4, only to move from that stable a to g, holding the latter in a fermata. The stems especially connect the initial a to the final a and g. If confirmation is wanted of other Beethoven passages in which similar stemming is found over considerable stretches, one can cite, for example, the cello solo at the opening of the Quartet Op. 59 No. 1. Here in the autograph the entire stemming of the melodic line is downward, although much of it could have alternated between upward and downward stems.

The next example deals with another facet of Beethoven's notational practice that seems to have resulted in a kind of traffic accident in the performance history of one of his most powerful keyboard chamber works—the first movement of the "Ghost" Trio, Op. 70 No. 1.[19] The autograph, acquired some years ago as part of the Mary Flagler Cary Collection of music manuscripts at the Morgan Library in New York, is a major source of insight into the genesis of the work and its performance. In Example 11.7 I show the first

bar of the first movement as it appears in the autograph. The key point is that Beethoven uses a slur to bind together not the first four notes of the motive but only its first three, with the fourth note detached. After the slur he not only puts dots over each note in all instruments but carefully writes "staccato" in all parts. Now in the first edition this opening is found to be articulated in the same way as in the autograph, but in many other editions, including the standard Breitkopf complete works edition of 1862–1865 (and all modern editions to date), the slur covers the first four notes, with a dot still found over the fourth note, a. Probably a careless copyist or engraver failed to notice that Beethoven's slur embraced the first three notes, not the first four. This articulation is consistent throughout the movement whenever the opening motive of an eighth plus two sixteenth notes is followed by eighth notes; when the motive is isolated, as in the development section, and is presented simply as two sixteenths and an eighth followed by a rest, then normally the two sixteenths only are slurred, with the eighth note detached. One result of the correct articulation of the opening measures is that it almost certainly requires a change of bow for the violin and cello on the fourth note of measure 1, either starting up-bow and continuing down-bow (then alternating on each eighth), or beginning down-bow, *martellato,* and then continuing in up and down alternation.

This change of bow tends to reinforce strongly the a on the second beat of m. 1, and it has interesting consequences for the linear and harmonic implications of the phrase. With the a stressed, the principal quarter-beats of m. 1 consist of the three notes of the D major triad (d, a, f♯), and the same is true of m. 2. But at the same time there is a rich ambiguity in this phrase, since the four-note descending groups stress the pitches d,g,b—that is, the members of the subdominant triad—and this in a movement in which the IV harmony plays a significant role as basic harmonic contrast to I as well as having other important syntactic functions.

In a draft document about the editions of his works that Beethoven left among his posthumous papers, we find a powerful statement that captures the bitterness he felt as he witnessed the ever-widening dissemination of his works in imperfect editions, brought out by publishers over whom he could exert too little control. The text of this document was published in an appendix in Anderson's English edition of the Beethoven letters.[20] It reads in part as follows:

> The law-books begin without further ado with the question of human rights; which nevertheless the executors trample underfoot; thus the author begins in the same manner.
>
> An author has the right to arrange for a revised edition of his works. But since there are so many greedy brainpickers and lovers of that noble dish—since all kinds of preserves, ragouts, and fricassees are made from it, which go to fill the pockets of the chefs—and since the author would be glad to have as many *groschen* as are sometimes paid out for his work—the author is determined to show that the *human brain* cannot be sold either like coffee beans or like any form of cheese, which as everyone knows, must first be made from milk, urine, and so forth . . .
>
> The human brain is not a saleable commodity . . .

After this hardly anything remains to be said, but the larger point of this essay can be briefly summed up. We live in a society in which musical scholarship and musical performance are like two parts of a divided country. For reasons apparently beyond anyone's control, they maintain territories, inhabitants, institutions, and activities that could profit greatly from close contact with one another but are largely prevented from achieving this by professional interests that remain in conflict. Yet both groups, performers and scholars, who are devoted to serious music and serious musical thought, are themselves members of an endangered species, living in a society monumentally dominated by the mass media and by the commercial interests that govern the artistic marketplace. So there is good reason to advocate change. One direction of such change should be toward increasing contact between musicologists and performers, who are among each other's most valuable clients and colleagues. Another is that the training of performers should as much as possible include some exposure to serious aspects of music history, to source studies, and to analysis in its creative and historical framework. In this way performers may become more aware of the inevitable limitations of the editions from which they perform, and can become increasingly cognizant that music history, as a living discipline, is in fact the field they are in. Although the past twenty years have witnessed a greatly improved climate for the kind of interaction I am talking about, it has yet to be reflected in our institutional life.

In the meantime we can take Beethoven's angry message to heart—"the human brain is not for sale." Whether the listener pays a few dollars for a recording of a Beethoven work or hundreds of thousands of dollars to own an autograph manuscript, he really possesses neither until he begins to feel a responsibility to understand the work in more than its superficial features. Beethoven's simple sentence puts the case in a nutshell: the work of art is precisely the object that can be communicated and received but that cannot be bought and sold, because its producer, the artist, is by definition a maker unwilling to conform to standards not of his own making. I take it that the recognition, acceptance, and defense of such standards constitute the true business of education, at whatever level, and that the spreading of Beethoven's homely message is the business of all who are involved in music, in whatever way.[21] The message may be blunt and simple but it states the case, and the present condition of artistic values and of public awareness of such values suggests that we never needed it more.

Appendixes · Notes · Credits
Index of Compositions · General Index

Physical Features of the Autograph Manuscript of Opus 69, First Movement

Paper. Nine leaves, uniform size and type. Oblong format, average size of page, 21.5 × 31.5 cm. Sixteen staves per page. Gatherings: folios 1–4; 5–8; 9 attached to second gathering. Watermark: letters (cut off at upper edge) with fleur-de-lis surmounting shield with oblique band (left to right). Apparently identical to the watermark described by Dagmar Weise as belonging to the paper used for the "Pastoral Symphony" sketchbook (source C). This further corroborates the musical connection between the autograph and this sketchbook described earlier.

Writing and Implements. With the trivial exception of the penciled folio numberings, all the writing in the MS appears to be in Beethoven's own hand, to judge from comparative evidence and from special studies such as M. Unger, *Beethoven's Handschrift.* The two folio numberings are in pencil, one in the upper right-hand corner (recto only), the other in both lower left- and right-hand corners ("1" and "1a" for recto and verso). The main musical content is written throughout in brownish ink with occasional use of a darker black ink to make complex corrections more prominent. Folios 1v, 2r–v, and 3r–v also show the use of red pencil (Emily Anderson called it "Beethoven's famous red pencil, of monstrous size"), partly to add new notational elements as corrections and partly to write over certain elements either crossed out or preserved and made more prominent. The special meaning of the red-penciled wavy lines on folio 2r is discussed on p. 41. It should be mentioned that the corresponding wavy lines on folio 6v are in brown ink, not red pencil. On his use of the red pencil, see A. Tyson, "The Text of Beethoven's Op. 61," *Music and Letters,* XLIII (1962), and Beethoven's note to his publisher Haslinger (1818?), Anderson No. 925: "You are requested to send red pencils for marking."

Heading of the ms. The heading on folio 1r is all in ink, with no over-writing visible. In dark ink: (1) "ma non tanto" in large letters, canceled; (2) "Violoncello" and "piano" at left of Vcl staff. All other words in the heading are in lighter ink of fairly uniform quality. I interpret the mixture of words and cancellations in the heading as follows: Beethoven apparently began by writing "Son" (for "Sonata") at the upper left, but realized almost at once that he would leave himself no room to insert the tempo marking in its usual place at the upper left-hand corner. So he canceled "Son" and wrote

"All°." Later he must have decided to change "Allegro" to "Allegro ma non tanto" and so added these three additional words in bold strokes and dark ink. At a still later stage he may have been disturbed by the discrepancy in appearance between "Allegro" and the remainder, so he canceled the bold strokes and squeezed in the same words in smaller writing above them. With the tempo markings and cancellations occupying the upper left-hand area, the upper middle and right-hand side is now the place for the title of the work and his signature in German script: "Sonate für Piano und Violonzell von LvBthwn." (On his signature see Unger, *Beethoven's Handschrift,* pp. 15f.; and Anderson, I, 20, who notes that in early letters he "frequently signs his name in abbreviated forms of this type.") Compare his signature in the right-hand margin of folio 6r.

Words and Letters Inserted in the Autograph (excluding dynamic and expression markings). As previously, each reference is in terms of folio/staff/bar number.

1v/5–6/1:	"in 8va"	4v/14/2:	"e e"
1v/5/2:	"loco"	5r/5–6/3:	"in 8〰〰〰"
2v/9/3:	"h"	5r/9–10/1–5:	"in 8〰〰〰"
3r/1–2/3:	"pizz"	5r/10/1,5:	"siml"
3r/bet. 8 and 9:	"arco" [?]	5r/13–14/1:	"loco" (canceled)
3r/12/below 3:	"l.h." [*linke Hand*]	5v/10/1:	"loco"
3r/14–15/1:	"16tel/in 8en"/"col	6r/6/ r. margin:	"e"
	Violoncell in 8 [a]"	6r/7/ r. margin:	signature "LvBthwn"
3v/5/3:	"e f g a h c d e f g a h"	6r/below 8/4:	letter "F" superimposed
3v/6/2:	"d e g"		upon letter "h"
3v/14/1:	"8———loco"	6r/11/3:	"in 8en"
4v/1/1 and 2:	"F"; "F"	7r/7/2:	"g"
4v/3/2,4; 4v/7/2:	"siml"	7r/7/3:	"h g a"
4v/9/3; 4v/11/1:	"siml"	7v/below 8/3:	"l.h. col Vcllo in 8va"
4v/below 16/2–3:	"c h a g a fis" fol-	7v/11/1:	"in 8ven"
	lowed by "f f a a"; at	8r/1/1:	"a h c d e f g a h"
	end of st. 16: "e"	8r/9–10/1:	"in 8———loco"
4v/10/2:	"g e g e" (canceled)	8v/below 5/1–2:	"g h a g a e"
4v/10/4:	"f a f"	8v/10, 11, 14, 15:	"siml"
4v/13/1:	"a"	9r/1–2/2:	"a"

On the use of the letters "Vi-de" throughout the MS, see pp. 4–5 in this volume and Unger, *Beethoven's Handschrift,* p. 17.

Beethoven's Correspondence on the Text of Opus 69

Source M. Letter to Breitkopf and Härtel of July 26, 1809 (Anderson No. 220). German text from E. Kastner, *Briefe,* No. 222 (translation given in text, p. 32). This excerpt begins the second paragraph of the letter.

Hier eine gute Portion Druckfehler, auf die ich, da ich mich mein Leben nicht mehr bekümmere um das, was ich schon geschrieben habe, durch einen guten Freund von mir aufmerksam gemacht wurde (nämlich in der Violoncellsonate). Ich lasse hier dieses Verzeichnis schreiben oder drucken und in der Zeitung ankündigen, dass alle diejenigen, welche sie schon gekauft, dieses holen können. Dieses bringt mich wieder auf die Bestätigung der von mir gemachten Erfahrung, dass nach meinen von meiner eigenen Handschrift geschriebenen Sachen am richtigsten gestochen wird. Vermutlich dürften sich auch in der Abschrift, die Sie haben, manche Fehler finden; aber bei dem Übersehen übersieht wirklich der Verfasser die Fehler.

Source N. Letter and misprint list (undated; Anderson dates both items "Vienna, August 1, 1809," on the basis of internal evidence). See Figures 2.2 and 2.3.*

Letter

Here are the misprints in the violoncello sonata. Czerny [Traeg?]† has corrected them in the copies which he still possessed. By the next post I will send the song I promised you and perhaps a few more songs as well. You can do what you like with them.

In haste
Beethoven

---

*Earlier publication of letter or list, or both: Frimmel, *Beethoven-Handbuch,* II, 187 (wrongly dated "11 August"); Kalischer, No. 449 (misprint list only, wrongly assigned to the year 1815, which in turn was followed by Tovey in the Augener edition); Fritz Prelinger, ed., *Sämtliche Briefe und Aufzeichnungen* (Vienna and Leipzig, Stern, 1907–1911), No. 1252 (letter only); Emerich Kastner, ed., *Sämtliche Briefe* (Leipzig, Hesse, 1910), No. 228 (letter only); Emerich Kastner, ed., *Sämtliche Briefe* (new edition by Julius Kapp; Leipzig, Hesse and Becker, 1923), No. 204 (letter only); MacArdle-Misch, *New Beethoven Letters,* No. 65 (letter only); Anderson No. 221 (letter and misprint list); Unger, *Zeitschrift fur Musik,* CII (1935), 635–642, 744–750 (second part quotes all correspondence on Op. 69 in full and lists errors; except for the fact that Unger did not have access at this time to the earliest editions, his commentary is the most complete to date).

† All earlier editors of this letter read this name as "Czerny," but Anderson reads it as "Traeg."

Misprint List

["Ex." in brackets indicates a musical example. The examples are given in the translation that follows.]

Fehler in der Klavierstimme.

[1] Erstes Allegro im 7ten Takt [Ex.] das mit x bezeichnete E muss c sejn, nemlich [Ex.].

[2] Eilfter Takt fehlen zwei triller auf h [Ex.].

[3] 12ter Takt fehlt auf dem zweiten A ein Auflösungszeichen, nemlich [Ex.].

[4] Im 22ten Takt des zweiten Theils des ersten Allegro fehlt gleich auf der ersten Note das ffmo (fortissimo).

[5] Im Hundert ein und fünfzigsten (151) Takt muss (im Bass) statt [Ex.] der mit x bezeichneten Noten so heissen [Ex.] wie hier, wo sich das Zeichen x befindet.

2tes Stück. Scherzo Allo molto.

[6] Gleich im ersten Takt muss das ff weggestrichen werden.

[7] Wo da nach die Vorzeichnung der [Ex.] sich wieder auflöset [Ex.] ist der nemliche Fall und muss nebst dem dass das ff weggestrichen wird gleich auf die erste Note piano gesezt werde.

[8] das zweitemal als sich die Vorzeichnung der [Ex.] wieder in [Ex.] auflöset, wird wieder das ff weggestrichen und gleich auf die erste Note p gesezet.

Adagio Cantabile. Klavierstimme.

[9] Im (17) Siebzehnten Takt muss statt so wie hier [Ex.] so heissen bej denen mit x bezeichneten Noten [Ex.] nemlich der ⌢ Bogen von den zwene E muss weggestrichen werden und oben im Diskant ⌢ und unten ⌣ im Bass so, wie hier angezeigt, bezeichnet werden.

[10] Im 18ten Takt desselben Stücks ist das arpeggio Zeichen ausgelassen, welches da sejn muss, nemlich so [Ex.].

Letztes Allegro vivace in der Klavierstimme.

[11] (NB) 3ter Takt sind zwei Bindungen [Ex.] ausgelassen, welche mit ^x_x bezeichnet sind.

Fehler in der Violonschell Stimme.

[12] Erstes Allegro im 27ten Takt steht ein Punkt hinter der halben Note A, welcher weggestrichen werden muss.

[13] Im 64ten Takt ist ein ♯ ausgelassen nemlich [Ex.] vor D.

[14] Zwischen dem 77ten und 78ten Takt muss eine Bindung angebracht werden, welche ausgelassen, nemlich: [Ex.] sie ist hier mit x bezeichnet.

[15] (NB) im zweiten Theil, im 72ten Takt steht ein ♯ statt einem Auflösungszeichen—nemlich so muss es heissen [Ex.].

[16] Im 125 Takt muss statt E c gesetzt werden nemlich [Ex.].

[17] Im Adagio Cantabile im 5ten Takt ist der Bogen ausgelassen über den 2 Staccato Zeichen **' '** nemlich [Ex.].

[18] Wo hier das x steht, im 17ten Takt ist in der Manier eine Note nemlich D, welches hier mit einem x bezeichnet ist, ausgelassen [Ex.].

[19] Im Allo Vivace muss im 4ten Takt [Ex.] von dort an, wo das x ist ein Bogen über 5 Noten getzogen worden.

[20] Im 56 Takt ist Dolce ausgelassen, welches hingesetzt werden muss.

[21] Im zweiten Theil des nemlichen Stücks im 9ten Takt muss statt fis, gis stehen, nemlich hier, wo das x ist [Ex.].

[22] Im 58ten Takt des nemlichen Stückes ist *c r s* vergessen.

[23] Im 116ten (hundert Sechzehnten Takt) ist die ˆ und **' '** Staccato Zeichen ausgelassen nemlich: [Ex.].

Mistakes in the pianoforte part.

[1] In the 7th measure of the first Allegro, the E marked with x should be C, namely:

[2] In the 11th measure, two trills over B are missing, namely:

[3] In the 12th measure, a natural on the second A is missing, namely:

[4] In the 22d measure of the second part of the first Allegro [bar 115], the *ffmo* (fortissimo) is missing on the very first note.

[5] In the 151st measure (151) in the bass [bar 244], instead of the notes marked with x

there should be
exactly as it is here where the x has been placed.

Second movement. Scherzo Allegro Molto.

[6] In the very first measure, the *ff* should be removed.

[7] Afterwards, when the key signature

is again altered to
the *ff* should again be removed and *p* should be
inserted for the very first note

[8] and similarly the second time that the key signature changes, the *ff* should be removed and *p*
should be inserted for the very first note.

Adagio Cantabile. Pianoforte part.

[9] In the 17th measure instead of the passage
there should be this passage for the notes marked
with x, i.e., the ⌢ slur over the two notes E must
be removed and marked above in the treble ⌢ and
below in the bass ⌣, as has been indicated here.

[10] In the 18th measure of the same movement, the
arpeggio mark has been omitted. It should be inserted, i.e., in the following way:

The final movement. Allegro Vivace.

[11] The pianoforte part, NB: in the 3d measure, two
ties have been omitted which have been marked
with x.

Mistakes in the violoncello part.

[12] In the 27th measure of the first Allegro, there is a
dot after the minim A which must be deleted.

[13] In the 64th measure a ♯ before D has been omitted, i.e.,

[14] A tie which has been omitted should be inserted
between the 77th and 78th measure, i.e.,
This has been marked here with x.

[15] In the 72d measure (NB, in the second half of the
movement) [bar 165], there is a ♯ instead of a natural, i.e., it should be thus:

[16] In the 125th measure [bar 218] instead of an E, there should be a C, i.e.,

[17] In the 5th measure of the Adagio Cantabile, the slur has been omitted over the two staccato marks, i.e., where the x is

[18] In the 17th measure, a note, i.e., D, has been omitted in the grace notes. It is marked with an x.

[19] In the Allegro Vivace in the 4th measure from the point where the x has been put, the slur should be drawn over 5 notes.

[20] In the 56th measure, Dolce has been omitted. It should be added.

[21] In the second half of the same movement, in the 9th measure, there should be G sharp instead of F sharp, i.e., where the x has been put.

[22] In the 58th measure of the same movement, Cresc has been forgotten.

[23] In the 116th (one hundred and sixteenth) measure, the ⌢ and staccato marks have been omitted, i.e.,

Source O. Letter to Breitkopf and Härtel of August 3, 1809.

Lachen Sie über meine autormässige Ängstlichkeit. Stellen Sie sich vor, ich finde gestern, dass ich im Verbessern der Fehler von der Violoncellsonate selbst wieder neue Fehler gemacht habe. Also im Scherzo allegro molto bleibt dieses ff* gleich anfangs

*Nämlich wie es anfangs gestanden hat, so ist es recht.

Laugh at my author's anxiety. Imagine, I find that yesterday, in correcting the errors in the violoncello sonata, I myself made new errors. Thus, in the Scherzo allegro molto let this *ff** remain at the very beginning just as it was indicated, and also the other times—only in the ninth measure should the first note have *piano,* and similarly the other times, at the ninth measure, where the signature ♯♯♯ resolves to ♮♮♮. This is the way it should be. You may see from this that I really am in a situation about which one could say, "Lord into Thy hands I deliver my soul!"

*That is, the way it stood in the first place is correct.

wie es angezeigt war und auch die übrigen Male, nur muss im neunten Takt vor die erste Note *piano* gesetzt werden und ebenfalls die beiden anderen Male, beim neunten Takt, wo die ♯ ♯ ♯ sich in ♮ ♮ ♮ auflösen. So ist die Sache. Sie mögen hieraus sehen, dass ich in einem wirklichen solchen Zustande bin, wo es heisst: "Herr, in deine Hände befehle ich meinen Geist!"

Use of Additional Staves in the Autograph of Opus 69

Note: *A* means used as alternative; *R* means as replacement.

    1r: None.

    1v: None.

    2r: None (at 2r red pencil and ink corrections go into extra staff below; there is evidently no concern here to save space).

    2v: None.

  3r/8: St. 8 as Vide *A* for Pfte r.h. in st. 10.

 3r/12: St. 12 as Vide *A* for Pfte l.h.; marked "l.h." to clarify.

 3r/16: St. 16 as Vide *R* at m. 2 for clarification of Pfte l.h. on st. 15; and again at m. 4 to replace Pfte r.h. on st. 14.

  3v/8: St. 8 used for m. 1 to sketch in later version of Vcl figure.

 3v/12: St. 12 used to sketch in later version of Pfte. l.h. on st. 11, m. 1 (Vide *A*); and again in the same way at st. 11, m. 3.

 4r/12: St. 12 as Vide *R* for Pfte l.h. on st. 11, for change of octave only.

  4v/4: St. 4 as Vide *R* for Vcl on st. 5/1–3; also revises within st. 4.

  4v/8: St. 8 as Vide *R* for Vcl on st. 9/4.

 4v/12: St. 12 as Vide *R* for Vcl on st. 13/2–4.

 4v/16: St. 16 as Vide *R* for Pfte r.h. on st. 14/2–4, and revises heavily within st. 16.

  5r/4: Vide *R* for Pfte r.h. on st. 2/1–3.

  5r/8: Vide *R* for Vcl on st. 9/2–5.

 5r/12: Vide *R* for Pfte r.h. on st. 10/1–5.

 5r/16: Vide *R* for Pfte r.h. on st. 14/3–4.

  5v/4: Vide *R* for Pfte r.h. on st. 2/1–4 *and also* for sketch for Pfte l.h. on st. 3/5–7.

 5v/12: Vide *R* for Pfte r.h. on st. 10/5.

    6r: None.

    6v: None.

 7r/12: St. 12 as replacement for Vcl figuration on st. 13/2–3.

  7v/8: St. 8 as alternative to Pfte r.h. at st. 6/3.

7v/12: St. 12, continuing st. 8; alternative for Pfte r.h. at st. 10/1 (cf. fol. 3r/st. 8–12).

7v/16: Clarification of Pfte r.h. at st. 14/1.

8r: None.

8v: None.

9r/16: Clarification of Pfte r.h. at st. 14/5.

9v/8: New version of Pfte r.h. at st. 6/1–3.

Provisional List of Variants in the Autograph of Opus 69 (excluding variants discussed in text)

Note: Aut = autograph; GA = Gesamtausgabe.

Measure

1   Time signature "C" in all staves (GA has "₵"); early editions are inconsistent.

12   Pfte: cadenza has no ♮ before a in descent (see Beethoven's own misprint list in Appendix II).

13–16   Vcl: in octaves with Pfte in Aut (sketch handwriting).

18   Vcl: an octave too high in Aut even with treble clef implying pitch an octave lower, as it does throughout the MS.

19   Vcl: "dolce" in Aut.

21   Pfte l.h., third quarter: three-note chord (from bottom, c♯–e–a) in Aut.

23–24   Vcl: below its notes has "in 8va. . . . ." with "loco" at bar 24. The Vcl notation at mm. 18–22 had been treble clef implying pitch an octave lower; in m. 24, if not changed, it would involve too many ledger lines in cadenza; accordingly, m. 23 is clarified for the sake of the "loco" in m. 24.

24   Aut has neither "ad libitum" as in GA nor any other verbal additions. Note too that "6" appears only over the second group of sixteenths in the Vcl cadenza.

27/1–3   Pfte: lower octave A crossed out.

28/1   Pfte: lower octave A crossed out.

29/1–2   Pfte: lower octave B's crossed out in favor of low B only.

30/4   Pfte, r.h.: repetition sign for fourth quarter note omitted from Aut; phrasing for l.h. not in GA.

31–34   Vcl: two stages in Aut, first an octave lower than second, in mm. 31–32/3 and 33/2–34/3.

45/4–46/1   Pfte: I interpret the l.h. as simply a quarter rest crossed out by a swirling motion—not as a string of notes.

47/4   Vcl: apparent erasure below last eighth note in measure is simply rubbing of red pencil from facing page.

47/4	Pfte: last f♯ in measure correctly notated with natural plus sharp, to cancel previous double-sharp in measure; but in the apparently identical preceding measure Beethoven had forgotten to cancel the double-sharp; or is it possible that the two measures are not identical?
48/1	Vcl: erroneous repetition of d♯ canceled.
49	Pfte: heavily inked c♯ evidently added later.
51	Vcl: no slur in Aut.
53	Pfte: double sharp written over what appears to be f♯ eighth-note followed by canceled g♯ eighth-note.
54	Pfte, l.h.: has rhythm of half note followed by quarter note, not dot.
55–56	Pfte: both hands in octaves in Aut.
56	Vcl: correction made to bring Vcl into conformity with Pfte at m. 43.
58–59/1	Vcl: neither reading in Aut contains connecting eighth notes for Vcl at end of m. 58.
62	Vcl: first note in Aut is quarter, not eighth note; eighth rest and sharp crossed out on beats immediately following first note.
63	Pfte, r.h.: overlaid with red pencil for emphasis.
77	Pfte: marking below l.h. in m. 1 is *ff*.
81	Pfte: triplet gone over heavily and note-names written in below: "d e g."
94b	Pfte: second ending has only octave e's in Aut.
152	Pfte and Vcl: *fp* is written over *p* in both parts. Only Vcl has "dolce," corresponding to m. 1.
155	Pfte: has "vi-de" correction of first two triplets.
155/4–156	Pfte, l.h.: rests until m. 156/4; in GA supports Vcl an octave higher.
157–163	Pfte, l.h.: repeats E octaves (parallel to mm. 19ff.); in GA has triplets with r.h. throughout.
161/4	Vcl: has two eighth notes instead of dotted eighth and sixteenth (c.f. mm. 10, 22).
163	Vcl: no verbal indications over cadenza (as at m. 24).
167/4	Pfte: complex set of changes, of which the last visible reading produces the explicit "e" in the r.h. against the explicit "f" (changed from "h") in l.h.; both of these are confirmed by the letters written in. To this Beethoven adds his signature in the r. margin as an indication to the copyist that the dissonant reading is his true intention.
168–169	Vcl: dynamic in m. 168 was originally *f* with "cresc" written in over it. The same is found in the Pfte part at m. 168.
169/4–170/1	Pfte l.h.: doubles r.h. an octave lower (see GA reading).
171/4–172/1	Vcl: f-triplet instead of GA reading (c–b–a–e).
183–184	Pfte: originally in l.h. reading was ⁴₄ moving to ²₂; changed to d–a an octave higher. Originally an initial eighth rest in r.h. in each measure.
186/3	Pfte: f♯ added later (cf. m. 49).
190	Pfte: last four eighth notes in l.h. are b♯–c♯e–c♯ (e canceled and replaced by a); GA has earlier reading!

191   Vcl: low e changed to quarter notes rising an octave; put entirely in upper octave in GA reading.

192   Erased scale in Vcl was apparently the result of momentary lapse, immediately corrected.

196–197   Vcl: group of three eighth notes leading to each first beat is added later to each measure.

218   Pfte, l.h.: triplet was originally c♯–e–a, changed to g♮–a–c♯.

224–225   Pfte: no dynamic markings on trills.

230–231   Vcl: a slur over each measure, not over both.

238–239   Vcl: revision results from double change of octave, pitch sequence remaining in each case the same.

238–250   Pfte, l.h.: in Aut not yet elaborated into final continuous eighth-note figures.

240–250   Vcl: first reading an octave higher than final reading as given in GA.

253   Vcl: originally had .

257   Vcl: earlier reading appears to have been written a step too low, then clarified by thickening of note heads up to correct pitches. The problem of notes apparently written a step too low is rampant throughout many of the sketchbooks.

270   Pfte: original reading brought back in r.h. the motive earlier introduced at mm. 140–141 and subsequently suppressed there. See text, pp. 67–68.

278   Pfte, r.h.: originally had four quarter notes: a–f♯–e–g♯ ♭.

Notes

Additions to the notes made in order to update material in previously published essays are given in square brackets.

1. On Beethoven's Sketches and Autographs

1. On Beethoven's use of "Vi-de," see Max Unger, "Beethoven's Handschrift," in *Veröffentlichungen des Beethovenhauses in Bonn,* Vol. IV (Bonn, 1926), pp. 17 and 25.

2. Two other explanations of this sequence of entries and corrections might be mentioned: (1) Beethoven wrote A1 and decided to change to A2; then he determined to effect a notational distinction between A2 and B1; after writing B1 he decided to suppress this distinction and write B2. This can neither be fully refuted nor adequately supported; it can only be said that the final version reinforces the exact parallelism established by the theme and the other variations at this point. This view therefore seems unlikely on musical grounds. (2) Another view might be that Beethoven wrote A1, then left a space to accommodate another version, since he had not yet made up his mind which he wanted; then he wrote B1, left another space, and then crossed out both A1 and B1, adding A2 and B2. But this seems even more far-fetched than the preceding theory, and it derives no support whatever from the spacing of the material or the character of its writing. It goes without saying that in order to judge the graphic aspects of the example, the reader should compare the musical example given here with the published facsimile.

3. In connection with text-critical problems in works of Beethoven and other composers, the variable meaning of the term "autograph" has had some attention from several scholars, especially H. Unverricht in *Die Eigenschriften und die Originalausgaben von Werken Beethovens in ihrer Bedeutung für die moderne Textkritik* (Kassel, 1960), p. 13, and earlier studies cited there. From a rather different standpoint, the very idea of a "final version" of a composition was explored by G. von Dadelsen, "Die 'Fassung letzter Hand' in der Musik," *Acta Musicologica,* XXXIII (1961), pp. 1–14. But thorough and detailed studies of even the published Beethoven autographs, as documents of the composition process, are few and far between. The

preface to the autograph of Op. 27, No. 2 by Heinrich Schenker (Vienna, 1921) points in this direction but is primarily concerned with analytical observations on the finished work.

4. In addition to the piano sonatas, autographs of the following works have been issued in full facsimile: the Fifth Symphony, ed. G. Schünemann (Berlin, 1942); the Ninth Symphony (Leipzig, 1924); the *Missa Solemnis, Kyrie,* ed. W. Virneisel (Tutzing, 1965); the Sonata in A Major for Violoncello and Piano, Op. 69, with introductory note by Lewis Lockwood (New York, 1970); the song cycle *An die ferne Geliebte,* Op. 98 (Munich, 1970); the excerpt "Gott welch' Dunkel hier . . . In des Lebens Frühlingstagen" from *Fidelio* (Leipzig, 1976); the Sonata for Violin and Piano in G Major, Op. 96, with notes by Martin Staehelin (Munich, 1977); the Violin Concerto in D Major, Op. 61 (Graz, 1977); the complete cadenzas for Beethoven's Piano Concertos 1–4 and his cadenza for Mozart's D Minor Piano Concerto, K. 466, with Introduction by Willy Hess (Zurich, 1979); the String Quartets Op. 59, Nos. 1 and 2, with Introduction by Alan Tyson (London, 1980); the Sonata in G Major for Violin and Piano, Op. 30, No. 3, with Introduction by Alan Tyson (London, 1980); the Six Bagatelles for Piano, Op. 126, with Introduction by Sieghard Brandenburg (Bonn, 1984); and the two Romances for Violin and Orchestra, Op. 40 and Op. 50, ed. Willy Hess (Winterthur, 1990).

5. Schlemmer was mentioned as having been in Beethoven's employ from at least 1811 on by T. von Frimmel in "Beethovens Kopisten," *Beethoven-Studien,* Vol. II (Munich and Leipzig, 1906), pp. 3–19. But thanks to the additional Beethoven letters that have become known since then, we can now find further evidence for him. The earliest reference to Schlemmer in Beethoven's correspondence seems to be a letter assigned by Emily Anderson to September 1807 (Anderson No. 152). He is mentioned again in letters of March 1811 (Anderson No. 301); November 1816 (Anderson No. 675); March 1819 (Anderson No. 938): "Schlemmer, my copyist, is getting old and he is a poor devil." In 1823 several letters mention Schlemmer as being still in service, although he was apparently becoming blind (see Anderson No. 1158), and in a letter attributed to February 1824 (Anderson No. 1268) Beethoven mentioned the death of his "regular copyist"—presumably Schlemmer. Doubtless exaggerated is the estimate of "thirty years" of Schlemmer's service to Beethoven given by Gerhard von Breuning in *Aus dem Schwarzspanierhause,* p. 49, a figure that von Breuning reported he had heard from his mother. But the estimate shows that some of Beethoven's contemporaries took Schlemmer to be Beethoven's steady and regular copyist for the greater part of his career. If it is Schlemmer who is meant in a letter attributed to March 1812 (Anderson No. 359), we can judge his value to Beethoven; after mentioning that his copyist is ill, he writes: "I cannot entrust my works to anyone else." For important biographical information on Schlemmer, see Vol. 4 of the Beethoven *Konversationshefte,* edited by Karl-Heinz Köhler (Leipzig, 1968), p. 336, n. 40. Thanks to archival research carried out by Ignaz Weinmann in Vienna, we know that the copyist's full name was Wenzel Schlemmer, that he was born in 1760 and died on August 6, 1823, and that after his death his second wife took over the task of distributing some of Beethoven's copying work to other copyists. [After the orig-

inal publication of this essay, further important material on Schlemmer and other copyists appeared in Alan Tyson, "Notes on Five of Beethoven's Copyists," *JAMS*, XXIII (1970), pp. 439–471. Tyson showed, among other things, that Schlemmer's work for Beethoven began as early as 1799 and extended in at least a supervisory role to 1823.]

6. On this point see Unverricht, *Die Eigenschriften und die Originalausgaben von Werken Beethovens*, p. 21.

7. As early as April of 1805, Beethoven complains of delay in the preparation of two works because of the "lack of a copyist familiar with my handwriting"; he also mentions that the other copyist is extremely busy—this may be Schlemmer (Anderson No. 111). In 1816 Beethoven writes to Hauschka to explain that he cannot send a score because his own is written in "too small a hand for anyone but myself to read" (Anderson No. 716). In April of 1820 we find the most revealing of his remarks on his own handwriting, expressed with characteristic wry humor and a pun. He had been forced to take on a copyist other than his usual one (Schlemmer), and "the one I employed for the variations was not familiar enough with my handwriting" "die öfter nur [string of small notes] usw. flüchtig kaum Nötchen macht; die gewöhnlichen Kopisten sind meistens in Not und wollen lieber tüchtige saftige Noten haben" (Anderson No. 1019). In 1824, after Schlemmer's death, Beethoven complained to Schott that he now had no dependable copyist, "and it takes time to train one" (Anderson No. 1325). The famous difficulties in his last years with copyists, including the unfortunate Gläser and Wolanek, occurred after Schlemmer's death in 1823.

8. On these aspects of his notation, see above all Heinrich Schenker, *Erläuterungs-Ausgabe der letzten fünf Sonaten* (1913–1920); P. Mies, *Textkritische Untersuchungen bei Beethoven* (Munich, 1957), pp. 28ff.; H. Unverricht, *Die Eigenschriften und die Originalausgaben von Werken Beethovens*, pp. 17–20.

9. In a letter attributed to March 1811 (Anderson No. 301), he mentions the difficulty of finding a copyist "who will copy at my home"; and in another letter attributed to the same year he considers the possibility of taking on a servant who could copy music for him (Anderson No. 340).

10. The autograph of Op. 26, like those of all but one of the other published autographs of piano sonatas, is written on oblong eight-staff paper with all staves filled on each page. It therefore had no blank staff available between systems or, normally, at the bottom of the page for corrections (except at the end of a movement). This practice implies that in beginning the manuscript, Beethoven did not think it necessary to allow for such staves. The exception is the autograph of Op. 57, in which a blank staff is left between systems on a twelve-staff page, and in which the corrections are consequently much clearer.

11. See Chapter 2.

12. See *MQ*, LIII (1967), p. 135. For a similar interpretation of a sketchbook passage from a later period, see J. Kerman, "Beethoven Sketchbooks in the British Museum," *Proceedings of the Royal Musical Association*, Vol. 93 (1966–1967), pp. 80–81.

13. The point at issue here is not the quality and importance of Nottebohm's contributions—which were, nevertheless, limited in scope, unsystematic in method,

and anything but abundantly documented—but rather their creation of a view of the subject that remained substantially unchanged since Nottebohm's time. Although the importance of his essays can hardly be overestimated, both intrinsically and in relation to the changing interpretation of Beethoven in the nineteenth century, it is ironic that they should have supplied the bulk of the musical examples for popular accounts of the subject since then. For the fact is that we do not have a truly critical edition of the majority of Nottebohm's essays on the sketchbooks—those published posthumously in his *Zweite Beethoveniana*, edited by E. Mandyczewski in 1887, six years after Nottebohm's death. A comparison of the *Zweite Beethoveniana* essays with the earlier versions of the same essays published in periodicals shows a considerable number of cases in which readings had been changed in the 1887 versions and in which question marks over individual notes had been suppressed. Lacking an editorial apparatus of any kind, we have no way of knowing whether these changes were made by Nottebohm or by Mandyczewski. For a survey of the subsequent publications of sketchbooks in facsimile and transcription, see my review of the Beethoven-Haus edition of the Pastoral Symphony sketchbook in *MQ*, LIII (1967), pp. 128–136. [Fifteen years after the original publication of this essay, there appeared the first comprehensive catalogue raisonné of the sketchbooks: Douglas Johnson, Alan Tyson, Robert Winter, *The Beethoven Sketchbooks* (Berkeley, 1985); see the review by Richard Kramer in *JAMS*, XL (1987), pp. 361–367.]

14. In addition to the remarks quoted in note 7, there is other evidence of Beethoven's awareness of the difficulties created by his handwriting. As early as 1801 he remarked to Hoffmeister concerning the solo part of the Second Piano Concerto, Op. 19: "I have only written it out now so that, as I am in a hurry, you will receive that part in my own not very legible handwriting" (Anderson No. 47). Much later, in 1821, he wrote to Franz Brentano, "Publishers who are not in Vienna will certainly not be able to make head or tail of my manuscript, as I know from experience" (Anderson No. 1059).

15. This distinction goes back to the original auction of Beethoven's property held after his death, in 1827, in which the sketch materials were first divided among various purchasers—the beginning of their dispersion on a vast scale. The distinction was further emphasized by Nottebohm and was also discussed by Joseph Braunstein, *Beethovens Leonore-Ouverturen* (Leipzig, 1927), pp. 26f.; also by Kerman in *Proceedings of the Royal Music Association*, Vol. 93 (1966–1967), pp. 78, 85.

16. For the term "continuity draft" I am indebted to Joshua Rifkin. The term seems to me to be a distinct improvement over such other English terms as "sectional draft" or "composition draft" that have been in circulation in the Beethoven literature for some time.

17. The former was edited by K. M. Mikulicz as *Ein Notierungsbuch von Beethoven* (Berlin, 1927); the portion of the Pastoral Symphony sketchbook in the British Library (Add. 31766) was edited by Dagmar Weise as *Ein Skizzenbuch zur Pastoralsymphonie Op. 68 und zu den Trios Op. 70, 1 und 2*, in *Veröffentlichungen des Beethovenhauses in Bonn, Neue Folge, Erste Reihe* . . . (Bonn, 1961). [For the structure and contents of the entire Pastoral Symphony sketchbook, see A. Tyson's article in *BS*, 1, pp. 67–96; also *JTW*, pp. 166–173.]

18. See Chapter 3. This sketchbook was ably described by Nottebohm, N II, pp. 321–348, at a time when it belonged to Eugen von Miller. Later it passed into the collection of Louis Koch, and it was described by Georg Kinsky in his catalogue of that collection, pp. 69–71. It is now a part of the Scheide Library in Princeton, N.J., and is the only large-scale Beethoven sketchbook known to be located in the Western hemisphere.

19. As cited by A. Leitzmann, *Ludwig van Beethoven, Berichte der Zeitgenossen, Briefe und persönliche Aufzeichnungen*, Vol. I (Leipzig, 1921), p. 333, Beethoven's words to von Breuning were: "Ich trage solch' ein Heft immer bei mir, und kommt mir ein Gedanke, so notiere ich ihn gleich. Ich stehe selbst des nachts auf, wenn mir etwas einfällt, da ich den Gedanken sonst vergessen möchte."

20. The tenacity with which Beethoven preserved his sketchbooks contrasts strikingly with the free and generous manner in which his own scores circulated in later years among his friends and acquaintances. In October of 1810, while correcting errors in Op. 74, he remarked to Breitkopf & Härtel that he hardly possessed any of his own manuscripts, "no doubt because some good friend here and there asks me for them" (Anderson No. 281). In 1815 he asked Steiner for the manuscript of Op. 90 because Archduke Rudolph wanted it *"again"* (Anderson No. 535; italics mine). Occasionally Beethoven's living habits created additional problems in his finding scores when he wanted them; witness this letter to Johann Baptist Rupprecht, probably of mid-1815: "A very long time ago I jotted down two melodies for your 'Merkenstein.' But both these compositions were buried under a pile of other papers. The day before yesterday I found the one I am enclosing. The other one is for two voices and in my opinion is a better work. But I have not been able to find it. Since, however, in spite of my great untidiness nothing in my house is ever lost as a rule, I will let you have the other setting, too, as soon as I find it" (Anderson No. 553). For a similar problem see Anderson No. 592, probably also of 1815.

21. This work was briefly described by Nottebohm in several passages in N II (Chapters 33 and 34, pp. 312, 314f., 321f.), and in the essay "Ein unvollendetes Clavierconcert," pp. 223–224 (with brief transcription of the opening measures in reduced score). It is listed by Willy Hess as No. 15 in his *Verzeichniss der nicht in der Gesamtausgabe veröffentlichten Werke Beethovens* (Wiesbaden, 1957). [In 1970 I published a preliminary overview of the relationship between this rudimentary score and a number of the surviving sketches, in an essay, "Beethoven's Unfinished Piano Concerto of 1815: Sources and Problems," *MQ*, LVI (1970), pp. 624–646, reprinted in P. H. Lang, ed., *The Creative World of Beethoven* (New York, 1970), pp. 122–144. A revised view of this score and associated sketches, based on a more recent study of the physical properties of the autograph and on newly available sketches, was offered by Nicholas Cook, "Beethoven's Unfinished Piano Concerto: A Case of Double Vision?" *JAMS*, XLII (1989), pp. 338–374; to which see my reply in "Communications," *JAMS*, XLIII (1990), pp. 376–382, and Cook's reply, ibid., pp. 382–385.]

22. This would reinforce the remark attributed by D. F. Tovey to the publisher André; see Tovey's *The Integrity of Music* (London, 1941), p. 112: "The publisher André once told Mendelssohn in shocked tones that he had seen Beethoven's Sev-

enth Symphony in progress in manuscript, and that Beethoven was evidently composing in a manner that could not but produce disconnected results, by leaving many pages blank and skipping from one part of a work to another." [For an excellent study of this aspect of the autograph and related matters, see Benito Rivera, "Rhythmic Organization in Beethoven's Seventh Symphony: A Study of Cancelled Measures in the Autograph," *19th-Century Music,* VI (1983), pp. 241–251.]

23. Alan Tyson, "The Textual Problems of Beethoven's Violin Concerto," *MQ,* LIII (1967), p. 484.

24. For certain aspects of this discussion I am indebted to a close study of the facsimile of the Kyrie autograph that was carried out in a seminar at Princeton University in 1968 by Joel Lester. [See J. Lester, "Revisions in the Autograph of the *Missa Solemnis Kyrie," JAMS,* XXIII (1970), pp. 420–438.]

25. In 1986 William Drabkin kindly called my attention to some entries that Beethoven made in a sketchbook of 1822, mainly devoted to the *Missa Solemnis.* Some of these were published by Nottebohm in N II, pp. 471f. They include a reminder by Beethoven to "write all future scores with pencil and have the lines drawn in beforehand"; also a reminder to have "not more than three measures per page"; and a reminder to himself about the "little notes that should be put into the violin part in the score" (*in die Violin Partitur Stimme die kleinen Noten*).

26. This essay was published in German translation in the volume *Ludwig van Beethoven* in the series *Wege der Forschung,* Vol. CXXVIII, ed. Ludwig Finscher (Darmstadt, 1983), pp. 113–138; see also the Editor's *Vorwort,* p. xi.

2. The Autograph of the First Movement of Opus 69

1. Op. 26, Erich Prieger, ed. (Berlin, Cohen, 1895); Op. 27 No. 2, Heinrich Schenker, ed., in "Musikalische Seltenheiten," Vol. 1 (Vienna, Universal-Edition, 1921); Op. 53, Dagmar Weise, ed. (Bonn, Beethoven-Haus, 1954); see also her article in *Beethoven Jahrbuch,* Jg. 1955/56, 102–111; Op. 57 (Paris, Piazza, 1927); Op. 78 (Munich, Drei Masken, 1923); Op. 109, O. Jonas, ed. (New York, Lehman Foundation, 1965); Op. 110, K. M. Komma, ed. (Stuttgart, Ichthys, 1967); Op. 111, (Munich, Drei Masken, 1922). Fifth Symphony, G. Schünemann, ed. (Berlin, Maximilian, 1942); Ninth Symphony (Leipzig, Kistner and Siegel, 1924); *Missa Solemnis: Kyrie,* W. Virneisel, ed. (Tutzing, Schneider, 1965). [For additional autographs published in facsimile, see Chapter 1, note 4.]

2. The "Engelmann" sketchbook of 1822–23, published as "Ludwig van Beethoven, Skizzenbuch" (Leipzig, Röder, 1913); the "Moscow" sketchbook of 1825, published by M. Ivanov-Boretzky in *Muzykalnoye Obrazovanie (Musikalische Bildung),* Nos. 1/2 of the 1927 volume; the "Wielhorsky" sketchbook of 1802–03, published by N. Fishman as *Kniga Eskizov Beethovena* . . . (3 vols.; Moscow, State Publishing House, 1962). [On these and other sketchbooks published in facsimile and transcription since 1970, see JTW, passim.]

3. Gesamtausgabe: *Ludwig van Beethoven's Werke* (Leipzig, Breitkopf and Härtel, 1864–90); hereafter cited as GA. Even in the large specialized literature, studies of the autographs themselves have not been plentiful, despite the pioneering work of

Heinrich Schenker in calling attention to their great value as musical documents. Schenker's own studies of Beethoven autographs, embodied in his *Erläuterungsausgaben der letzten Sonaten Beethovens* (Vienna, Universal-Edition, 1913–20) and in other writings, were followed by important studies by O. Jonas on Op. 61 (*Zeitschrift für Musikwissenschaft*, XIII [1931], 443–450) and Op. 93 (*Music and Letters*, XX [1939], 177–182), as well as more recent writings; see also Paul Mies, *Textkritische Untersuchungen bei Beethoven* (Munich, Henle, 1957) and Hubert Unverricht, *Die Eigenschriften und Originalausgaben von Werken Beethovens in ihrer Bedeutung für die moderne Textkritik* (Kassel, Bärenreiter, 1960); also studies by Alan Tyson, especially his painstaking and significant contributions to Beethoven textual criticism, in which the autographs naturally play a vital role. These include the important book *The Authentic English Editions of Beethoven* (London, Faber and Faber, 1963) and numerous articles, including "The Textual Problems of Beethoven's Violin Concerto," *MQ*, LIII (October, 1967), 482–502.

4. I should like to thank the late Felix Salzer, former owner of the manuscript, for repeatedly placing it at my disposal for the close examination of detailed problems. [On May 17, 1990, the manuscript was sold at auction by Sotheby's, London, to an unidentified purchaser. In the fall of 1990 it was obtained by the Beethoven-Archiv in Bonn. Its shelf mark is NE 179.]

5. For further discussion of this point, see Unverricht, pp. 12–13, and Chapter 1 in this volume.

6. Kinsky-Halm, p. 164. [In 1973, Douglas Johnson was able to show through a newly found document that Artaria had only the first movement; see Johnson, "The Artaria Collection of Beethoven Manuscripts: A New Source," *BS*, p. 200.]

7. *Fachkatalog der Wiener Musikausstellung 1892*, p. 287, No. 20; "Sonate (A-Dur) für Pianoforte und Violoncell. Op. 69, Erster Satz. Autogr. (1807–08). Dr. Heinrich Steger, Wien." Steger was also the owner of the autographs of other Beethoven works, including Opp. 28, 33, 53, 59/3, 62, 96, 98, 102/2, 120, and WoO 20. It seems that in this same year the manuscript (explicitly only the first movement) was given to Brahms for his scrutiny and, possibly, his acquisition. This is clear from a letter Brahms wrote to Joachim on April 2, 1892: "Der erste Satz der A-dur-Cello-Sonate von Beethoven liegt bei mir, und ich habe die heimliche Angst, dass mein bescheidenes Sträuben, ihn für ein Manuskript von mir(!) zu erwerben, mich schliesslich um den Schatz bringt!" For the entire letter see *Johannes Brahms im Briefwechsel mit Joseph Joachim*, Andreas Moser, ed. (Berlin, Deutsche Brahms-Gesellschaft, 1912) II, 275, Letter No. 506. For this reference I am indebted to Felix Salzer.

8. Max Unger, "Die Beethoven-Handschriften der Familie W. in Wien," *Neues Beethoven Jahrbuch*, VII (1937), 160f.

9. In addition to what is indicated for the piano sonatas, the following autographs also used oblong format: all the quartets from Op. 59 to 95; all the piano trios (except part of Op. 97); the Fourth to Eighth Symphonies (except part of the Eighth); the accompanied sonatas (including Op. 102, Nos. 1 and 2). The only exception seems to be the Violin Sonata, Op. 96, which has received a good deal of attention from American scholars because it is owned by the Morgan Library in New York; actually its format is highly exceptional among the chamber works.

For facsimiles see E. Winternitz, *Musical Autographs from Monteverdi to Hindemith* (Princeton, Princeton University Press, 1955), Facs. Nos. 83–86.

10. Of the piano sonata autographs thus far published, only that of Op. 78 could reasonably be described as a true example of what we would call a fair copy. On the other hand, none of the others contains revisions as far-reaching as those of the middle folios of Op. 69; all of them represent their material at a more nearly final stage of composition.

11. Kinsky-Halm, p. 164; a brief description by Max Unger in *Neues Beethoven Jahrbuch*, VII, 160–161.

12. G. Nottebohm, *Thematisches Verzeichnis der im Druck erschienenen Werke von Ludwig van Beethoven* (Leipzig, Breitkopf and Härtel, 1868), p. 63. This is the same Consul Clauss who once owned the autograph of Bach's C-Major Organ Prelude and Fugue, BWV 545, and a Bach canon, BWV 1073.

13. Kinsky-Halm, p. 164.

14. In December 1984 I learned from Dr. Albert Dunning of his discovery of the "Clauss copy" of Op. 69 in a library in the Netherlands. Dr. Dunning kindly placed a complete xerox copy at my disposal. My preliminary study of this source reveals that it strongly confirms the hypotheses advanced in this study. This is particularly true with regard to the textual problems presented by mm. 35–36 and 172–173 and also the process by which Beethoven composed the final version of the principal second subject of the movement (mm. 38–45 and 174–182). Further particulars will be given in future discussions of this vitally important source.

15. Dagmar Weise, *Ein Skizzenbuch zur Pastoralsymphonie und zu den Trios Op. 70, 1 und 2* (2 vols.; Bonn, Beethoven-Haus, 1961), I, 14; see my review in *MQ*, LIII (January 1967), 128–36. Figure 2.1 is reproduced by permission of the Trustees of the British Museum. [See Alan Tyson, "A Reconstruction of the Pastoral Symphony Sketchbook," *BS 1*, pp. 67–96; and JTW, pp. 166–173.]

16. N II, p. 253.

17. N I, pp. 68–69.

18. I am greatly indebted to Dr. Hans Schmidt of the Beethoven-Archiv, Bonn, for help in obtaining photographs of this source and of others used for this study, as well as for much valuable information.

19. Max Unger, *Eine Schweizer Beethovensammlung* (Zurich, Corona, 1939), p. 170.

20. Firm of K. E. Henrici, Versteigerung CXLII (Auction of November 7, 1928 [Berlin, 1928]), p. 1, No. 3; p. 3 (facsimile).

21. N I, pp. 531f.

22. Max Unger, "Die Beethovenhandschriften der Pariser Konservatoriumsbibliothek," *Neues Beethoven Jahrbuch*, VI (1935), 100f. (brief description).

23. N II, pp. 533–534; see also note 15.

24. Kinsky-Halm, pp. 164f.: "April, 1809."

25. Kinsky-Halm, p. 165. Facsimile of title page in Robert Bory, *Ludwig van Beethoven, sein Leben und sein Werk in Bildern* (Zurich, Atlantis, 1960), p. 118. According to Kinsky-Halm, this printing contains the corrections submitted by Beethoven at the end of July 1809. The copies I have seen contain no such corrections, or at most a tiny fraction of them and not necessarily made in 1809.

26. Kinsky-Halm, p. 165, where this printing is dated as early as the end of April, 1809.

   Later editions listed by Kinsky-Halm include the following: Paris, Pleyel, n.d.; Hamburg, Böhme, 1828 (also as "Op. 59"); Frankfurt, Dunst (as part of "Oeuvres Complets de Piano," according to Kinsky-Halm the first edition in which the piano part contains the entire score); London, Monzani ("um 1815"), according to Kinsky-Halm no copy known.

   To these can be added: Hamburg, Cranz, n.d.; Bonn, Simrock, n.d.; Mainz, Schott (all listed in Nottebohm, *Thematisches Verzeichnis*). Also: Offenbach, J. André (c. 1840), Publisher's No. 6464 (copy in New York Public Library).

27. Emily Anderson, ed. and trans., *The Letters of Beethoven* (3 vols.; London, Macmillan, 1961; New York, St. Martin's Press, 1961).

28. On Schlemmer as copyist see T. von Frimmel, "Beethovens Kopisten," *Beethoven-Studien* (Munich, Müller, 1906), II, 3–19; also G. Schünemann, preface to facsimile edition of the Fifth Symphony; A. Tyson, "Notes on Five of Beethoven's Copyists," *JAMS*, XXIII (1970), pp. 439–471.

29. Alexander Wheelock Thayer, *Ludwig van Beethoven's Leben,* translated into German and edited by Herman Deiters; newly revised and completed by Hugo Riemann (5 vols.; Leipzig, Breitkopf and Härtel, 1901–1911), III, 112.

30. The evidence connecting Gleichenstein with the sonata convincingly explains its dedication to him as an intimate friend. But the general inference by biographers and earlier writers that it was intended for Gleichenstein in recognition of his ability as a cellist is not borne out by clear evidence. It is evident from Beethoven's letters to him that they were on close terms from at least 1804 (possibly earlier— see Frimmel, *Beethoven-Handbuch I* [Leipzig, Breitkopf and Härtel, 1926], art. "Gleichenstein") until 1812, and that Gleichenstein was one who Beethoven expected to take care of business and everyday tasks for him. That Beethoven originally intended to dedicate Op. 58 to him and later substituted Op. 69 is also clear enough from correspondence (see Anderson No. 172). But it is also evident that Gleichenstein was "no connoisseur," as Beethoven himself puts it in a recommendation written for him at just this time (see Anderson No. 173). It is much more interesting to realize that Beethoven himself, in 1809, suggested to Zmeskall that Op. 69, "which has not yet been performed well in public," be played by Baroness Ertmann and the famous cellist Nikolaus Kraft (son of Anton Kraft). Nikolaus apparently played the first performance of Op. 69 on March 5, 1809 (see *Thayer's Life of Beethoven,* revised and edited by Elliot Forbes [Princeton, Princeton University Press, 1964], p. 467; hereafter cited as Thayer-Forbes). The level of difficulty represented by the cello part surely demands a performer of more than average caliber, just as the cello part in the Triple Concerto had (first performed by Anton Kraft, according to Schindler). In this connection, note Beethoven's reference to [N.] Kraft in a message to Zmeskall (who was also an "able cellist" by all accounts): "Kraft has offered to play with us today. It would be imperious not to accept his offer; and I myself do not deny, just as you will admit, that his playing affords us all the greatest pleasure." (Anderson No. 210, perhaps written April 1809.) Another performance of Op. 69, by Lincke and Czerny, is reported to have taken place in 1816 (Thayer-Forbes, p. 641).

31. N I, p. 70; N II, p. 254.

32. See, for example, these letters: Anderson Nos. 72, 79, 228, 230, 272, 278, 281, 294.

33. Letter to Breitkopf and Härtel of February 19, 1811 (Anderson No. 297): "At last you have adopted the sensible procedure of sending me the proofs of the Fantasia to correct, and you should always do so." But by no more than three months later he was incensed again by the publisher's actions; see Anderson No. 305 and especially No. 306: "Fehler—Fehler! Sie sind selbst ein einziger Fehler" (apropos of the Fifth Piano Concerto).

34. The most important lists or references to them, apart from the Op. 69 letters, are these: Anderson No. 5 (on WoO 40); Nos. 76–78 (on Op. 31); No. 199 (on Fifth and Sixth Symphonies); No. 218 (on Op. 70 No. 2); No. 228 (on Op. 70 and Fifth and Sixth Symphonies); No. 230 (on Op. 70 No. 2); No. 306 (Pfte arr. of Egmont Overture); No. 496 (on ariettas for George Thomson); No. 649 (on Op. 95); No. 675 (on Op. 92: "a list of all the mistakes will have to be printed"); No. 691 (corrections had *not* been made in Op. 95 copies, as promised); Nos. 938–939 (on Opp. 104 and 106); No. 1053 (on Op. 108); No. 1060 (on Op. 109); No. 1061 (on Op. 109); No. 1187 (on Opp. 120 and 111); Nos. 1190–1190a (on Op. 111); No. 1548 (on Opp. 125 and 127).

35. Beethoven's own more general impression of the situation is shown in a letter to Simrock of February 15, 1817: ". . . so many inaccurate editions of my works are prancing about in the world"; also in his draft proposal regarding a complete edition of his works (Anderson, III, 1450f.): ". . . seeing that so many inaccurate and forged editions are wandering about . . ."

36. Anderson Nos. 192, 197, 199, 203, 204.

37. With the kind permission of the Beethoven-Haus authorities it is published here in complete facsimile for the first time, along with the covering note that accompanied it to Breitkopf and Härtel in Leipzig.

38. A. C. Kalischer, ed., *Beethoven's Sämtliche Briefe* (2nd ed., newly revised by Frimmel; Berlin and Leipzig, Schuster and Loeffler, 1909–1911), No. 449.

39. Especially those given by Donald W. MacArdle and Ludwig Misch, *New Beethoven Letters* (Norman, University of Oklahoma Press, 1957), No. 65, and by Emily Anderson.

40. Unger, "Stichfehler und fragliche Stellen bei Beethoven," *Zeitschrift für Musik*, CII (1935), 635–642 and 744–750.

41. In the Library of Congress copy these errors (numbered according to the misprint list in Appendix II and Anderson No. 221) are written in: Nos. 4 (the *ff*) and 11 only. The British Museum copy is entirely uncorrected, as is a copy of the piano part alone recently possessed by Scientific Library Service, New York. I have also compared the Vienna Nationalbibliothek copy of the first Vienna edition by Artaria and find it to contain all but three of the errors in Beethoven's list.

42. The right-hand reading *p—ff* in the upbeat to m. 1 and to m. 2 is found in at least these early editions: Breitkopf and Härtel, 2d ed. of 1809 ("Op. 69"); Artaria's first Vienna edition of 1809 ("Op. 59"); J. André, undated edition, evidently of the 1840s, Plate 6464; Breitkopf and Härtel ("Nouvelle Edition"), Plate 6870 of c. 1843. In the GA and in editions of the later nineteenth century that followed it,

puzzled editors evidently "solved" the apparent problem of this reading by converting the *p—ff* into an innocuous *p—sf*. This in turn was changed by Tovey in his Augener edition, with a reproving note: "The sforzando given in all editions (including the 'critical' Breitkopf and Härtel) at the second bar is an attempt to make sense of a bad misprint pointed out by Beethoven in the letter mentioned above."

The "letter mentioned above" is the misprint list alone, and by following it Tovey makes the passage simply *p* in the piano part each time it appears. The situation illustrates what can happen when one has only a part of the source material: if Tovey had had Beethoven's letter of August 3, 1809, as well (my source O), he would have been compelled to let the *ff* stand, and most modern performances would consequently differ drastically in this important detail.

The chain of errors is extended by the modern Peters edition (C. F. Peters, No. 748), ed. Walter Schulz. Schulz is the only editor I know of who gives the "last corrected reading"—the opening *ff*—but he follows it with an undocumented *sff* and then writes in a note: "In the manuscript, the reading of which was also taken over by the Gesamtausgabe, the reading is *p* and *sf*." While Schulz knows the letter of August 3, 1809, I doubt that he really knows the "Manuskript" of the Scherzo; for no one since Beethoven's lifetime has ever reported its existence or whereabouts. Almost certainly Schulz is working from the confusions of the early prints, as all other editors have also been forced to do.

[The same mistake was still perpetuated in both the Beethoven Werke edition of 1971 and the Henle "Urtext" edition of 1971, both edited by Bernard Van der Linde. In the preface to the latter, Van der Linde apparently misreads the letter of August 3, 1809, inferring from it that Beethoven "restored the *ff* that had been cut out in all these places but without withdrawing the preceding *p*." This last point is incorrect. Beethoven's intention was to have all the pianoforte statements *fortissimo* and all the following violoncello statements *piano*. Performers should correct these editions accordingly.]

43. Perhaps distantly relevant to this aspect of the score is a much later reference by Beethoven to his own procedure of writing, in a letter to A. M. Schlesinger (Anderson No. 1060) of November 13, 1821. Beethoven explains that to send both his own MS and a copy of a work would be too risky, for they might be lost. "This is what happened the last time when on account of my ailing condition I had written down the draft more fully than usual. But now that my health appears to be better, I merely jot down certain ideas as I used to do, and when I have completed the whole in my head everything is written down, but *only once*" (my italics). The German text was published for the first time in *Music and Letters*, XX (1939), 236–238: ". . . das Vorigemal geschah es, indem ich, meiner kränklichen Umstände wegen, mein *Concept* weitläufiger aufgeschrieben als gewöhnlich, jezt aber wo wie es scheint meine Gesundheit besser ist, zeige ich wie sonst auch nur gewisse Ideen an, u. bin ich mit dem Ganzen fertig im Kopf (?), so wird alles nur einmal aufgeschrieben" (question mark by the editors, B. Schofield and D. Wilson).

44. On comparable problems regarding parallel passages see Unverricht, pp. 67–70, and Mies, p. 14 (on Op. 96), p. 51 (on Op. 27 No. 2).

45. Noteworthy too is the fact that the Pfte at m. 172 is an octave higher than in the final version, in which the parallel passages agree in register.

46. The modern C. F. Peters edition differs in giving c♮ at mm. 35–36 and f♮ at both m. 172 and m. 173, without notice of any kind. Exactly the same arrangement then appears in the International Music Co. edition (Leonard Rose, ed.), which is identical in every typographical detail with that of Peters. This compound error seems to have begun with the G. Schirmer edition by Leo Schulz, copyright 1905, which is still being issued in unrevised form.

47. Augener edition, No. 7660. Despite its shortcomings this is still the best edition yet available, since it represents at least an honest attempt to grasp the text-critical nettles. Of all the recorded performances I know of, however, only that made by Emanuel Feuermann and Myra Hess appears to be based on this edition—perhaps because it was made in England?

48. Notably, he did not take the trouble to make the parallel change at m. 181. But again one must either assume that the copyist did so or that Beethoven corrected the copy before the first printing.

49. On the distinctions between these methods of writing, see Max Unger, *Beethovens Handschrift* (Bonn, Beethoven-Haus, 1926), pp. 22f. Some relevant comments of his own appear in later letters, for example, Anderson No. 1019 (of 1820) and No. 1402 (of 1825): ". . . tell him [the copyist Rampel] that I write quite differently now, much more legibly than during my illness."

50. See my remarks in *MQ*, LIII (January 1967), 133f.

51. Compare the following indications of "pizz" in published facsimiles: Fifth Symphony autograph, p. 22, m. 2; p. 87, m. 1; p. 91, m. 1; p. 95, mm. 1–2; p. 99, m. 2; p. 107, m. 2; p. 119, m. 1; p. 184, m. 6; and others. Also in the sketchbook Add. 31766: fol. 47v/3/2; 45r/3/ right margin; 45r/6–7/3–4; 42v/10; 43r/above st. 4: "Violoncello pizzicato."

52. Compare the autograph of Op. 57, 14v/1/1, where the sequence of indications is "bleibt——in 8va——loco."

53. For an example of the opposite procedure, altering groups of four sixteenths to triplets, see N II, p. 279 (on Op. 95).

54. For a similar addition on an intervening staff in the Op. 96 autograph, see E. Winternitz, Plate 85, which also exhibits the significant words "klein geschrieben" as an indication to the copyist, as is pointed out by Winternitz, 1, 84. See also the Fifth Symphony autograph, pp. 173–177 (trio of the Scherzo), bottom of each page. Valuable here is the letter to N. Simrock of April 23, 1820 (Anderson No. 1019), in which he himself remarks on the problems a copyist encountered who was unfamiliar with his hand: "which frequently produces only very sketchy [notes] [B. gives sample note-shapes], etc., and these might hardly be described even as *little notes*."

55. Above mm. 1 and 2 at the top of 4v is the letter "F" to clarify the Vcl reading.

56. The extended published analyses, representing different periods of Schenker's work, include the monograph on the Ninth Symphony (Vienna, Universal-Edition, 1912); that on the Fifth Symphony in *Der Tonwille* (1921 and 1923) and also published separately; also the *Erläuterungsausgaben* of Opp. 101, 109, 110, and

111; and the exhaustive analysis of the Eroica Symphony in *Das Meisterwerk in der Musik,* Vol. III (Munich, Drei Masken, 1930). In addition to other essays on piano sonatas (Op. 2 No. 1; Op. 49 No. 2; and Op. 57) important material is also presented in the analyses in *Neue Musikalische Theorien und Phantasien,* Vol. III: *Der Freie Satz* (Vienna, Universal-Edition; 2d ed., revised and edited by Oswald Jonas, 1956).

57. Schenker, *Der Freie Satz,* Fig. 109e2.

58. Schenker, *Der Freie Satz,* Anhang, No. 128, 5a; text-volume, p. 169, Section No. 273.

59. Mies, *Textkritische Untersuchungen,* p. 51.

3. Beethoven's Sketches for Sehnsucht

1. Stephen Spender, "The Making of a Poem," originally published in *Partisan Review* (Summer 1946) and reprinted in B. Ghiselin, ed., *The Creative Process* (New York, 1955), p. 114. For a balanced and informed view of the evidence for Mozart's methods of composition, see Erich Hertzmann, "Mozart's Creative Process," in P. H. Lang, ed., *The Creative World of Mozart* (New York, 1963), pp. 17–30. To the generally known indications of Mozart's rapidity in composition and the apparent absence of drafts (Hertzmann believes that Constanze Mozart may have disposed of a good many after his death) one may add this line from a letter of Mozart's to his father, dated July 31, 1778: "You know that I am, so to speak, soaked in music, that I am immersed in it all day long and that I love to plan works, study and meditate."

2. N I and especially N II. To these must be added Nottebohm's valuable extended essays on single sketchbooks: N 1865, on the "Kessler" Sketchbook, and N 1880, on the "Eroica" Sketchbook.

3. For a brief review of publications in facsimile or transcription up to 1967 see Lewis Lockwood, review of the Beethovenhaus edition of the Pastoral Symphony Sketchbook, in *MQ,* LIII (1967), 128–136. [For a more recent survey see JTW, passim.]

4. In a letter of January 26, 1793, Beethoven's Bonn acquaintance Bartolomäus Fischenich sent Beethoven's song *Feuerfarb'* (later published as Op. 52 No. 2) to Charlotte von Schiller and described it as "by a young man whose musical talents are universally praised and whom the Elector has sent to Haydn in Vienna. He also proposes to set Schiller's 'Freude' and indeed all stanzas of it"; see Ludwig Schiedermair, *Der Junge Beethoven* (Leipzig, 1925), pp. 221f., and Thayer-Forbes, I, 121f. The first sketches directly attributable to the Ninth Symphony are also found in the "Scheide" Sketchbook and refer to the opening of the scherzo.

5. On Reissig see Otto Erich Deutsch, "Der Liederdichter Reissig, Bestimmung einer merkwürdigen Persönlichkeit," *Neues Beethoven-Jahrbuch,* VI (1936), 59–65; also Kinsky-Halm, pp. 602f. Beethoven's settings of Reissig texts are the songs WoO 137, 138, 139; Op. 75, Nos. 5 and 6; WoO 143 and 146.

6. Hans Boettcher, *Beethoven als Liederkomponist* (Augsburg, 1928), pp. 64f., 95f. Boettcher's few remarks on Beethoven's treatment of meter in *Sehnsucht* sketches are based entirely on Nottebohm's examples.

7. Op. 52 No. 1 probably dates from the early 1790s; the date of Op. 52 No. 8 is still in doubt.
8. For sketches for Op. 75 No. 3 (perhaps from 1791–1793), see N II, p. 563, and Joseph Kerman, ed., *Beethoven: Autograph Miscellany from circa 1786–1799* (London, 1970), II, 69; for references to sketches for Op. 75 No. 6 (written in 1809), see N II, pp. 274f. and 281.
9. Boettcher, *Beethoven als Liederkomponist*, p. 64.
10. Most recently by Leslie Orrey in his chapter, "The Songs," in Denis Arnold and Nigel Fortune, eds., *The Beethoven Companion* (London, 1971), p. 432. The sketches quoted by Orrey are also based wholly on Nottebohm.
11. N II, pp. 332–333.
12. The sketchbook is extensively described in N II, pp. 321–348, and more briefly in G. Kinsky, *Manuskripte, Briefe, Dokumente . . . Katalog der Musikautographen-Sammlung Louis Koch* (Stuttgart, 1953), pp. 69–71. It is now housed in the Scheide Library at Princeton University.
13. For Kerman on Op. 98 see Alan Tyson, ed., *Beethoven Studies* (New York, 1973). On the D-major concerto see Lewis Lockwood, "Beethoven's Unfinished Piano Concerto of 1815: Sources and Problems," *MQ*, LVI (1970), 624–646, reprinted in Paul Henry Lang, ed., *The Creative World of Beethoven* (New York, 1970), pp. 122–144.
14. On the problem of the original and later versions of Nottebohm's essays, see the brief remarks in Chapter 1, n. 13; see also the "Papers of the Colloque at Saint-Germain-en-Laye: Studies on Music of the 19th Century," *Acta Musicologica*, XLIII (1971), 86f. For an extensive account of many of the textual differences see my "Nottebohm Revisited," in J. Grubbs, ed., *Current Thought in Musicology* (Austin and London, 1976), pp. 139–191.
15. On this point see Lockwood, review in *MQ*, LIII (1967), 128–136.
16. The "Scheide" Sketchbook is one of the large type used at the writing table, in which Beethoven normally wrote in ink—as opposed to the folded or smaller notebooks or sheaves which he was accustomed to carrying in his pockets while out of doors and in which he normally wrote in pencil.
17. Little, if anything, can actually be said about the length of time Beethoven devoted to any particular body of sketches. The exact chronology of the "Scheide" Sketchbook is still uncertain in details and is based on a few relatively fixed external points, such as the dating of the autograph manuscripts of Op. 102 No. 2 ("anfangs August 1815"), of Op. 98 ("1816 im Monath April"), of the March in D Major, WoO 24 ("3ten Juni 1816"), and of Op. 101 ("1816 im Monath November"). One song in the sketchbook, WoO 145 (*Wo blüht das Blümchen*), was published in a Vienna periodical as early as February 28, 1816, just four months before the publication of *Sehnsucht* (WoO 146) by Artaria. While Nottebohm attributed the entire sketchbook to the period "May 1815 to May 1816," he then emended this hypothesis to limit the sketchbook to 1815 (N II, p. 348). For critical comments on this view of the dating and especially on the date of Op. 101, see A. Levinsohn, in *Vierteljahrsschrift für Musikwissenschaft*, IX (1893), 163–165.
18. For an approach to the meter of *Sehnsucht*, largely derived from the standpoint of Riemann's theory of "Vierhebigkeit," see Arnold Schering, "Metrische Studien zu

Beethovens Liedern," *Neues Beethoven-Jahrbuch,* II (1925), 30–31. The predictable result of this approach is that the final $\frac{3}{4}$ meter is considered "really" a series of $\frac{2}{4}$ measures in which mm. 2, 4, 6, and 8 are shortened by half—that is, each bar consists of $\frac{2}{4} + \frac{1}{4}$, and Beethoven chose the $\frac{3}{4}$ notation only to avoid an awkward change of meter signature too frequently. From this standpoint the $\frac{2}{4}$ of the sketches is regarded not merely as the "original" conception but as the underlying one, transformed only for notational convenience.

19. See E. Bartlitz, *Die Beethoven-Sammlung in der Musikabteilung der Deutschen Staatsbibliothek* (Berlin, 1970), p. 37.

20. N II, p. 332.

4. Eroica Perspectives

1. Wagner's published comments on the *Eroica* are found in the following writings (references to volume and page numbers are those of *Richard Wagner: Gesammelte Schriften und Dichtungen,* ed. Julius Kapp, 12 vols., Leipzig, 1914): "Ein glücklicher Abend," vol. VII, pp. 154–156; "Ueber das Dirigieren," vol. VIII, p. 182; "Beethoven," vol. IX, pp. 110–114; "Ueber die Anwendung der Musik auf das Drama," vol. XIII, pp. 284–286. Wagner's program note for the symphony is in vol: IX, pp. 110–112, written for his performance of the work at a subscription concert in Zurich on February 25, 1851.

2. F. G. Wegeler and F. Ries, *Biographische Notizen über Ludwig van Beethoven* (Koblenz, 1838), pp. 77–79; Anton Schindler, *Biographie von Ludwig van Beethoven* (Münster, 1840), pp. 55–57; A. W. Thayer, *Ludwig van Beethovens Leben, nach dem Original-Manuskript deutsch bearbeitet von Hermann Deiters . . . Revision . . . von Hugo Riemann* (Leipzig, 1917), Vol. II, pp. 418–419. For a sample of a more recent biography in which the older evidence is repeated uncritically, see George R. Marek, *Beethoven: Biography of a Genius* (New York, 1969), p. 343.

3. Maynard Solomon, "Beethoven and Bonaparte," *Music Review,* XXIX (1968), 96–105.

4. Alan Tyson, "Beethoven's Heroic Phase," *Musical Times,* CX (1969), 139–141.

5. See Berlioz's discussion in his *À travers chants* (2nd ed., Paris, 1872), pp. 22–29; Alexandre Oulibicheff, *Beethoven, ses critiques et ses glossateurs* (Leipzig and Paris, 1875), pp. 173–187; on Wagner's program note, see note 1 above.

6. Adolph Bernhard Marx, "Die Sinfonia eroica und die Idealmusik," in *Ludwig van Beethoven: Leben und Schaffen* (6th ed., Leipzig, 1902), vol. I, pp. 203–218.

7. Paul Bekker, *Beethoven* (2nd ed., Berlin, 1912), p. 223; Eng. trans. (London, 1925), p. 163.

8. N 1880; the most recent reprint was issued by Johnson Reprint Corp. (New York, 1970).

9. George Grove, *Beethoven and His Nine Symphonies* (3rd ed., London, 1898; reprinted New York, 1962), pp. 49–95. Donald Francis Tovey, *Essays in Musical Analysis,* vol. I (London, 1935), pp. 29–33; "Sonata Forms," *Musical Articles from the Encyclopaedia Britannica* (London, 1944), pp. 221–228; *Beethoven* (London, 1944), passim.

10. Fritz Cassirer, *Beethoven und die Gestalt* (Stuttgart, 1925); the first chapter had been issued separately in *Der Dreiklang*, IV (1922), 192ff.

11. Alfred Lorenz, "Worauf beruht die bekannte Wirkung der Durchführung im I. Eroica-satze?" *Neues Beethoven-Jahrbuch*, I (1924), 159–183; "Betrachtungen über Beethovens Eroica-Skizzen," *Zeitschrift für Musikwissenschaft*, VII (1924–25), 409–422.

12. August Halm, "Der Fremdkörper im ersten Satz der Eroica," *Die Musik*, XXI (1928–29), 481–484.

13. "Beethovens Dritte Sinfonie zum erstenmal in ihrem wahren Inhalt dargestellt," in *Das Meisterwerk in der Musik: ein Jahrbuch von Heinrich Schenker*, vol. III (Munich, 1930), pp. 25–101; the three volumes of this yearbook were reprinted in one volume by Georg Olms Verlag (Hildesheim and New York, 1974).

14. Walter Engelsmann, "Beethovens Werkthematik, dargestellt an der 'Eroica,'" *Archiv für Musikforschung*, V (1940), 104–113.

15. Walter Riezler, *Beethoven* (8th ed., rev. Zurich, 1962), pp. 289–324; Eng. trans. (New York, 1938; reprinted 1962), pp. 247–281.

16. Hoffmann's essay appeared in *Allgemeine musikalische Zeitung*, XII (1810), cols. 630–642, 652–659; it is conveniently available in English translation in *Beethoven, Symphony No. 5 in C Minor*, ed. Elliot Forbes, Norton Critical Scores (New York, 1971), pp. 150–163.

17. Erich Roeder, *Felix Draeseke, Der Lebens- und Leidensweg eines deutschen Meisters*, vol. I (Dresden and Berlin, 1932), p. 106; Roeder quotes Draeseke's words from the latter's essay, "Was tut der heutigen musikalischen Produktion not?" *Signale*, LXV (1907), 1–12. The translation of this passage is by Lewis Lockwood. The episode is also described in Otto zur Nedden, *Felix Draeseke* (Pforzheim, 1952), p. 7, and mentioned in Fritz Reckow, "Zur Wagners Begriff der unendlichen Melodie," in *Das Drama Richard Wagners als musikalische Kunstwerk*, ed. Carl Dahlhaus (Regensburg, 1970), pp. 87f. As cited by Engelsmann in "Beethovens Werkthematik," p. 112, the story was given a different twist of meaning: according to Engelsmann, "Richard Wagner . . . zeigte Felix Draeseke bei einer Zusammenkunft in Luzern, dass im Werk-Anfang der Eroica die Melodie der ganzen Sinfonie enthalten ist."

18. "Ueber die Anwendung der Musik auf das Drama," in *Richard Wagner: Gesammelte Schriften*, ed. Kapp, vol. XIII, pp. 290f, cited in *Die Musik in Geschichte und Gegenwart* [hereafter cited as *MGG*], ed. Friedrich Blume, vol. XIV (Kassel, 1968), col. 113.

19. Cited in *MGG*, vol. XIV, col. 113.

20. Grove, *Beethoven and His Nine Symphonies*, p. 50.

21. Engelsmann, "Beethovens Werkthematik," p. 112.

22. The central early writing by Goethe on this subject is his *Versuch die Metamorphose der Pflanzen zu erklären* (Gotha, 1790). For more on Goethe's views on organic form, in relation to German scientific thought of his time, see Hugh Barr Nisbet, *Goethe and the Scientific Tradition* (London, 1972); for an attempt to apply the same views to analysis of Goethe's *Faust*, see Peter Salm, *The Poem as Plant: A Biological View of Goethe's Faust* (Cleveland, 1971). And for a wide-ranging study of the

entire concept of organic form in literature and in the history of ideas, see the essays by G. N. Giordano Orsini, Philip C. Ritterbush, and William K. Wimsatt collected in G. S. Rousseau, ed., *Organic Form: The Life of an Idea* (London, 1972); the volume has an extended bibliography of writings on the subject, but lacks references to publications of any kind on music. Although the issue has yet to be seriously studied by musicologists, it would be extremely profitable to trace the ways in which this idea, gathering force in the nineteenth century following Goethe, Coleridge, and other writers, found its way readily into writings on music and became deeply embedded in analytic procedures. [For recent views on the role of organicism in musical thinking, see Ruth Solie, "The Living Work: Organicism and Musical Analysis," *19th-Century Music*, IV (1980), pp. 147–156; and Joseph Kerman, *Contemplating Music* (Cambridge, Mass., 1985), pp. 65, 73, 76, 79.]

23. Heinrich Schenker, *Beethovens Neunte Sinfonie: eine Darstellung des musikalischen Inhalts unter fortlaufender Berücksichtigung auch des Vortrags und der Literatur* (Vienna, 1912; reprinted 1969). "Beethovens Fünfte Sinfonie," *Der Tonwille*, I (1922), 27–37; II (1923), no. 5, pp. 10–42, no. 6, pp. 9–35; this was separately published (Vienna, 1925; reprinted 1969) and is partly available in English translation in Forbes's edition of the symphony for the Norton Critical Scores, pp. 164–182. *Der freie Satz* (Vienna, 1935), ed. Oswald Jonas (2nd ed., rev., Vienna, 1956); Ernst Oster's complete translation of Schenker's *Der freie Satz* was issued in two volumes under the title *Free Composition* (New York and London, 1979).

24. From the extensive literature pursuing, explicating, or developing the Schenkerian approach, at times in ways that would not be likely to have met with Schenker's approval, I should mention the following, which seem to me especially significant: Felix Salzer, *Structural Hearing*, 2 vols. (New York, 1952; reprinted 1962); the immensely important review of Salzer's work by Milton Babbitt, *Journal of the American Musicological Society*, V (1952), 260–265; and the yearbook *The Music Forum*, ed. William J. Mitchell and Felix Salzer (New York and London, 1967–), which contains a number of important articles written along Schenkerian lines. For a convenient and extensive listing of writings by Heinrich Schenker and of works written about him and his theoretical views, up to 1969, see David Beach, "A Schenker Bibliography," *Journal of Music Theory*, XIII (1969), 2–37.

25. "Diminution," in *Der freie Satz*, Part III, Chap. 3, no. 7.

26. Schenker himself contributed to the literature on this enormous field in his early study, *Ein Beitrag zur Ornamentik* (Vienna, c. 1902), translated into English by Hedi Siegel as "A Contribution to the Study of Ornamentation," in *The Music Forum*, vol. IV (1976), pp. 1–40. Only after the completion of this article, in the spring of 1977, did I become aware of David Epstein's analytic discussion of the *Eroica* in his book *Beyond Orpheus* (Cambridge, Mass., 1979), pp. 111–138. Epstein attempts to utilize Schenker's analytic views of various portions of the work and to relate them to aspects of the motivic structure.

27. Schenker's essay not only provides a thoroughgoing analysis but also a partial *Revisionbericht* for the symphony, offering some comparisons of readings between the earliest surviving sources (the corrected copy of the full score and the first edition of the performing parts); there is, as well, a very brief discussion of the literature, mentioning only Halm and Nottebohm. [For some valuable sugges-

tions on Schenker's essay in relation to my remarks in this essay, see William Drabkin, review of *BS 3* in *19th-Century Music,* VII/2 (1983), pp. 167–169.]

28. An example of an earlier commentary that does take note of the G-minor implication at the beginning is Marx, *Ludwig van Beethoven,* vol. I, p. 189.

29. Riezler, *Beethoven,* Eng. trans., p. 251; Philip Downs, "Beethoven's 'New Way' and the *Eroica,*" *MQ,* LVI (1970), 598–599 (especially Example 8), reprinted in *The Creative World of Beethoven,* ed. Paul Henry Lang (New York, 1970), pp. 96–97; Charles Rosen, *The Classical Style* (New York and London, 1971), p. 393.

30. See Kinsky-Halm, pp. 129–130. There is also the testimony of Carl van Beethoven that "my brother at first believed, before he had heard the Symphony, that it would be too long if the first part of the first movement were repeated, but after frequent performances he found that it is detrimental if the first part is not repeated." See Carl's letter of February 12, 1805, in Thayer-Deiters-Riemann, vol. II, pp. 625f.

31. In Op. 16 the formal structure of the first movement is unexceptional in its thematic and harmonic design. The middle section employs as a central articulation merely a restatement of the opening theme on the subdominant (A♭ major) in mm. 175–186, and in much of the middle section the piano routinely hammers out eighth-note triplets against arpeggiated quarter-note figures in the winds; the whole is entirely within the scope established by the first movement of the Clarinet Trio, Op. 11, and consolidated in the Septet, Op. 20. The Cello Sonata, Op. 5 No. 2, on the other hand, has always been recognized as a much more ambitious work, and comparison of some features with the Quintet shows why: the segments of its first movement are much larger than those of Op. 16 not merely in length but in material; the typical piano triplet figurations are here vastly richer and more linear in character; and the middle section even has room for a new subject, presented in D minor, G minor, and E♭ major (mm. 264–294). This last may be unique in early works before the *Eroica* first movement, which in a formal sense the Cello Sonata foreshadows.

32. Downs, "Beethoven's 'New Way,'" in *The Creative World of Beethoven,* ed. Lang, p. 100; Downs further says of three appearances of this subject that Beethoven uses them in the same form, "nowhere modifying a note and only slightly strengthening the color in the final appearance." He makes no reference to the alteration of the harmonic goal that occurs in m. 681.

33. See Leo Spitzer, *Studies in English and American Literature* (Princeton, 1962).

34. I refer here to mm. 5–7, 161–163, and 251–258.

35. For aspects of this view of the first movement of Op. 57, I am indebted in a very long-range sense to the teachings, years ago, of Edward Lowinsky and of the late composer and teacher Hugo Kauder.

36. The background of this discussion is a seminar on the sketches for the first movement of the *Eroica* which I conducted at Princeton University in the autumn of 1975; to the careful and assiduous work of the graduate students in that seminar I am indebted in ways that go far beyond the present essay.

37. Donald Francis Tovey, *The Integrity of Music* (London, 1941), pp. 79–81.

38. The four exposition continuity drafts are on these pages in Landsberg 6: no. 1, pp. 10, 11; no. 2, pp. 12–13; no. 3, pp. 14–15; no. 4, pp. 20–21.

39. For a study of the sketches of the coda and middle section I am especially indebted to Lawrence Earp, who took part in the seminar mentioned in note 36.

5. The Earliest Sketches for the Eroica Symphony

1. *Ein Skizzenbuch von Beethoven aus dem Jahre 1803* (Leipzig, 1880; most recent reprint, New York, 1970). A thorough inventory of the *Eroica* sketchbook was provided by Rachel Wade, "Beethoven's *Eroica* Sketchbook," *Fontes Artis Musicae*, XXIV (1977), 254–289. [A new and authoritative physical description of the sketchbook is provided by Alan Tyson in JTW, pp. 137–145.]

   Although the *Eroica* sketchbook indeed contains the vast bulk of the known sketches for the symphony, apart from the early sketch in the Wielhorsky sketchbook that is the central element in this discussion, there remains one further outside sketch leaf, so far identified, that contains a single item of material for this work. It is a brief pair of sketches for the coda of the Scherzo, on one page of the bifolium Berlin, Deutsche Staatsbibliothek, MS Artaria 153, described by Alan Tyson in his essay, "The Problem of Beethoven's 'First' *Leonore* Overture," *JAMS*, XXVIII (1975), 299, 307, and fig. 3.

2. *Kniga eskizov Beethovena za 1802–1803 gody,* ed. and transcribed by Nathan L. Fishman, 3 vols. (Moscow, 1962). On the contents and importance of this publication, see especially the review by Boris Schwarz in *The Musical Quarterly*, XLIX (1963), 518–526. [See JTW, pp. 130–136.]

3. Fishman, *Kniga eskizov,* commentary volume, especially pp. 110–118; see also Fishman's article (in German), "Das Skizzenbuch Beethovens aus dem Jahren 1802–03 aus dem Familienarchiv Wielhorsky und die ersten Skizzen zur 'Eroica,'" Gesellschaft für Musikforschung, *Bericht über den internationalen musikwissenschaftlichen Kongress: Bonn 1970* (Kassel, 1971), pp. 104–107. Fishman returned to the subject in his contribution, "Das Moskauer Skizzenbuch Beethovens aus dem Archiv von M. J. Wielhorsky," in K. Dorfmüller, *Beiträge zur Beethoven-Bibliographie* (Munich, 1978), pp. 61–67.

4. *Beethovens Eroica und Prometheus-Musik: Sujet-Studien* (Wilhelmshaven, 1978), pp. 73–81.

5. Although this interpretation of the term *festeggiare* in the final title seems to me entirely exaggerated and farfetched, I would concede that Beethoven's use of the same basic material (upper line and bass) in four categories—the orchestral dance, the ballet, the piano variations, and the symphony—clearly does show a desire to adapt the same content deliberately and tendentiously to diversified musical categories. On the other hand, the obvious difference in the scale, purpose, weight, and complexity of the four treatments of this material tends to underscore his awareness of the aesthetic boundaries that separate the categories from one another. The glass is either half empty or half full.

6. Floros, *Beethovens Eroica*, pp. 78f.

7. Robert Winter, "Plans for the Structure of the String Quartet in C Sharp Minor, Op. 131," *BS 2* (London and New York, 1977), pp. 110ff.

8. Alan Tyson, "The 1803 Version of Beethoven's *Christus am Oelberge*," *MQ*, LVI (1970), 554, 572.

9. Ludwig Nohl, *Beethoven, Liszt, Wagner* (Vienna, 1874); see also Nohl's account of this sketchbook in the *Neue Zeitschrift für Musik*, LXVIII (1872), 117f. Fishman attributes the page numbering of the manuscript to Nohl, but the penciled attribution "Eroica" on p. 44 to Wilhelm von Lenz, who described the sketchbook in his *Kritischer Katalog sämmtlicher Werke Ludwig van Beethovens . . .* (Hamburg, 1860), pp. 221f.

10. Philip Gossett, "Beethoven's Sixth Symphony: Sketches for the First Movement," *JAMS*, XXVII (1974), 248–284.

11. Christopher Reynolds, "Beethoven's Sketches for the Piano Variations Opus 35," *BS 3*, pp. 47–84; and Sieghard Brandenburg, *Kesslersches Skizzenbuch* (Bonn, 1978), Part I: Übertragung, pp. 33–34.

12. Kurt von Fischer, "'Never to be performed in public.' Zu Beethovens Streichquartett Opus 95," *BJ*, Jg. 1973–77 (1977), p. 87.

13. See the facsimile of the sketchbook Berlin, Stiftung Preussischer Kulturbesitz, MS Grasnick 2, and its transcription by W. Virneisel (Bonn, 1972–1974), p. 8, staves 13–16, and p. 9, stave 1.

14. The finale sketches in Landsberg 6 occupy pages 70 to 90; cf. N 1880, pp. 50f., for a brief account.

15. N 1880, p. 50. A new transcription of these leaves was made by Steven Huebner during a seminar on the *Eroica* sketchbook that I carried out at Princeton University in 1979.

16. See Karl Mikulicz, ed., *Ein Notierungsbuch von Beethoven* (Leipzig, 1927), p. 56.

17. On the form of the finale see Donald Francis Tovey, *Essays in Musical Analysis,* vol. I (London, 1935), p. 32: "a form which was unique when it appeared and has remained unique ever since"; and Heinrich Schenker, "Beethovens Dritte Sinfonie," in *Das Meisterwerk in der Musik,* vol. III (Munich, 1930), pp. 75f. and fig. 45. Admittedly, the position of the Poco Andante suggests that it also constitutes the formal equivalent of the slow variation that often appeared just before the end of a traditional variations movement. For this point I am indebted to Charles Rosen.

18. In his essay on the "first" *Leonore* Overture (see note 1), p. 330, Alan Tyson shows that in 1804 Beethoven went a step further with his rudimentary plan for a C-Minor Symphony (later the Fifth) than Nottebohm's published transcriptions had revealed. For present purposes it suffices to note that at this very early stage of formulating ideas for the work, Beethoven experimented considerably with the slow movement and finale; the third movement was apparently arrived at quite early but was probably completed late, to judge from the autograph score; and the basic idea for the first movement remained the primary element of stability.

6. The Compositional Genesis of the Eroica Finale

1. For a recent account of the structure of the sketchbook, see JTW, pp. 137–145, and the further bibliography listed there. My edition of the sketchbook is currently in progress.

2. D. F. Tovey, *Essays in Musical Analysis* (Oxford, 1935), Vol. I, p. 32.

3. D. F. Tovey, *Beethoven* (New York, 1945), p. 124.

4. H. Schenker, *Das Meisterwerk in der Musik,* Vol. III (Vienna, 1930), p. 75. "A close connection to the form of Opus 35 is so clear in the Finale of the Third Symphony that Beethoven's express indications can also be used here. Thus, one can call the group of bars 1–76 the 'Introduzione col Basso del Tema;' the 'Tema' follows in bars 76–107. Instead of the chain of fifteen variations in the main key, which it would be impossible to translate into an orchestral work—and surely not in a symphony—there appears in its place a fugal passage, which, like that of the 'Finale alla fuga' in Opus 35, has the function of presenting as many contrasting other sonorities to the E-flat major main sonority as possible."

5. K. von Fischer, "Eroica-Variationen Op. 35 und Eroica-Finale," *Schweizerische Musikzeitung,* 89 (1949), pp. 282–286.

6. N 1880, pp. 50–51.

7. Pages 80–102.

8. The most recent boundary dates advanced for Landsberg 6, by Tyson in JTW, pp. 139f., are between June 1803 and April 1804. In a valuable recent study, Reinhold Brinkmann has established from newly discovered archival evidence in the Lobkowitz Archive in Litomerice, Czechoslovakia, that a private rehearsal of a Beethoven symphony that required a third horn—accordingly the Third Symphony, without a doubt—took place on June 9, 1804. This is the earliest known date for the completion of the work. See Reinhold Brinkmann, "Kleine 'Eroica'-Lese," *Österreichische Musikzeitung* (1984), pp. 634–638.

9. P. Cahn, "Aspekte der Schlussgestaltung in Beethovens Instrumentalwerken," *Archiv für Musikwissenschaft,* XXXIX (1982), pp. 19–31.

10. Philip Gossett, "Beethoven's Sixth Symphony: Sketches for the First Movement," *JAMS,* XXVII (1974), pp. 248–284.

11. See N 1880, p. 44. The phrase occurs in the sketchbook on page 10, above an early entry for the third movement of the symphony. The last word is abbreviated, but Nottebohm's reading is "St(?)," that is, "Stimme" (voice).

12. In a recent article, entitled "A Structural Model for the *Eroica* Finale," *College Music Symposium,* 22/2 (1982), pp. 138–147, David Eiseman proposes that J. S. Bach's motet *Jesu, meine Freude* may have served as a model for the *Eroica* finale. Although Beethoven's veneration of Bach is well attested, I am unable to accept the hypothesis in the absence of any specific and other than circumstantial evidence.

7. Planning the Unexpected

1. F. G. Wegeler and F. Ries, *Biographische Notizen über Ludwig van Beethoven* (Koblenz, 1838), p. 79. For some aspects of this essay, I am indebted to Jonathan Glixon.

2. D. F. Tovey, *Essays in Musical Analysis* (London, 1935), Vol. I, p. 31. For a review of these "corrections" and the reference to Wagner's practice, see F. Weingartner, *Ratschläge für Aufführungen klassischer Symphonien,* Vol. I, 4th ed. (Wiesbaden, 1958), pp. 40–41.

3. D. Newlin, *Schoenberg Remembered* (New York, 1980), p. 294.

4. Stephen Paul, "Comedy, Wit, and Humor in Haydn's Instrumental Music," in J. P. Larsen, H. Serwer, and J. Webster, eds., *Haydn Studies; Proceedings of the Inter-*

national Haydn Conference, Washington, D.C., 1975 (New York, 1981), pp. 450–456.

5. G. A. Griesinger, *Biographische Notizen über Joseph Haydn* (1980), ed. F. Grasberger (Vienna, 1954), p. 32; English translation in V. Gotwals, *Joseph Haydn, Eighteenth-Century Gentleman and Genius* (Madison, 1963), p. 33 (Griesinger); pp. 130f. (the same anecdote from Dies, *Biographische Notizen über Joseph Haydn*). H. C. Robbins Landon, *Joseph Haydn, Critical Edition of the Complete Symphonies,* Vol. XI, Philarmonia No. 599, 2nd rev. ed. (1981), p. 116, prints an original version of the Andante of Symphony No. 94 without the drum-stroke.

6. See note 4 above.

7. Rey Longyear, "Beethoven and Romantic Irony," in P. H. Lang, ed., *The Creative World of Beethoven* (New York, 1970), pp. 145–162.

8. Examples are especially frequent in his letters to Zmeskall; for example, see Anderson Nos. 28 and 29 and especially 30 (perhaps 1798?) in which the play on "Baron" . . . "ron ron/nor/orn/ rno/onr" furnishes a partial verbal equivalent of motivic inversion, retrograde, and "interversion" found in certain Beethovenian musical situations.

9. *Essays,* Vol. I, p. 31.

10. W. Riezler, *Beethoven,* 8th ed. (Zurich, 1962), pp. 289–323, especially p. 313–314; English translation (New York, 1938), pp. 271f.; H. Schenker, *Harmonielehre* (Vienna, 1906), p. 208; English translation (Chicago, 1954), pp. 162f.; D. Epstein, *Beyond Orpheus: Studies in Musical Structure* (Cambridge, Mass., 1979), pp. 119–120.

11. A still more developed example of a massive dissonance that possesses large-scale structural importance is the opening chord of the Finale of the Ninth Symphony, in which the B♭ major and D minor triad members are attacked simultaneously. Although one may say that the pitches B♭, *d,* and *f* are in a sense overhung from the last chord of the third movement, this is scarcely the same as a contrapuntal preparation of a dissonance in normal tonal syntax.

12. H. Schenker, *Beethovens Dritte Sinfonie,* in *Das Meisterwerk in der Musik, Ein Jahrbuch von Heinrich Schenker,* Vol. III (Munich, 1930), p. 52.

13. Epstein, *Beyond Orpheus,* p. 120.

14. For a recent review of some major textual aspects of the symphony, see Michael Tusa, "Die authentischen Quellen der 'Eroica,'" *Archiv für Musikwissenschaft,* XLII (1985), pp. 121–150. It is curious that in the earliest surviving score copy (that in the Gesellschaft der Musikfreunde, Vienna), in m. 394 the horn entrance was originally entered in the trumpet stave, then corrected to the horn. There is no reason to assume that this is anything other than a copyist's slip that was immediately corrected to the proper instrument. My remarks on the first edition of the parts are based on the copy in the Gesellschaft der Musikfreunde.

15. See Chapter 4.

16. I am grateful to the former Director of the Biblioteka Jagiellońska in Krakow, Dr. Jan Pirozsyński, for facilitating my research during my visit to the library in 1984. For an excellent inventory of the sketchbook, made before its survival in Krakow became known in 1980, see Rachel Wade, "Beethoven's Eroica Sketchbook," *Fontes Artis Musicae,* XXIV (1977), pp. 254–289.

17. D. Johnson, "Beethoven Scholars and Beethoven's Sketches," *19th Century Music,* II (1978–79), pp. 3–17; see also the replies to Johnson by Sieghard Brandenburg and William Drabkin, ibid., II (1978–79), pp. 270–279, and by Richard Kramer, ibid., III (1979–80), pp. 187f.; all with replies by Johnson.

18. See Chapter 3; see also the review by Peter Cahn in *Die Musikforschung,* 30 (1977), pp. 523–525. An important further statement on this controversy was offered by Robert Winter, in his book, *Compositional Origins of Beethoven's Opus 131* (Ann Arbor, 1982), pp. xxi–xxiv. Further developments on both sides of this issue are to be expected as Beethoven scholarship on the sketches continues to grow in range and, one hopes, in depth.

8. The Problem of Closure

1. J. Kerman, "Notes on Beethoven's Codas," in *BS 3,* pp. 141–160; P. Cahn, "Aspekte der Schlussgestaltung in Beetovens Instrumentalwerken," *Archiv für Musikwissenschaft,* XXXIX (1982), pp. 19–31. For reference to some earlier studies bearing on Beethoven's codas, see Cahn's article, p. 23, note 7.

2. An obvious precursor of Beethoven's procedure here is the great Haydn keyboard sonata in E♭ Major, Hoboken XVI:52, in which the slow movement in E major gives way to the Finale, in E♭ Major, abruptly shifting downward a semitone. As pointed out by Lawrence Moss in *Haydn Studies,* ed. J. P. Larsen et al. (New York, 1981), p. 501, the ending of the first movement of the sonata clearly foreshadows the E major of the second movement at mm. 109–110; to which one can add that the abrupt return of E♭ Major at m. 111 of the first movement also anticipates the way in which the later shift is brought about to start the Finale. In the Beethoven Third Piano Concerto, the *ff* dynamic for the final chord is extremely unusual, matched in early- and middle-period works only in the Fourth Symphony slow movement ending.

3. The autograph of Opus 96 was issued in complete facsimile by Henle Verlag (Munich, 1977), edited by Martin Staehelin; it was also discussed by Sieghard Brandenburg, "Bemerkungen zu Beethovens Op. 96," *B J,* IX (1973/77), pp. 11–25.

4. P. Mies, "Quasi una fantasia . . . ," in S. Kross and H. Schmidt, eds., *Colloquium Amicorum, Joseph Schmidt-Görg zum 70. Geburtstag* (Bonn, 1967), pp. 239–249.

5. See P. Gülke, "Introduktion als Widerspruch im System," *Deutsches Jahrbuch der Musikwissenschaft für 1969,* edited by R. Eller, 14 (1970), pp. 5–40; reprinted in L. Finscher, ed., *Ludwig van Beethoven* (Darmstadt, 1983), pp. 338–387.

6. See Paul Mies, "Die Bedeutung der Pauke in den Werken Ludwig van Beethovens," *B J,* VIII (1975), p. 50.

7. A. Tyson, "Stages in the Composition of Beethoven's Piano Trio Op. 70 No. 1," *Proceedings of the Royal Musical Association,* XCVII (1970–71), pp. 1–19; R. Taub, "The Autograph of the First Movement of Beethoven's Piano Trio Op. 70 No. 1," Doctor of Musical Arts Thesis, The Juilliard School (April 1981), 84 pp.

8. This view is strongly stated by E. T. A. Hoffmann in his review of both trios of Opus 70, which appeared in the *Allgemeine Musikalische Zeitung,* XV, No. 9, dated March 3, 1813, cols. 141–154, with four pages of music examples; it is available in

modern reprint in E. T. A. Hoffmann, *Schriften zur Musik* (Munich, 1963), pp. 118–144.

9. As translated by Oliver Strunk, *Source Readings in Music History* (New York, 1950), p. 779, from the composite version of Hoffmann's review that was published under the title *Beethovens Instrumental-Musik,* in his *Fantasiestücke in Callot's Manier (1813).*

10. Carl Czerny, *Ueber den Richtigen Vortrag der Sämtlichen Beethoven'schen Klavierwerke,* ed. P. Badura-Skoda (Vienna, Universal-Ed., No. 13340), p. 99.

11. See mm. 12, 14, and above all the *ff/p* contrast at m. 45, which ends the first part of the movement and is thus structurally analogous to the final close, in that both end in the tonic.

12. On the format and makeup of the manuscript, see the essay by Tyson mentioned in note 7 above.

9. Process versus Limits

1. For this anecdote see Thayer-Forbes, Vol. I, p. 409.

2. See, for example, the remarks of the critic of the *Allgemeine Musikalische Zeitung,* February 27, 1807, who begins his review, "Three new, very long, and difficult Beethoven string quartets, dedicated to the Russian ambassador Count Razumovsky, are attracting the attention of all connoisseurs" (cited in Thayer-Forbes, Vol. I, p. 409). A characteristic modern reflection of the same view is found in Joseph Kerman, *The Beethoven Quartets* (New York, 1967), in which the chapter on this quartet is entitled "After the *Eroica.*"

3. See Chapter 5. There are of course substantial differences between the two situations, first of all that in the case of the *Eroica* finale Beethoven had already worked out the compositional elaboration of the theme in three different ways by the time he came to use it as a symphonic finale.

4. For a brief discussion of Beethoven's apparent indebtedness to the Prach collection for this and other Russian melodies, see N II, p. 90.

5. Steven Lubin, "Techniques for the Analysis of Development in Middle-Period Beethoven" (dissertation, New York University, 1974), pp. 134–135.

6. D. F. Tovey, *Beethoven* (Oxford, 1935), p. 104; quoted by Lubin, ibid., p. 104.

7. A facsimile edition of the autograph, now in Berlin, was edited by Alan Tyson for Scolar Press (London, 1980). For a valuable study of some of the revisions in the manuscript, with special emphasis on the fugato in the development section, see Richard Kramer, " 'Das Organische der Fuge': On the Autograph of Beethoven's Quartet in F Major, Opus 59 No. 1," in C. Wolff, ed., *The String Quartets of Haydn, Mozart, and Beethoven: Studies of the Autograph Manuscripts* (Cambridge, Mass: Harvard University Press, 1980), pp. 223–265. See also Kramer's review of the Scolar Press facsimiles, in *19th-Century Music,* VI (1982), pp. 76–81.

8. Florence Moog, "Gulliver Was a Bad Biologist," *Scientific American,* 179/5 (1948), pp. 52–56.

9. Bertram Jessup, "Aesthetic Size," *Journal of Aesthetics and Art Criticism,* IX (1950), pp. 31–38. The point of departure for Jessup is, appropriately, Aristotle's *Poetics,*

50b34, where the length of a tragedy is brought forward as a factor in determining its quality.

10. A preliminary account of some of the autograph changes in the second movement and finale is given by Kramer, "'Das Organische der Fuge,'" pp. 237–238 and Example 1.

10. On the Cavatina of Beethoven's String Quartet in B-flat Major

1. *The New Grove Dictionary of Music and Musicians* (London, 1980), Vol. 2, p. 385; see also J. Kerman and A. Tyson, *The New Grove Beethoven* (New York, 1983), p. 121.

2. K. H. Köhler and G. Herre, eds., *Ludwig van Beethovens Konversationshefte,* Vol. VIII (Leipzig, 1981), p. 246 (January 2–8, 1826).

3. W. Osthoff, "Mozarts Cavatinen und ihre Tradition," in W. Stauder et al., eds., *Helmuth Osthoff zu seinem siebzigsten Geburtstag* (Tutzing, 1969), pp. 139–177.

4. I am indebted here to recent scholarship on German romantic opera, especially the operas of Weber, and particularly to David Kilroy and Michael Tusa. See Tusa, "Carl Maria von Weber's *Euryanthe:* A Study of Its Historical Context, Genesis, and Reception" (dissertation, Princeton University, 1983), pp. 103ff. As Tusa notes, cavatinas in German opera of this period were generally "single-movement compositions of predominantly elegiac character"; he notes that Mozart's "Porgi amor" stood as a model for the comparable cavatina in *Euryanthe,* and also cites Agathe's cavatina in *Der Freischütz,* "Und ob die Wolke," as a sample of the genre. Cited by Tusa as well is the definition of the genre by C. F. D. Schubart, *Ideen zu einer Aesthetik der Tonkunst* (Vienna, 1806), who says that a cavatina must have no coloratura, and is an "einfacher kunstloser Ausdruck *einer* Empfindung, und hat deswegen nur einen Satz. Das Motiv einer Cavatine muss gefühlvoll, rührend, verständlich, und leicht sein." It is important in this connection to realize that in the years 1823–1824 Beethoven was considering various possible operatic ventures, and that these included settings of libretti by Rellstab and Grillparzer. On the German romantic operatic literature and its classes of compositional categories, see S. Gosling, *Die Deutsche Romantische Oper* (Tutzing, 1975), pp. 267–284.

5. See Gosling, *Die Deutsche Romantische Oper,* p. 269.

6. W. von Lenz, *Beethoven: Eine Kunststudie* (Hamburg, 1860), Part 5, p. 217.

7. On the transcendent aspects of Beethoven's later works, see Maynard Solomon, *Beethoven* (New York, 1977), pp. 309f.

8. See K. L. Mikulicz, *Ein Notierungsbuch von Beethoven* (Leipzig, 1927), p. 30. This idea for a slow movement seems to be related to the first theme of Opus 18 No. 1, first movement, and the theme of the slow movement of Opus 24.

9. Osthoff, "Mozarts Cavatinen," p. 176, n. 37.

10. SV 387 is a single, detached oblong leaf of 12-staff paper, preserved in the Library of Congress, Washington, D.C., as ML 96. B44 Case. See Douglas Johnson, *Beethoven's Early Sketches in the "Fischof Miscellany," Berlin Autograph 28* (UMI Press, Ann Arbor, 1980), Vol. 1, pp. 45, 50, 124–126, 351, 356.

11. The autograph of Opus 83 is dated 1810, and the songs were published in the

following year. There is no apparent thematic or motivic connection between the setting of 1794–1795 and that of Opus 83.

12. See Hans-Günter Klein, *Ludwig van Beethoven: Autographe und Abschriften; Staatsbibliothek Preussischer Kulturbesitz, Kataloge der Musikabteilung, Erste Reihe, Handschriften*, Vol. II (Berlin, 1975), p. 220. Klein mentions that the recomposed last nine bars of the movement (the Coda) were pasted into the MS but that the original version can still be read. It would be most valuable to have this earlier reading correctly read and made available, along with the surviving sketches for the Cavatina. Klein makes no reference to Beethoven's cancellation of the original bar 39 in the autograph.

13. See Heinrich Schenker, *Der freie Satz* (Vienna, 1935; reprinted 1956), p. 212.

14. An example of a vocal piece in which the vocal phrases are repeatedly echoed in the accompaniment is *An die ferne Geliebte*, No. 2.

15. In an early copy of the parts to Opus 130, which still has the *Grosse Fuge* as finale, this bar is already omitted; see the reproductions of two pages of the Viola part in I. Mahaim, *Beethoven: Naissance et Renaissance des Derniers Quattuors* (Paris, 1964), Vol. II, Figs. 259–260.

16. On the larger pitch structure and framework of the entire work, as well as of its individual movements, see Stefania de Kenessey, "The Quartet, the Finale, and the Fugue: A Study of Beethoven's Opus 130/133" (dissertation, Princeton University, 1984).

11. Beethoven's Autograph Manuscripts and the Modern Performer

1. Artur Schnabel, *My Life and Music* (New York, 1964), pp. 15, 63.

2. Schnabel's edition was originally published in Germany in the 1920s (Ullstein Verlag) and later in the United States (New York: Simon and Schuster, 1935). See *My Life and Music*, pp. 96, 131.

3. A notable exception in the United States over many years has been the teaching of Jacob Lateiner at the Juilliard School. His deeply informed knowledge of the autographs and other relevant sources of the classics of tonal music has certainly influenced many of his students.

4. *JTW.* Since the early 1950s the Beethoven-Archiv in Bonn has had in progress a long-range project aimed at producing a "complete critical edition" of the Beethoven sketches. Begun under the leadership of Dr. Joseph Schmidt-Görg, the series is entitled *Beethoven: Skizzen und Entwurfe: Erste Kritische Gesamtausgabe*. Continued by Schmidt-Görg's successors, Martin Staehelin and then Sieghard Brandenburg, this series has produced a handful of volumes of varying quality. For a sample view of the earlier volumes, see my review of Dagmar Weise's edition of the London portion of the "Pastoral-Symphony" Sketchbook, in *MQ*, LIII (1967), pp. 128–135. The most recently published volume, which raises the Bonn series to a higher level, is Sieghard Brandenburg's edition of the "Kessler Sketchbook" of 1801–1802, entitled *Ludwig van Beethoven: Kesslersches Skizzenbuch*, 2 vols. (Bonn: Beethovenhaus, 1978). Since 1978 no further volumes have appeared; it is to be hoped that more will soon be forthcoming.

5. An example of a fair copy is the autograph of the Piano Sonata in F-sharp Major,

Op. 78, issued in facsimile in 1923 (Munich, Drei Masken Verlag). An autograph that lapsed into the status of a composing score is, clearly, that of the first movement of the Violoncello Sonata in A Major, Op. 69 (see Chapter 2). Many other autographs contain strategic changes and modifications of material that represent revision at a very late stage, as Beethoven reserved certain decisions until he had come to a final phase of work on a given composition. In addition to voice-leading details, there are substantial changes in many autographs, including those of the Symphonies Nos. 5, 6, 7, 8, and 9; and the Quartets Op. 59 No. 1 (see Chapter 9); 59 No. 2; 74; 95; and all of the late quartets.

6. See Chapter 1.

7. The autograph of the Eighth Symphony, which has yet to be studied in full detail, is preserved in its entirety but is presently dispersed among several locations. The first and second movement autographs are in Berlin, SPK (Mus. ms. autogr. Beethoven 20. I and II); that of the third movement is in Krakow, Biblioteka Jagiellońska; and that of the finale is in Berlin, DSB. In this passage in the finale autograph, Beethoven sought to clarify his final intentions by appending a leaf showing only the wind parts that play in each measure of the revised passage, leaving the string parts as before.

8. A subtle touch is the support of the successively changing wind octaves by changes in the octave spacing of the strings (mm. 458–469), while at the same time the string choir as a whole sustains the basic major third interval over the lower and middle octaves of the string registers.

9. The autograph of the "Waldstein" Sonata, Op. 53, formerly in the Bodmer collection, is in Bonn, Beethoven-Archiv, under the signature H. C. Bodmer Mh 7. It has been issued by the Beethoven-Haus twice in full facsimile: (1) *Veroffentlichungen des Beethoven-Hauses in Bonn,* Neue Folge, Dritte Reihe, Vol. II (n.d., [1954]); for a subsidiary commentary see Dagmar Weise, "Zum Faksimiledruck von Beethovens Waldsteinsonate," in *BJ,* II (1955/56), pp. 102–111; (2) same series, same series title, Neuauflage, ed. Martin Staehelin (Bonn, 1984), with Introduction in German and English by Staehelin. On the genesis of the first movement see Barry Cooper, "The Evolution of the First Movement of Beethoven's 'Waldstein' Sonata," *Music and Letters,* LVIII (1977), pp. 170–191.

10. Compare this with the f♯/f♮ and c♯/c♮ problem in the first movement of the Violoncello Sonata Op. 69 (see Chapter 2); in Op. 69 the autograph reading differs from that of the first edition but turns out to be both more convincing and more authoritative, as is now confirmed by the recently discovered corrected copy of the work—which agrees with the autograph in these particulars.

11. See Paul Mies, *Textkritische Untersuchungen bei Beethoven* (Bonn, 1957), p. 51.

12. *Beethoven: Die Letzten Sonaten; Kritische Einführung und Erläuterung von Heinrich Schenker,* 2nd ed., ed. Oswald Jonas (Vienna: Universal-Edition, 1970), p. 4.

13. Studies devoted specifically to Beethoven's uses of dynamic markings began with Gustav Nottebohm's article "cresc—", in N I, pp. 104–106, and also include Mies, *Textkritische Untersuchungen,"* pp. 96–129. For the most part this topic receives attention in studies of individual works, their sources, and their text-critical and performance problems. A larger study of the entire subject is badly needed.

14. A facsimile edition of Op. 27 No. 2 was first issued by Heinrich Schenker in the

series *Musikalische Seltenheiten . . .* , ed. O. E. Deutsch; the facsimile is Volume I of this series, with the title *Ludwig van Beethoven, Sonate Op. 27 Nr. 2 . . . mit drei Skizzenblättern des Meisters,* edited by Heinrich Schenker (Vienna: Universal-Edition, 1921). A second and technically better reproduced facsimile was issued in Japan in the series Ongaku No Tomo Edition (Tokyo, 1970), under the general editorship of Keisei Sakka, and with an introduction by Joseph Schmidt-Görg. The Japanese edition also included a facsimile of the first published edition of the sonata, issued by Cappi in 1802.

15. See N I, pp. 107–125.

16. Anderson No. 1421, probably of August 1825.

17. See Mies, *Textkritische Untersuchungen,"* p. 40. The passage is from the third movement of the Ninth Symphony, first violin part, mm. 57–58. The passage is readily visible in the published facsimile of the Ninth Symphony autograph, first issued in 1924 in a magnificent reproduction, and reprinted by Edition Peters (Leipzig, 1975).

18. For reproductions of the opening page of the Pastoral Symphony autograph, see Kinsky-Halm, p. 162; for the published facsimile of the complete autograph of Op. 59 No. 1, see Chapter 9.

19. On the autograph of Op. 70 No. 1 see Alan Tyson, "Stages in the Composition of Beethoven's Piano Trio Op. 70 No. 1," *Proceedings of the Royal Musical Association,* 97 (1970–71), pp. 1–19; also Robert Taub, "The Autograph of the First Movement of Beethoven's Piano Trio Op. 70 No. 1" (Doctor of Musical Arts thesis, The Juilliard School, 1981), 84 pp.; and Chapter 8 of the present volume.

20. Anderson, Vol. III, Appendix I, p. 1450–51.

21. On the broader context of this problem see my essay, "Communicating Musicology: A Personal View," in *College Music Symposium,* 28 (1989), pp. 1–9. Of course, the rapid growth of the "early instrument" movement in recent years has accelerated such contact to some degree. At the same time, I cannot stress too much that the performance of older music on period instruments, whether originals or replicas, although it brings modern ears closer to the sound-world in which the music was first heard, remains by itself no guarantee whatever of the kind of serious approach to sources, content, and structure to which I mean to refer. What is needed is the addition of such an approach, through rigorous and required courses, in the conservatories which are the fundamental training grounds for younger performers.

Credits

Several of the chapters in this volume have been previously published, as indicated below.

Chapter 1   Originally published in *Acta Musicologica*, XLII (1970), pp. 32–47. Reproduced by permission of Bärenreiter-Verlag.

Chapter 2   Originally published in *The Music Forum*, II (1980), pp. 1–109. Reproduced by permission of Columbia University Press.

Chapter 3   Reprinted from *Beethoven Studies*, ed. Alan Tyson (New York: W. W. Norton, 1973), pp. 97–122, with the permission of W. W. Norton & Company. Copyright © 1973 by W. W. Norton & Company.

Chapter 4   Originally published in *Beethoven Studies 3*, ed. Alan Tyson (Cambridge: Cambridge University Press, 1982), pp. 85–106. Reproduced by permission of Cambridge University Press.

Chapter 5   Originally published in *The Musical Quarterly*, LXVII (1981), pp. 457–478. Reproduced by permission of Oxford University Press, New York. An Italian translation of this essay was published in *Beethoven*, ed. Giorgio Pestelli (Bologna, 1988), pp. 163–184.

Chapter 6   Reprinted from *Beethoven's Compositional Process*, ed. William Kinderman, by permission of University of Nebraska Press. Copyright © 1991 by the University of Nebraska Press.

Chapter 7   Hitherto unpublished.

Chapter 8   Originally published in *Beiträge zu Beethovens Kammermusik: Symposion Bonn 1984*. Copyright © 1987 by G. Henle Verlag, Munich. Reproduced by permission of G. Henle Verlag.

Chapter 9   Originally presented as the annual Martin Bernstein Lecture at New York University on October 9, 1986; hitherto unpublished.

Chapter 10   Originally published in *Liedstudien: Wolfgang Osthoff zum 60. Geburtstag*, ed. Martin Just and Reinhard Wiesend (Tutzing: Hans Schneider Verlag, 1989), pp. 293–306. Reproduced by permission of Hans Schneider Verlag.

Chapter 11   Originally presented at the University of British Columbia, Vancouver, in 1971; hitherto unpublished.

Permission to reproduce the facsimiles in this volume has been given by the following:

Figure 2.1   Folio 31v of sketchbook Landsberg 10. Reproduced by permission of the Trustees of the British Library.

Figures 2.2, 2.3   Letter of August 1, 1809, and misprint list reproduced by permission of the Beethovenhaus, Bonn.

Figure 2.4   Autograph manuscript of the first movement of the Violoncello Sonata, Op. 69. Reproduced by permission of the Beethovenhaus, Bonn.

Figures 3.1 and 3.2   Pages 60 and 61 of the Scheide Sketchbook. Reproduced by permission of Mr. William H. Scheide.

Figure 10.1   Page from autograph manuscript of the Cavatina of the Quartet Op. 130. Reproduced by permission of the Staatsbibliothek Preussischer Kulturbesitz, Berlin.

Index of Compositions, Sketches, and Other Documents

Compositions are listed first, followed by sketches, sketchbooks, and sketch leaves and bundles. SV represents the numbering of sketch items in Hans Schmidt, *Verzeichnis der Skizzen Beethovens,* in *BJ,* VI (1969). Citations of letters published in Emily Anderson, *The Letters of Beethoven,* 3 vols. (New York, 1961) are not indexed.

Hess 76–85 Cadenzas to Piano Concertos, 249n4

Sketch

Sketch for unfinished Piano Trio in F Minor (in Scheide sketchbook, SV 364), 99

Sketchbooks

SV 107 Sketchbook (Engelmann), 253n2
SV 47 Sketchbook (Grasnick 2), 267n13
SV 263 Sketchbook (Kessler), 144f, 146f, 273n4
SV 60 Sketchbook (Landsberg 6), 130–133, 134, 143, 265n38, 266n1, 268n8
SV 61 Sketchbook (Landsberg 7), 11, 141, 148f
SV 64 Sketchbook (Landsberg 10), 24
SV 342 Sketchbook (Moscow), 253n2
SV 188 Sketchbook (Pastoral Symphony), 11, 21, 24, 30, 39
SV 364 Sketchbook (Scheide), 99ff; facsimiles, 102f; transcriptions, 112–116, 260n4; dating, 261n17
SV 343 Sketchbook (Wielhorsky), 134–150, 199, 253n2, 266n2

Sketch Leaves and Bundles

[Not in SV] Berlin, Deutsche Staatsbibliotheck, MS Artaria 153, 266n1
SV 162 Bonn, BSk 57, 23, 70f
SV 123 Bonn, Bodmer Collection, Mh 76, 23, 66
SV 332 Copenhagen, Royal Danish Conservator, n.s., 24
SV 195 Paris, Bibl. Nat., MS 45, 23f, 72f
SV 289 Vienna, Gesellschaft der Musikfreunde, MS A 59, 22f
SV 387 Washington, Library of Congress, ML 96.B44 Case, 212, 272n10

General Index